The Struggle to Constitute and Sustain Productive Orders

About the Cover Art by Katherine Meyers:

The daily tasks of families, associations, and communities aspire toward order. Sustaining a high productive order demands effort, and this was evident as I stood at the edge of Vincent Ostrom's quest to understand human affairs. My cover art plays on the order of architecture and the ideas of a kindred soul to Ostrom. Architect and philosopher Louis Kahn wrote: "Order is all the designs of construction both mechanical and spiritual. Design is the process of fitting theme into conditions and coming up with certain experiences which will strengthen and enrich the order." The buildings represented in the cover art place hut, ruin, and skyscraper in the intellectual landscape of productive human orders.

Permission is granted by Duke University Press for material in chapter 9 of this book from Brian Loveman and Elizabeth Lira, "Truth, Justice, Reconciliation, and Impunity as Historical Themes: Chile, 1814–2006," which appeared in *Radical History Review*, Volume 97 (Winter 2007): 43–76.

Interior design and typesetting by Patty Lezotte.

The Struggle to Constitute and Sustain Productive Orders

Vincent Ostrom's Quest to Understand Human Affairs

EDITED BY MARK SPROULE-JONES,
BARBARA ALLEN, AND FILIPPO SABETTI

LEXINGTON BOOKS

A division of
ROWMAN & LITTLEFIELD PUBLISHERS, INC.
Lanham • Boulder • New York • Toronto • Plymouth, UK

LEXINGTON BOOKS

A division of Rowman & Littlefield Publishers, Inc.
A wholly owned subsidiary of The Rowman & Littlefield Publishing Group, Inc.
4501 Forbes Boulevard, Suite 200
Lanham, MD 20706

Estover Road
Plymouth PL6 7PY
United Kingdom

Copyright © 2008 by Lexington Books

All rights reserved. No part of this publication may be reproduced, stored in a retrieval system, or transmitted in any form or by any means, electronic, mechanical, photocopying, recording, or otherwise, without the prior permission of the publisher.

British Library Cataloguing in Publication Information Available

Library of Congress Cataloging-in-Publication Data

The struggle to constitute and sustain productive orders : Vincent Ostrom's quest to understand human affairs / edited by Mark Sproule-Jones, Barbara Allen, and Filippo Sabetti.
     p. cm.
  Includes bibliographical references and index.
  ISBN-13: 978-0-7391-2627-1 (cloth : alk. paper)
  ISBN-10: 0-7391-2627-X (cloth : alk. paper)
  ISBN-13: 978-0-7391-2628-8 (pbk. : alk. paper)
  ISBN-10: 0-7391-2628-8 (pbk. : alk. paper)
  1. Constitutions. 2. Comparative government. 3. Separation of powers. 4. Democracy. I. Ostrom, Vincent, 1919– II. Sproule-Jones, Mark, 1941– III. Allen, Barbara, 1953– IV. Sabetti, Filippo, 1940–
  JF128.S77 2008
  320.3—dc22   2008009187

Printed in the United States of America

∞™ The paper used in this publication meets the minimum requirements of American National Standard for Information Sciences—Permanence of Paper for Printed Library Materials, ANSI/NISO Z39.48–1992.

To Gayle Higgins
in gratitude for her unfailing energy and talent
in bringing the writings of Vincent Ostrom
to readers on every continent

Contents

Preface ix

PART I: Introduction

1. Normative and Empirical Inquiries into Systems of Governance 3
   Mark Sproule-Jones, Barbara Allen, and Filippo Sabetti

2. Constitutional Foundations for a Theory of System Comparisons 11
   Vincent Ostrom

PART II: Foundations for a Normative Assessment of Governance

3. The Normative and Limiting Conditions in a Polycentric Political Order 29
   Vincent Ostrom

4. Legal Pluralism, Polycentricity, and Faith-Based Organizations in Global Governance 45
   Michael D. McGinnis

5. Challenges to Interreligious Liberative Collective Action between Muslims and Christians 65
   Anas Malik

6. Democratization without Violence: Can Political Order be Achieved through Peaceful Means? 85
   Filippo Sabetti

7. The Man Who Heated Up Economic Discussion with a Stove: Walter Eucken's Method of Institutional Design 111
   Stephan Kuhnert

PART III: Struggles for Polycentric Governance in Diverse Continents

8. Malawi's Lake Chiuta Fisheries: Intelligent Burden-Shedding to Foster Renewable Resources Stewardship 125
   Jamie Thomson

9. From the *Cheyenne Way* to the *Chilean Way* (of Political Reconciliation and Impunity): A Retrospective on Political Architecture, Political Culture, and Institutional Design 151
   Brian Loveman

10. Challenges Facing "State" Building in Burma 183
    Tun Myint

11. American Experience in Metropolitan Governance 201
    Vincent Ostrom

Index 217
Contributors 225

Preface

This is a book that honors the intellectual contributions of Vincent Ostrom to politics and community living. It consists of papers presented at a Conference in Honor of Vincent Ostrom, held at Indiana University in June 2006. It also includes some unpublished papers of Vincent Ostrom.

A second book entitled *The Practice of Constitutional Development: Vincent Ostrom's Quest to Understand Human Affairs* is also being published by Lexington Press. It has a similar content. Both books are designed to reflect the range of thinking of one of America's greatest modern thinkers on governance and the human condition.

Vincent Ostrom's works are founded on the ontological and ethical values of individuals in society. Individual and collective actions are thus advanced in this context. Complex governance must and can be disaggregated in terms of these criteria. These basic assumptions are challenges for both political science and for practical politics. The articles in these two volumes explicate the dilemmas in melding complex individuals with complex governance arrangements.

Vincent Ostrom's works have touched many lives and many studies of governance in America and abroad. He has established an agenda. His readers will find the answers.

PART I
Introduction

1

Normative and Empirical Inquiries into Systems of Governance

Mark Sproule-Jones, Barbara Allen, and Filippo Sabetti

The Struggle to Constitute and Sustain Productive Orders joins its companion volume, *The Practice of Constitutional Development* (Sabetti, Allen, and Sproule-Jones 2008), in examining the intellectual traditions pioneered by Vincent Ostrom. Together, they form a two-book set whose scope is signaled by their common subtitle: *Vincent Ostrom's Quest to Understand Human Affairs*. Common to all of the chapters of the present volume is the thesis that human communities struggle to devise and sustain productive relationships internally among their members and externally with other communities. When successful, they achieve this aim by learning from experiences, reflecting on these experiences, engaging in argumentations and discussions of these experiences and, finally, by developing principles of governance that can be applied and revised over time. These are recurring themes in Ostrom's scholarship.

Vincent Ostrom wrote extensively on the principles of governance advanced in early modern political thought, finding inspiration and catalysis from Thomas Hobbes, David Hume, Adam Smith, James Madison, Alexander Hamilton, and Alexis de Tocqueville. Ostrom extended his work into a close scrutiny of more modern theorists like Walter Bagehot, Woodrow Wilson, and a range of institutional economists like John R. Commons in the United States, Walter Eucken and Paul Hensel in Germany, and Friedrich von Hayek in Austria and England. Out of these thinkers, he discerned two enduring patterns of order. One pattern received its fullest articulation in the works of Hobbes and Wilson. It was the pattern of hierarchical order exemplified in practice in a sovereign Leviathan. The other pattern was polycentric, institutions of variety and redundancies. It was first best understood in the pages of Madison and Hamilton, but it could be found in practice in the self-governing communities of New England towns described by Tocqueville. Between the Leviathan and full polycentricity were a range of alternative systems of order, fashioned by different communities to deal with their physical environments and their particular histories. One could expect different communities to enjoy different epistemic orders or understandings about their governance systems.

With this context of ordered relationships in different patterns for different communities, the stage was set for Ostrom and his students and colleagues to depict the relationships as rules and to develop theoretical and empirical studies of all kinds of rule configurations that make up governance regimes. This volume contains three unpublished essays by Ostrom (chapters 2, 3, and 11) that amplify and develop some of the dilemmas in making comparisons across governance systems. The volume also contains seven original essays by scholars who shared ideas at a conference in honor of Vincent Ostrom at Indiana University in May 2006. The companion volume contains three further unpublished articles by Ostrom and eight more revised conference papers. The theme of the companion volume is on the formulation and revisions of the constitutional rules for governance systems.

Rule Configurations

Vincent Ostrom's early works recognized that patterns of order among individuals, organizations, and communities could take on different configurations depending on context. His work on the California water "industry" in the 1940s and local democracy in Oregon in the 1950s acknowledged that informal rules and social norms could form the central organizing principles for communities—including place-based communities like a town or interest-based communities like water producers, consumers, and regulators. This theme recurs in many of the chapters in this volume. For example, in chapter 9, Brian Loveman describes "the Chilean Way" of reabsorbing governmental and military elites back into the new revolutionary governments over a series of revolutions in two centuries of struggle.

The theme of socially organized rules at the center of communities set the agenda for Ostrom and his students for five decades. First, they directed attention to the possibilities of conflicts between the rules of the authorized governments and the rules or social norms of the populace. Sometimes they could develop into open conflicts, like Chile. Sometimes they spawned silent acquiescence like the post-colonial Burma described by Tun Myint in chapter 10. Sometimes they meshed into a fruitful partnership like the connections between the fishing villages in Lake Malawi and the Malawi national government described by Jamie Thomson in chapter 8.

A second implication of Ostrom's seminal insights on rule configurations was that the socially organized norms or rules could claim co-equal status with the formal rules of a political regime. The term "the state"—meaning the rules of a political (often national) community that established the incentives and the limits of behavior for members of that community—need not be confined to formal political regimes. Authorized governments rarely possessed a monopoly of power, suggesting much greater complexity than Max Weber's aphorism—that "a state is that human community which (successfully) lays claim to the *monopoly of legitimate physical violence* within a certain territory" ([1919] 2007, 310–11; Weber's emphasis)—seemed to suggest to many scholars. In chapter 4, Michael McGinnis provides modern examples of the power of religious communities, thus challenging the assumption in political thought that the government regimes trumped religious organizations in the Reformation and post-Reformation centuries.

A third implication of the rule bases of communities is that of self-governance or, more broadly, that of constitutional choice. Social norms or legal norms could, on occasion, be used as weapons for suppression or conformity. The task is to develop rules about rules through which these possibilities are structured and limited. "Constitutional rules" is the name given to rules about collective choices. In *The Practice of Constitutional Development*, the companion volume to the present text, stress is placed on the design of constitutions and ongoing practices of constitutional choice in constitutional revision. In the present volume, we see how these design issues were gradually conceptualized and accepted as rules about rules.

Third, social norms or even religious-based norms may also be critical metaphysical elements in diverse societies. Communities can accept such norms as realities that drive their epistemic views of governance. In chapter 5, Anas Malik dissects the diverse religious differences within Christian and Muslim thought and some of the implications of these differences for cooperation in plural societies. As we shall see below, Ostrom argues for universalistic standards of evaluation of governance systems that can integrate (at least partially) differing norms of behavior.

Evaluating Rules

Ostrom deepened his understanding of governance by addressing the question of "how can one evaluate governance arrangements?" in a series of books beginning in the 1970s. These included *The Political Theory of a Compound Republic* ([1971] 2008b), *The Intellectual Crisis in American Public Administration* ([1973] 2008a), *The Meaning of American Federalism* (1991), and *The Meaning of Democracy and the Vulnerability of Democracies* (1997).

Ostrom began to answer the question of evaluation by returning to the analysis of the two polar extremes of ordered relationships: the sovereign or hierarchical form, and the polycentric or dispersed form of governance. From Hobbes, he derived the proposition that sovereign power could be subject to natural punishments if sovereign powers were to be exercised with "intemperance," "rashness," "injustice," and other moral failings (Hobbes [1651] 1960, 68). From *The Federalist* (Hamilton, Jay, and Madison [1787–1788] 1941), he derived the proposition that constitutional rules could be developed to make sovereign power subject to enforceable laws of governance. From his examination of the conduct of American federalism, he reasoned that centralized executive powers could jeopardize the rules of constitutional law. These propositions were consistent with the prima facie superiority of polycentric systems.

However, any examination of governance arrangements around the world could reveal both productive and unproductive communities. A political theorist had two major tasks. One was to understand the epistemologies practiced by members of diverse communities—epistemic orders, if you will—that gave meaning to their social norms and rules of behavior. Through these norms, the real nature of governance systems could be revealed. Languages and translations of languages could be misleading.

The second task of the political theorist was to discover whether there were common standards of behavior among different epistemic orders. Was it possible to make interpersonal comparisons of diverse behaviors and hence diverse rules? Working through the intellectual legacies of Hume and Smith, Ostrom found that the so-called "golden rule" whereby "we should do unto others as we would have them do unto us" was a common ethical standard in epistemic orders of diverse communities. In the present volume, Ostrom amplifies on this intellectual quest, and in chapter 6, Filippo Sabetti explicates the political theory of Carlo Cattaneo, the nineteenth-century Italian scholar who had been following similar reasoning in his own quest for a productive governance system.

The golden rule is a normative standard that could be used to make judgments about governance systems. It is, of course, a necessary but not a sufficient condition of evaluation. The agenda of this approach remains open, and students and colleagues are engaged in research that would elaborate on further sufficient conditions. For example, Elinor Ostrom (1990;

E. Ostrom, Gardner, and Walker 1994; National Research Council 2002) conducts foundational research on natural resources and living systems with the objectives (in part) of sustaining ecosystems in the face of potential "tragedies of the commons."

Besides the golden rule as a necessary condition of conduct in diverse epistemic orders, Ostrom also uses the concept of "requisite variety" developed by W. R. Ashby (1956) as a vital condition for understanding and evaluating the design of constitutional systems. Polycentric arrangements with their diversities and redundancies offer potential variety for adaptation, homeostasis, sustainability, and evolution only to the extent that these are valued attributes of governance. Tightly bounded and limited systems conversely may limit, constrain, and inhibit old and newer forms of human activities. There are prima facie grounds for preferring requisite variety in economic and political systems, as Stephan Kuhnert argues in chapter 7 on the economic thought of Walter Eucken. In this case, the concept of requisite variety refers to the relative success of designing complexity into human artifactual systems.

There are thus two conditions in Ostrom's thought that can be used as evaluating principles or methods of inquiry. One is the golden rule, a normative method of inquiry. The other is requisite variety, a positive or empirical method of inquiry. Neither principle constitutes the full set of necessary and sufficient conditions of assessment for scholars and citizens. Both offer, however, an approach or a rule of guidance for evaluating governance systems.

The Paradox of Polycentricity

Open systems of governance that disperse and check concentrated powers are to be valued in both a normative and a positive way. Citizens in such regimes develop their understandings of this kind of system and of its productive status. Their tasks are often to sustain this institutional and epistemic order in the face of challenges that can be beguiling and ambiguous. One such threat comes from the marshalling of executive powers for purposes of national defense. Another kind of threat might appear in the guise of centralizing the governance powers within cities into a single regime of authority purportedly to improve efficient and effective service delivery. A third threat might be found in declining social capital and the weakening resilience of governance regimes that no longer adapt to emerging socioeconomic and ecosystem parameters.

However, citizens may work and enjoy the fruits of their labor in governance systems that do not exhibit the requisite variety of institutional arrangements. They may be content with their own epistemic orderings of governance regimes, and these may contain elements of productive orders. A "Napoleonic" system of administration may be well designed for centralized tasks of governance and provide a paradigm for citizens and political elites to judge all institutional arrangements. The negative consequences, such as rigidity in the face of new circumstances and the consequent incentives for people to develop informal working rules, may be reassessed as the inadequacies of public servants as persons or the rigidities of gerontocracies. Epistemic orders may thus not foster an appropriate "struggle" for improved governance of a functional kind. People may learn to work around formal bureaucratic rules. Even more bleakly, citizens of autocratic regimes may lapse into states of karma without moving intellectually or practically toward self-governing regimes. The struggle to establish productive orders may be thwarted by tradition, loyalty, and lethargy that result from different epistemic orders and the governance systems they support.

In this sense, polycentric governance systems may contain a paradox. They may be seen as productive orders by many residents or by the occasional outside observer like a Tocqueville. Other governance systems may also be viewed as productive by residents of such differently structured systems. There may thus be stable "inadequate" governance systems coexisting with stable adequate ones in both of the two senses of evaluation.

The resolution of this paradox can emerge over time, however. The Holy Roman Empire in the century before the Thirty Years War (1618–1648), as well as decades after the war, provides an example of an open tolerant and diverse governance system (cf. Keating 2001, 11). The current European Union may augur a return to these traditions, after three centuries of distrust and warfare, albeit without some of the necessary linkages between the Commission and Parliament (on the one hand) and individual Europeans (on the other). What societies may need are opportunities to discuss, reflect, and intellectually contest the bases of their epistemic orders and governance regimes. As Anas Malik shrewdly discovers, much Muslim and Christian thought is antithetical to developing the trust through which cooperative games may be played. However, Ostrom is an optimist that the paradox can actually be resolved. The chapters in this volume share that optimism.

References

Ashby, W. R. 1956. *An Introduction to Cybernetics.* New York: Wiley.
Hamilton, Alexander, John Jay, and James Madison [1787–1788] 1941. *The Federalist.* Edward M. Earle, ed. New York: Modern Library.
Hobbes, Thomas. [1651] 1960. *Leviathan or the Matter, Forme and Power of a Commonwealth Ecclesiasticall and Civil.* Michael Oakeshott, ed. Oxford: Blackwell.
Keating, Michael. 2001. *Plurinational Democracy.* New York: Oxford University Press.
National Research Council. 2002. *The Drama of the Commons.* Committee on the Human Dimensions of Global Change. Elinor Ostrom, Thomas Dietz, Nives Dolšak, Paul Stern, Susan Stonich, and Elke Weber, eds. Washington, DC: National Academy Press.
Ostrom, Elinor. 1990. *Governing the Commons: The Evolution of Institutions for Collective Action.* New York: Cambridge University Press.
Ostrom, Elinor, Roy Gardner, and James Walker. 1994. *Rules, Games, and Common-Pool Resources.* Ann Arbor: University of Michigan Press.
Ostrom, Vincent. 1991. *The Meaning of American Federalism: Constituting a Self-Governing Society.* San Francisco, CA: ICS Press.
———. 1997. *The Meaning of Democracy and the Vulnerability of Democracies: A Response to Tocqueville's Challenge.* Ann Arbor: University of Michigan Press.
———. [1973] 2008a. *The Intellectual Crisis in American Public Administration.* 3rd ed. Tuscaloosa: University of Alabama Press.
———. [1971] 2008b. *The Political Theory of a Compound Republic: Designing the American Experiment.* 3rd ed. Lanham, MD: Lexington Books.
Sabetti, Filippo, Barbara Allen, and Mark Sproule-Jones, eds. 2008. *The Practice of Constitutional Development: Vincent Ostrom's Quest to Understand Human Affairs.* Lanham, MD: Lexington Books.
Weber, Max. [1919] 2007. "The Profession and Vocation of Politics." In *Weber: Political Writings,* ed. Peter Lassman and Ronald Speirs, 309–69. Cambridge: Cambridge University Press.

2

Constitutional Foundations for a Theory of System Comparisons

Vincent Ostrom

In attempting to establish the foundations for system comparisons, we confront serious difficulties in achieving commensurability across different systems. These are problems that we must confront, but they cannot have an ultimate resolution by fallible human beings. We have no absolute and final standard by which to judge the merit of the conceptualizations that we use as the basis for organizing ways of life and for thinking about such matters. The best we can do is to recognize the necessity of conceptualizations that we must make in order to undertake good, comparative assessments. So we need to press the frontiers of inquiry in order to deepen our understanding and extend the horizons of our conceptual formulations.

Given the pervasive pattern of incommensurabilities, a conjecture can be advanced that these incommensurabilities are indicative of an order having emerged that cannot appropriately be characterized as a state. Instead, the reiteration of principles of constitutional rule to apply to all enduring forms of human association may yield self-governing societies rather than state-governed societies. In such circumstances, state-centeredness is not an appropriate mode of inquiry with regard to self-governed societies. In light of this conjecture, the inquiry is extended to consider the conceptual and social foundations for the emergence of self-governing societies.

Distinguishing Types of Political Order

Two basic types of order were posited within the political theory of the seventeenth and eighteenth centuries. One is a unitary theory of sovereignty; the other is a theory of constitutional democracy as applicable to federal or compound republics. Hobbes's *Leviathan*, first published in 1651, provides us with the best articulation of a theory of sovereignty. Montesquieu, by contrast, in Book XI on the constitution of liberty, clarifies some of the rudiments of constitutional government. These conceptualizations were further elaborated in the essays written by Alexander Hamilton and James Madison in *The Federalist*. Together, Montesquieu and the American federalists can be viewed as conceptualizing the basis for a system of constitutional government in compound republics where the provisions of constitutions apply as enforceable rules to those who exercise governmental prerogatives (V. Ostrom 1997, [1971] 2008).

For contemporary scholars analyzing social policies, it is essential not to accept a single model of governance as "the only way." One needs to dig deeply into the constitutional foundations of a self-governing society to understand the diversity of institutional arrangements that are needed to address the diversity of problems facing modern societies.

The Sovereign State

Thomas Hobbes in *Leviathan* presents a fully elaborated theory of the sovereign state. Peace as an alternative to war depends upon the maintenance of rule-ordered relationships that provide the foundations for reciprocity in mutually-productive relationships in human societies. Rules to be effective must be enforced: "covenants, without the sword, are but words, and of no strength to secure a man at all" (Hobbes [1651] 1960, 109). For human beings to enjoy the conditions of peace requires a common, unified body of law to which people can have reference in ordering their relationships. A unity of law, in turn, is presumed to depend upon a unity of power in the governance of a commonwealth. A sovereign authority is one that exercises the ultimate authority to govern in a society.

This conception of sovereignty is consistent with a definition of a state as a monopoly of the legitimate use of force in a society. The sovereign in Hobbes's formulation exercises the ultimate authority to govern including supremacy over legislative, executive, and judicial matters and over all means that are necessary to the peace and the security of a commonwealth. A hierarchy of authority relationships culminates in a single center of supreme authority: the sovereign. Hobbes emphasizes that this characteristic of monopoly power, as applied to the authority to govern, is such that authority is unalterable, so far as subjects are concerned, unlimited, and indivisible.

From the attributes of a unitary sovereign, implications follow that pose a serious puzzle for human societies. As the source of law, a sovereign is above the law and cannot be held accountable to a rule of law in the governance of a society. A sovereign is beyond the reach of law. In some fundamental sense, a sovereign can, thus, be regarded potentially as an outlaw in relation to the rest of society. This circumstance gives rise to extraordinary opportunities for sovereigns, or those who act on their behalf, to use instruments of coercion and fashion rules of law so as to dominate the allocation of values in a society. Instruments of government, then, afford opportunities for a few to exploit the many.

Hobbes's concluding warning about the "natural punishments" that will be endured by a sovereign who fails to abide by the fundamental moral precepts that are necessary to peace in human societies is recognition of this difficulty in his theory of sovereignty: "And hereby it comes to pass, that intemperance is naturally punished with diseases; rashness, with mischances; injustice, with the violence of enemies; pride, with ruin; cowardice, with oppression; negligent government of princes, with rebellion; and rebellion, with slaughter" (Hobbes [1651] 1960, 241).

A necessary condition for Hobbes's sovereign to obtain peace and concord in the governance of a commonwealth is a sufficient measure of enlightenment and benevolence to conform to the moral precepts of peace that are grounded in the golden rule: Do not that to another, which thou wouldst not have done to thyself. While a sovereign is not accountable to other human beings, he is accountable to that which "men call God" (Hobbes [1651] 1960, 68).

Constitutional Government

Hobbes recognized that three different forms of government might exist. A monarchy is the form where one person is sovereign; an aristocracy when an assembly of a few exercise the sovereign prerogatives of governance; and a democracy where an assembly of all citizens governs society. The last alternative provides the basis for conceptualizing a system of constitutional government.

When citizens rule by assembly, two sets of rules are necessary. One set applies to the conduct of government—to the assembly itself; the other set applies to the other exigencies of life that occur outside an assembly. The former is constitutional; the latter, ordinary law. Rules of assembly are necessary conditions for there to exist rule by assembly. Citizens function in the process of government; but citizens are also subject to the rules that they as citizens adopt in assembly to order their way of life outside the assembly. Citizens are both rulers and subjects who act in accordance with the rules they establish for themselves. This principle might be generalized where individuals are both rulers and subjects in all social units. Such a system of governance might yield a self-governing society in contrast to a state-governed society.

The problem of how to make constitutional law enforceable in relation to those who exercise the prerogatives of government depends in a democracy upon placing limits upon all exercises of authority so that no one exercises unlimited authority. Two types of provisions are necessary. One pertains to the basic constitutional authority of citizens and persons and correlative limits upon the authority of government. The other pertains to a distribution of powers that creates a division of labor in the exercise of rule-making, rule-applying, and rule-enforcing functions of government. These types of provisions imply that law pertains to an open public realm (*res publica*) where the standards set in law can be publicly knowable by those who use these same standards in ordering their own conduct and by those who perform judicial and executive functions in applying and enforcing standards of law.

When principles of governance consistent with maintaining the enforceability of constitutional law are reiterated to apply to diverse, overlapping, and concurrent associations and communities to form multiple units of government in a compound system of republics, we can imagine circumstances where all authority is subject to limits. The basic integrity of constitutional government then turns upon the willingness of citizens to challenge any improper discharge of authority by those who exercise the prerogatives of government.

A system of governance grounded in principles of constitutional rule is one that manifests equilibrating tendencies where lawful conduct occurs within the bounds established by potential limits and veto capabilities exercised by diverse instrumentalities of government. The basic design principle uses "power . . . to check power," as Montesquieu has expressed the concept in Book XI in *The Spirit of the Laws* ([1748] 1966, 200), or "opposite and rival interests," as Madison expressed much the same concept in Federalist 51 ([1787–1788] 1941, 337). Something called *government* occurs in an open interpersonal, interorganizational, and intergovernmental milieu. The emphasis is upon sharing power with others rather than exercising power over others.

The Problem of Incommensurabilities and Emergent Orders

This brief allusion to these two different approaches to the organization of systems of governance has been more fully elaborated elsewhere (e.g., V. Ostrom

1997, [1971] 2008). These two approaches to governance organizations are at least as divergent in their basic characteristics as exists between a market economy and a centrally-administered economy. We now confront a difficult problem. We recognize that differences exist. How do we identify those differences? How do those differences enter into some form of calculation where we can achieve some measures of commensurability in making comparative assessments? Can we, for example, make direct straightforward comparisons between the government of India and the government of the United States of America, both of which are considered federal systems of government?

A sovereign exercises unlimited authority; officials in a system of constitutional government exercise limited authority. The peace and concord of Hobbes's commonwealth depends upon an obedience of subjects and upon a level of enlightenment by those who exercise sovereign authority so as to avoid what Hobbes refers to as the natural punishments. Residual levels of enlightenment are presumed to reside with citizens of constitutional republics so that officials are held accountable to appropriate standards of performance. Furthermore, when problems of institutional weakness and institutional failures arise, appropriate methods are required to identify the potential sources of difficulty and to institute appropriate changes in constitutional arrangements. Constitutional democratic republics, as Montesquieu emphasized, depend upon a sufficient level of enlightenment so that each individual is presumed to be first his or her own governor. This implies the existence of substantial self-governing capabilities on the part of each individual.

Wherever governance is achieved through multiple instrumentalities of government and among numerous units of government, equilibrating tendencies are presumed to exist among the diverse structural components, each of which is governed by rules of law subject to limits inherent in the veto positions exercised by others. Any system of equilibrating structures acquires operational characteristics from the way that the parts interact with one another rather than by the dominance of one part over all of the other parts. In an equilibrating system, the parts contribute to a systemic order that has emergent properties that are distinguishable from the parts. In a system of dominance, the dominating part, presumably, imparts an essential element of order to all other parts of the system by virtue of its domination and their subordination.

Such considerations led Tocqueville in *Democracy in America* ([1835–1840] 1945) to indicate that the system of constitutional rule that was used in the design of that system of governance yielded a political system of a distinct kind. He characterized three types of political order. One is where a state rules over society. Another is where "the ruling force is divided, being partly within and partly without the ranks of the people." The third, which he identified with American democracy, is one where "society governs itself for itself" (Tocqueville, I:57).

If we follow Tocqueville's conceptualization, we then have two basically different types that parallel the distinctions between Hobbes's theory of sovereignty and a theory of constitutional rule reiterated to apply to all associations in a society. Tocqueville's second category has elements of both other types: "the ruling force, being partly within and partly without the ranks of the people." This clue affords some measure of commensurability with regard to the forms of political order that occur among the nations of Western Europe.

An important issue then is whether the intermediate type where "the ruling force is divided, being partly within and partly without the ranks of the people," is an intermediate form manifesting emergent properties that have potentials of moving from a state-governed society to a self-governing society and if stable conditions cannot be achieved of moving again to a state-governed society. Such patterns of oscillation might occur amid historical exigencies of accident and force. Under such circumstances, the pulling and hauling of social forces might be expected to manifest cyclicity where history has strong tendencies to repeat itself, and where human beings cannot achieve an ordered way of life grounded in reflection, discussion, and choice.

An essential core in any system of government can be identified with an exercise of executive authority where authority to command prevails. Whenever a division of labor occurs in the exercise of governmental authority so that distinguishable judicial and legislative instrumentalities have an independent existence outside the executive apparatus, some degree of separation of powers can then be identified. To have separately identifiable legislative, executive, and judicial instrumentalities of government is to have a separation of powers articulated with a commensurate division of labor.

How these instrumentalities become linked to one another is an important consideration. Thus, the place of a cabinet in a parliamentary system of governance is an important link, especially in identifying the relationship of legislative to executive instrumentalities. But any such linkages simultaneously involve relationships to electoral processes and judicial processes where larger communities of people monitor events by an autonomous testing of the reality of their experience with one another. Once a division of labor is firmly institutionalized within institutions of governance, simple doctrines of supremacy will no longer suffice to explain the way that these diverse institutions are linked to one another.

The relationship of the institutions of a central government to the ranks of the people may not be confined to the election of representative officials who function in a central government. An important feature of European political thought has been its emphasis upon some significant measure of autonomy on the part of institutions that are constitutive of society as distinguished from the state. A significant measure of self-governing or self-administering capabilities is presumed within the confines of family, church, economic, commercial, and communal relationships apart from the institutions of the central government. These relationships may be grounded in broad latitudes of discretion inherent in code law adjudicable in private-law jurisprudence as contrasted to public-law jurisprudence. When such distinctions are given structural substance, authority is complexly differentiated in the governance of society. Latitude then exists for sufficient diversity to allow for different sources of influence to be articulated in the rules that apply to discrete circumstances.

We can then imagine the possibility that discrete political orders might exist along some continuum. One extreme is crudely equivalent to Hobbes's theory of sovereignty with an unlimited, indivisible, and absolute sovereign that rules over society. The other extreme is a constitutional system that interposes limits upon the exercise of governmental authority to such an extent that a society might be aptly characterized as a self-governing society. Switzerland might be viewed as a society that manifests strong self-governing capabilities, while France, until recently, continues to articulate a theory of public jurisprudence that justifies broad latitudes of state tutelage where people are presumed, in the context of public and communal affairs, to be wards of the state.

The degree of ordering by reference to state authority may be treated as a variable ranging from absolute states to stateless, self-governing societies. As soon as we recognize this possibility, we are then confronted with a further possibility. Stateless societies may become numerous enough to allow for diverse possibilities. The attribute of statelessness may be viewed as a step-function that opens up a new range of possibilities for human development. New forms of political order and new courses of cultural development in human civilization may emerge from societies that previously were thought to be dominated by absolutism in the exercise of state authority.

Forms of order may thus possess emergent characteristics that, when reiterated and amplified, may become the basis for new patterns of order. Life is itself a form of order that is self-reproducing. This form of order has been subject to reiteration and amplification, by allowing variation and selection to occur in different self-reproducing species to yield a great variety of life forms. Emergent properties characteristic of animals, as distinguished from plants, have yielded emergent capabilities for learning. When learning is again amplified through vocalization, communication, and language, the emergent properties of cultural evolution and human civilization occur.

Since the theoretical foundations for the constitution of what might be designated as self-governing societies was reasonably well-clarified by the end of the eighteenth century, we have access to interesting demonstrations by different political analysts of the difficulties in construing the nature of the political orders that they sought to explain. Walter Bagehot's *The English Constitution* ([1865–1867] 1964), for example, is a marked contrast to Tocqueville's *Democracy in America*. These two analysts show surprisingly few points of commensurability in the inquiries that they offer to their readers. Bagehot is exclusively preoccupied with the institutions of central government. Tocqueville devotes one chapter in a two-volume work to the institutions of American national government. Tocqueville places strong emphasis upon the institutions of local government.

In highlighting the relative importance of institutional arrangements, Bagehot sees the cabinet as the key institution that ties the English constitution into a unified whole. Tocqueville, by contrast, identified the federal form of government, township institutions, and the judiciary as the most important institutions contributing to the viability of American democracy. Tocqueville considered customs, as habits of the hearts and minds of the American people, to be of even more fundamental importance than the institution of government per se in the shaping of a democratic society (Allen 2005). Indeed, he characterizes religion as "the first of their political institutions" even though "[r]eligion in America takes no direct part in the government of society" (Tocqueville [1835–1840] 1945, I:305). Such a statement would be incoherent if "political institutions" were equivalent to "governments."

The problem of incommensurabilities in the studies offered by Bagehot and Tocqueville are not resolved by differences inherent in the American and English constitutional systems. Woodrow Wilson, working with the same framework used by Bagehot, provides us in *Congressional Government* ([1885] 1956) with an American counterpart of *The English Constitution*. Congress and its committees are viewed by Wilson as the key center of power in the operation of American government.

Conceptual and Social Foundations for the Emergence of Self-Governing Societies

Tocqueville, in chapter 2 of *Democracy in America*, addresses his readers directly to indicate: "The readers of this book will find in the present chapter the germ of all that is to follow and the key to almost the whole work" ([1835–1840] 1945, I:28).

The chapter that is "the germ of all that is to follow" is about the historical origins of the Anglo-Americans. The key resides in the religious beliefs and practices of the Puritans: "Puritanism was not merely a religious doctrine, but corresponded in many points with the most absolute democratic and republican theories" (Tocqueville [1835–1840] 1945, 32). They relied upon the Judaic concept of covenant to constitute a church organized as self-governing congregations and civil communities as self-governing republics. Each town was organized as a republic governed by an assembly of citizens. The town was organized before the county, the county before the state, and the state before the federal union. This tradition of self-governance characterized by Tocqueville as the sovereignty of the people became "the law of laws" (Tocqueville, 56), that is, the constitutive principle used to create a system of governance.

Something more than the human condition as genetically determined is required for the development of self-governing societies. Such societies are, instead, grounded in long-term cultural achievements that provide the basis for shared communities of understanding, open patterns of discourse, and ways of associating with one another. Self-governing societies depend upon a consensual basis for ordering relationships in accordance with general rules of law. This consensual basis forms "the law of laws," to use Tocqueville's expression. Where do we turn to find the emergence of ideas and patterns of organization that offered potentials for the emergence of self-governing societies among the peoples of Europe?

A Common Method of Normative Inquiry

A general system of law is grounded in norms, standards, or criteria of choice that distinguish between that which is forbidden as against that which is permitted and that which is required. Law in self-governing societies is not simply a matter of command and obedience. Rather, standards are set and used by people in ordering their relationships with one another (Gellar 2005). Since the use of standards to order relationships is itself a matter of choice, the rule-ruler-ruled relationship also implies that such standards need to be enforced. Temptations would exist for some to prey upon others if rules of law were not enforced. The proper application of standards both by users and enforcers of law requires impartial standards of judgments that maintain the publicness of law. The problem then is how to make interpersonal comparisons to achieve knowable standards, norms, or criteria of choice for distinguishing that which is permitted from that which is forbidden or required.

Gratian identified such a method when he indicated, as Tierney observes, that "a principal foundation of all law (is) the timeless principle that we should do unto others as we would have them do unto us" (1982, 13). This is one version of the so-called golden rule that is at the core of religious teachings in the Judaic-Christian tradition, and at the core of other moral teachings as well. The reference to all law, properly conceived, does not necessarily apply to all systems of social order. There may be other patterns of order that rely more upon command and obedience than upon general standards or norms for the ordering of human relationships. Gratian's generalization stands as the fundamental principle for constituting self-governing communities of relationships in human societies.

The golden rule, as a basic moral precept, is surprisingly devoid of moral content. Instead, the golden rule can better be conceived as a method of normative inquiry that enables human beings to come to a commonly shared understanding about the meaning of value terms used as norms or criteria of choice. When viewed as a method of normative inquiry, the golden rule is at the foundation of major intellectual efforts in the seventeenth and eighteenth centuries to develop a theory of sovereignty and a theory of constitutional rule.

The method of the golden rule taps a level of human emotional feeling that David Hume and Adam Smith identify with sympathy or fellow feeling. This is the foundation for Smith's *The Theory of Moral Sentiments* ([1759] n.d.) and what Hume (1948, 252) refers to as his "theory concerning the origin of morals." Methods of making interpersonal comparison form a basis for deriving an approximate understanding of norms that can be used for ordering relationships among human beings.

Such a method, if relied upon by members of a society, shapes the habits of the heart and mind as people think and act with reference to one another. It is not the letter of the law that is of essential importance but the meaning of the standards and criteria of choice that stand behind the letter of the law. These standards cannot be purely objective if we mean by objective to have reference only to the material objects. There are, instead, ways of making interpersonal comparisons for establishing general criteria for distinguishing right from wrong, justice from injustice, and all of the other standards that get built into a system of law. Where disagreement prevails, human beings then have the potential for communicating with one another about the appropriateness of norms or standards and what these imply.

The golden rule might then be considered as a "law of laws," and the method of normative inquiry grounded in the golden rule might also be viewed as a "road to knowledge" that "leads man to civil freedom" (Tocqueville [1835–1840] 1945, I:41). It is a method where human beings taking the perspective of others, and aspiring to impartiality, might formulate general rules to which each would agree to be bound in ordering their relationships with one another. These same standards might variously be used in setting rules, acting in accordance with rules, adjudicating rules, enforcing rules, and evaluating the conduct achieved by reference to rules.

The Problem of Positive Inquiry

The golden rule, as elaborated in a method of normative inquiry, provides a foundation for formulating rules, acting in accordance with rules, adjudicating disputes over rules, enforcing rules, and for evaluating performance in accordance with rule-ordered arrangements. Considerations pertaining to norms and their place in the modal logic of rules must, however, always be juxtaposed to the logic of problematical situations within which human beings typically find themselves. At a minimum, prototypical situations that occur in all human societies would have reference to: (1) exchange relationships; (2) teamwork, including the ordering of teams of teams; (3) the use and management of common-pool (property) resources and facilities; (4) the provision of goods subject to collective use (consumption); (5) conflict and conflict resolution; and (6) rule-ruler-ruled relationships. Understanding the logic of situations is important because the structure of situations and the incentives that motivate human conduct combine to create cognitive puzzles for those who find themselves in such situations.

The logic of situations—a combination of structures and incentives—may be counterintentional and counterintuitive. Intentions are not always sufficient to yield patterns of order consistent with results that human beings wish to achieve. The counterintuitive character of the situations in which human beings find themselves means that human perception and judgment about the implications that follow from patterns of order in human society may be subject to serious error. Potential for error should be accompanied by a substantial measure of modesty on the part of those who eat fruit from the tree of knowledge. Cautious attention needs to be given to procedures and processes that facilitate methods of inquiry where conflicting conjectures can be used to correct errors and enlighten further inquiry.

Counterintentionality and counterintuitivity pervade many aspects of human social relationships. An awareness of their existence means that human beings can become aware of potential traps that are inherent in the structure of typical situations and find ways for reordering those situations by modifying rules that help to restructure those situations.

The discrepancy between intentionality and the effects that occur in Hobbes's state of nature creates a puzzle that leads Hobbes to contemplate an alternative to war. His response is to formulate a series of rules that, if acted upon, would yield peace. These rules are his so-called laws of nature. It is these rules that are grounded in the golden rule as a method of normative inquiry. Having formulated a set of rules that would yield peace rather than war, Hobbes, however, warns his reader that problems still exist. Those problems pertain to making rules binding in human relationships. Peace may be possible, but the man of peace may simply make himself the prey of others, contrary to his intentions, if he acts in conformity to the rules of peace while others pursue temptations of availing themselves of whatever opportunities may be available.

The logic of the Prisoner's Dilemma and the Commons Problem indicates how individuals who seek their best advantage are motivated to pursue strategies that leave them worse off rather than better off. Human beings in many different societies with diverse cultural traditions have devised rule-ordered relationships so as to constrain the temptation strategies that yield tragedies of the commons and instead develop cooperative methods for productively managing common-pool resource systems and facilities. Competitive games that yield perverse results in relation to the common-pool resources can be transformed by an appropriate modification in rules to yield mutually productive relationships (E. Ostrom 1990, 2005).

Human activity is always mediated in relation to material conditions of life. Those conditions are also subject to transformations that affect human welfare. Knowledge of how to achieve such transformations depends upon the use of methods that are appropriate to yield desired effects. W. R. Ashby (1956) formulated in his law of requisite variety a principle that applies to regulative efforts inherent in human activity. Ashby's law of requisite variety was formulated as a fundamental law of cybernetics. This law is potentially relevant to all forms of regulation and adaptation.

Regulation and adaptation can be achieved only when regulatory or adaptive arrangements have access to as much variety as there is variety in the conditions that are subject to regulatory or adaptive efforts. To realize specified effects, there must exist as much variety in the strategies available as there is variety in the conditions that obtain. Those variables not subject to regulation remain sources of potential disturbance. If the range of regulatory effort is limited, disturbances beyond that range remain.

The law of requisite variety addresses regulatory efforts in light of the potential of affecting transformations in causal or quasi-causal relationships so as to achieve preferred states as against what would have occurred in the absence of human intervention. The law of requisite variety applies, thus, to all forms of artisanship and human productive efforts to achieve what economists might broadly conceive as goods defined as preferred events. The law of requisite variety implies that relationships of a causal and quasi-causal nature must be dealt with knowledgeably and on their own terms. Nature and the laws of nature that apply to the material and biological realms require knowledgeable and respectful efforts by human beings if human beings are to make constructive uses of the opportunities available to them.

The law of requisite variety becomes especially important in making the tie between universal rules that apply to the material and biological realms and the time-and-place exigencies that exist in the discrete world of human experience. Principles of hydrology and hydraulic engineering, for example, must always be applied to the unique characteristics of any particular hydrological system to be developed and managed as a water resource and supply system. The degree of regulation and utilization achieved for multiple uses depends upon the discrete application of the law of requisite variety to the characteristics of discrete hydrological systems and the pattern of uses to be made.

Uniform procedures applied across diverse ecological systems will not achieve the requisite variety that is necessary for more effective, rather than less effective, regulation. Modern societies drawing upon more extended bodies of knowledge and technological possibilities to yield greater productive potential require a great deal of organized complexity in making best use of adaptive potentials, or productive opportunities. Uniform measures do not suffice. Instead, increasing reliance upon self-organizing capabilities among the great diversity of productive-consumptive efforts and rule-ordered relationships is required in a modern society.

Ashby's law of requisite variety can thus be used as a methodological principle to address problems pertaining to the constitution of order in human societies. Human societies would seem to require recourse to increasing patterns of complexification as the horizons of human knowledge are extended to include reference to increasing productive potentials involving diverse environmental and cultural exigencies. Increasing patterns of complexification can be achieved so long as commensurate self-organizing and self-governing capabilities are also achieved.

The Challenge

Thus, two basic methodological foundations address patterns of order in human societies that are amenable to self-organizing, self-administering, or self-governing capabilities. The *law of laws* for calculating normative consideration is the golden rule. The *law of laws* for positive analysis is Ashby's law of requisite variety.

These, in turn, are set within cosmological and epistemological assumptions that presume that a universe exists in which universal rules apply to that universal order. Universal rules are subject to tests of coherence so as to yield a basic unity of knowledge. Aspects of this order may manifest patterns of adaptation subject to regulative, interactive patterns of relationships so that the universe is not a simple machine working upon mechanical cause and effect (one-one) relationships but manifests an openness to emergent properties in orders that include one-many and many-one relationships. One-many relationships imply potential variety; many-one relationships imply selection. Choice is a form of selection. Systems capable of generating variety and selecting from that potential variety by the use of appropriate methods and criteria of choice are adaptive systems capable of generating emergent properties in an evolving system of order. Systems of order grounded in combinations of one-many and many-one relationships yield greater developmental potentials than those characterized by one-one relationships.

The structure of opportunities in an emergent system of order is always tied to time-and-place exigencies that apply to the here and now. Patterns of social order, then, always exist "in-between" the universals as manifestations of an eternal order and the time-and-place exigencies in which human beings live their lives, order their relations with others, and pursue opportunities that are available to them. This condition of being "in-between" means that the human beings' aspiration to know that which is eternal can never fully be achieved. Humans can, however, draw upon one another's capabilities to achieve error-correcting capabilities by listening to and being informed by contestable arguments and by engaging in practical experiments to test the warrantability of theoretical conceptualizations.

Human beings can draw upon such potentials to become self-organizing and self-governing creatures subject to the constraints implied by both a golden rule and a law of requisite variety. Significant self-organizing, self-administering, and self-governing capabilities must exist for there to be tens or hundreds of millions of organized social units functioning autonomously from one another in societies such as Italy, China, and the United States. If these principles can be extended, as James Madison suggested, to the supreme offices of the state, we can begin to imagine possibilities that self-governing, rather than state-governed, societies can exist.

To achieve such a possibility, one further condition would need to be met. Structures of rule-ordered relationships would need to be extended to communities of relationships that reach beyond the boundaries of nation-states. These are the frontiers of human association that are being explored and debated in the European Community. Whether or not the European peoples can devise complex configurations of order sufficient to meet the requirements of the method of normative inquiry inherent in the golden rule and the positive contingencies inherent in the law of requisite variety remains to be seen.

Bibliographical Note

An earlier version of this chapter was presented at the Radein Seminar, Radein, Italy, February 14–25, 1987. A revised version was published in 2006 as "Fondamenti costituzionali per una teoria delle comparazioni tra sistemi" (Constitutional Foundations for a Theory of System Comparisons), *La Rivista delle Politiche Sociali* (Italian Journal of Social Policy), no. 2, pp. 127–43.

References

Allen, Barbara. 2005. *Tocqueville, Covenant, and the Democratic Revolution: Harmonizing Earth with Heaven.* Lanham, MD: Lexington Books.
Ashby, W. Ross. 1956. *An Introduction to Cybernetics.* New York: John Wiley.
Bagehot, Walter. [1865–1867] 1964. *The English Constitution.* R. H. S. Crossman, ed. London: C. A. Watts.
Gellar, Sheldon. 2005. *Democracy in Senegal: Tocquevillian Analytics in Africa.* New York: Palgrave Macmillan.
Hamilton, Alexander, John Jay, and James Madison. [1787–1788] 1941. *The Federalist.* Edward M. Earle, ed. New York: Modern Library.
Hobbes, Thomas. [1651] 1960. *Leviathan or the Matter, Forme and Power of a Commonwealth Ecclesiasticall and Civil.* Michael Oakeshott, ed. Oxford: Basil Blackwell.
Hume, David. 1948. *Hume's Moral and Political Philosophy.* Henry D. Aiken, ed. New York: Hafner.

Montesquieu, Charles-Louis de Secondat, baron de. [1748] 1966. *The Spirit of the Laws*. New York: Hafner.

Ostrom, Elinor. 1990. *Governing the Commons: The Evolution of Institutions for Collective Action*. New York: Cambridge University Press.

———. 2005. *Understanding Institutional Diversity*. Princeton, NJ: Princeton University Press.

Ostrom, Vincent. 1997. *The Meaning of Democracy and the Vulnerability of Democracies: A Response to Tocqueville's Challenge*. Ann Arbor: University of Michigan Press.

———. [1971] 2008. *The Political Theory of a Compound Republic: Designing the American Experiment*. 3rd ed. Lanham, MD: Lexington Books.

Smith, Adam. [1759] n.d. *The Theory of Moral Sentiments*. Indianapolis, IN: Liberty Classics.

Tierney, Brian. 1982. *Religion, Law and the Growth of Constitutional Thought, 1150–1650*. Cambridge: Cambridge University Press.

Tocqueville, Alexis de. [1835–1840] 1945. *Democracy in America*. 2 vols. Phillips Bradley, ed. New York: Alfred A. Knopf.

Wilson, Woodrow. [1885] 1956. *Congressional Government: A Study in American Politics*. New York: Meridian Books.

# PART II
Foundations for a Normative Assessment of Governance

3

The Normative and Limiting Conditions in a Polycentric Political Order

Vincent Ostrom

In exploring the interorganizational level of analysis, an issue of some importance is the conditions that bound or limit the patterns of interorganizational relationships. If there were no limiting conditions among organizations, we might anticipate that interorganizational relationships would be dominated by patterns of conflict that Boulding (1963) has elaborated in his essay on "Towards a Pure Theory of Threat Systems." The complete absence of limiting conditions both within and among organizations might be expected to yield the conditions that Hobbes ([1651] 1960) anticipated in his parable of man in a state of nature. We would expect conflict to escalate to a point where a struggle for dominance would foreclose mutually productive relationships.

To speak of limiting conditions requires one to address the central issue in political theory of how order is maintained in human relationships. In human societies, language is used to order relationships with reference to rules. Since rules are not self-formulating, self-applying, nor self-enforcing, it becomes necessary for human beings in creating ordered social relationships to rely upon some who exercise the extraordinary prerogatives of formulating, applying, and enforcing rules. Rules imply both rulers and ruled.

The exigencies of rule introduce radical inequalities into human societies. Those who exercise the prerogatives of rule have access to the legitimate use of coercive sanctions to enforce performance in accordance with the requirements of rules. An opportunity then exists for those who exercise the prerogatives of rule to dominate the allocation of values in a society and to exploit others to the advantage of those who rule. The fundamental class structure in human societies arises from the organization of rule with a ruling class exercising dominance over a subject class (i.e., those who are subject to rules).

The traditional theory of sovereignty does no more than to justify rulership as a necessary condition for the maintenance of order in human relationships. Since both the coherence of a system of law and the unity of a commonwealth are assumed to be derived from the existence of a single source of authority that exercises the ultimate prerogatives of rulership, the traditional theory of sovereignty holds that those who exercise such authority are the source of law. As such, they are above the law and cannot be held accountable to law. There comes a point where limiting conditions do not prevail in the traditional theory of sovereignty; the exercise of sovereign prerogative is unlimited. All exercises of subordinate authority are subject to limits, but the ultimate center of authority that interposes those limits of rule upon subordinate authorities is itself unlimited in its exercise of prerogative.

The traditional theory of sovereignty does recognize the existence of normative conditions that are essential to the maintenance of productive relationships in human societies. However, these normative conditions are viewed as elements of an eternal order where those who exercise sovereign prerogative are accountable only in their recognition of that eternal order. They are not accountable to their fellow human beings. Others are responsible to those who exercise sovereign prerogatives, but sovereigns have no legal or political responsibility to others. Their only responsibility is to God, and they suffer the natural punishment that follows from the neglect of God's law as those rules that form the basis for an eternal order in human relationships.

The traditional theory of sovereignty implies a monocentric order. There is a single center of authority that exercises ultimate authority over the governance of a society as a whole. All other relationships are subordinate to that authority. A polycentric political order, by contrast, is one that has recourse to many different centers of authority that exercise the prerogatives of government and where no single center of authority is dominant over the rest. Thus, the theoretical problems of specifying the normative and limiting conditions that apply to a polycentric order are quite different than those that apply to a unitary state as a monocentric order. In the case of a polycentric order, the relationships that apply to the governance of interorganizational arrangements are themselves multiorganizational in nature.

In specifying the normative and limiting conditions of a polycentric order, I shall first indicate the essential design characteristics that apply to such a political system. Second, I shall explore the normative conditions that might apply to such a system. Third, I shall indicate how structural conditions can be used to establish limits so that no exercise of governmental authority is unlimited. Finally, I shall indicate how these normative and limiting conditions provide a milieu within which interorganizational arrangements are free to develop within a public economy.

The Essential Design Characteristics of a Polycentric Order

The basic question confronting human beings is whether they are forever destined to bear the yoke of rulership and must passively submit to domination by others or whether they are capable of creating and participating in systems of government of their own making. The issue is a perplexing one because a theory of sovereignty, as Hobbes correctly emphasizes, implies that those who rule are not accountable to their subjects and subjects owe obedience to their rulers if order and well-being are to be realized in human societies. Political relationships are basically asymmetrical in nature (Greene 1978).

The possibility that human beings are capable of creating and participating in a government of their own making depends upon the organization of government itself in accordance with rules of law. Such a possibility would require that all exercise of governmental authority be limited and that no one center of authority be capable of exercising unlimited authority. This implies that no single center of authority be permitted to dominate the rest and that all centers of authority be limited by prerogatives that can be exercised by others.

Such conditions imply that authority can be distributed among diverse decision structures for any community of interest that human beings share in common and that authority can be distributed among multiple communities of interest. No single unit of government need exercise unlimited authority. Conflict arising from interdependent interests might be resolved by attaining political solutions to enable human beings to establish reciprocity among interdependent interests through the articulation of a perceived community of interest as the basis for collective organization. An extended circle of symmetrical relationships is then possible within a political community.

A distribution of authority among diverse decision structures in any one community of interest is a means of sharing power in the exercise of collective authority. Limits can be specified as veto points; but within those limits of reciprocal veto points, power is shared by all of those who have a voice in the taking of collective action.

The design of a polycentric order implies that the exercise of governmental prerogative can be subject to law so that no one is above the law and everyone is subject to the constraint of lawful authority. But such a possibility depends upon conditions that must be met before such a possibility can be realized. The first of these conditions is a shared community of understanding about basic normative and explanatory considerations. The second is the articulation of an appropriate set of instrumental conditions that permit the realization of the design objectives.

Normative Conditions

A basic presupposition in economic theory is that an interpersonal comparison of utility is not possible. People cannot read each other's minds and thus know each other's preference for specific goods, objects, or relationships. The best that can be done under this presupposition is to provide people with an opportunity to express their preferences through various types of institutional arrangements such as market structures or voting arrangements. The Arrow (1951) paradox, or impossibility theorem, derives from this and the related presumption that human beings have diverse preferences. No known arrangement exists for attaining a consistent ordering of preferences under assumptions that commonly are believed to apply in democratic societies.

An alternative approach has been suggested by Hobbes where he accepts the presupposition that human beings cannot know what preferences others have for particular things that are the object of their preferences. He then argues that there is, however, a basic "similitude of thoughts and passions" that characterizes all human beings in terms of how individuals think and feel. In this sense, human beings can make interpersonal comparisons about how human beings think and how they express their feelings even though they cannot know what they think or what feelings or passions are related to what particular objects or relationships.

Hobbes's position presumes certain characteristics that are shared in common by all human beings and, thus, are universal among human beings. By coming to know oneself and how one thinks and feels, one can come to understand others and how they think and feel without presuming to know *what* others are thinking and feeling. Arrangements are still needed for human beings to articulate their own thoughts and preferences as they relate to one another.

We might further assume that human beings who share a similitude of thoughts and passions characteristic of all mankind find themselves in circumstances where they exist among a community of individuals who use a common language to communicate with one another. Communication built upon a common genetic endowment permits human beings to reach a shared understanding about basic criteria of choice in ordering their relationships with one another. In such circumstances, human beings can be expected to come to a shared understanding for distinguishing what is right from wrong and forming a tentative basis for moral judgment.

This still leaves secure the presumption that human beings cannot read one another's preferences for particular objects or relationships but opens the possibility that human beings can apply a general classification in distinguishing between right and wrong. The capacity to distinguish right from wrong, conceding many ambiguities, is fundamental to human social relationships. Individuals could not be responsible for their own actions if they were incapable of distinguishing right from wrong. Guilt in criminal jurisprudence is without meaning unless there is some commonly agreed ground for distinguishing right from wrong. An individual who cannot distinguish right from wrong is presumed to be incompetent to make his or her own decisions. All individuals who are assumed to be competent to make their own decisions are presumed to distinguish right from wrong as a basis for moral judgment.

These circumstances imply a criterion of choice that serves as a foundation for an interpersonal comparison of values that is of fundamental importance in the organization of human societies. It can be argued that such standards are idiosyncratic among particular societies and do not hold across all human societies. Such unquestionably is the case, but this does not foreclose the possibilities that human beings might draw upon their basic similitude of thoughts and passions to engage in communication with one another about the appropriate grounds for human community and thus strive for a more universal understanding of the human condition and the criteria of choice that might apply to the human community in the most universal sense.

In assuming that there is a similitude of thoughts and passions characteristic of all mankind, we imply that there are elements of human nature that are common to all mankind. If human beings have the potential for understanding what is universal among human beings, they also have the potential for appreciating the criteria that are appropriate to ordering relationships with one another. Criteria based upon that which is universal among human beings presumably would be consistent with an eternal order. If we choose to call that eternal order "God," as Hobbes does, then human beings have the possibility of grounding their relationships with one another upon mutual consent and in conformity to their understanding of the eternal. Human beings might then aspire to governing themselves by covenanting with one another under terms and conditions that are consistent with an eternal order. A covenantal order based upon a common understanding and agreement would permit human beings to hold one another accountable to common standards of propriety, justice, and truth. What is good for an individual should be consistent with what is good for others. Human communities might then exist under conditions where individuals could maintain reciprocity with one another in mutually productive relationships.

This task of conceptualizing the grounds for human community is greatly confounded by the circumstance that the realization of a joint good of advantage to a community of individuals is the subject of a Faustian bargain where potential use of instruments of evil is necessary to the common good. The Faustian bargain inherent in all human societies is best symbolized by the sword of justice. To maintain a system of law requires potential recourse to coercive sanctions to enforce law and thus maintain ordered social relationships bounded by law. The imposition of punishment is in the nature of an evil even though that evil is done to maintain a commonly accepted understanding of what is right and wrong.

The use of instruments of evil to do good is the basic condition that applies in the exercise of governmental prerogatives. It is not enough to know what is right in the sense of what is broadly conceived to be good, but it is necessary to know when the use of instruments of evil is right in order to realize some greater good. This, of course, is compounded by the circumstance that those who can legitimately use instruments of evil to do good have access to powerful tools to dominate the allocation of values in a society and exploit others.

It is this potential that has enabled human beings to create political artifacts that then facilitate the systematic destruction of their own creators. The potential for one human being to destroy another in Hobbes's state of nature is hardly a match for the systematic genocide that has been practiced by those who exercise the prerogatives of government in human societies. This condition can be surmounted only if people in a society can develop appropriate criteria not only for determining what is right and wrong in their relationships with other human beings but what is right and wrong in their relationships with those who exercise the prerogatives of governance and in judging the conduct of those who exercise such prerogatives. Such criteria depend upon clarifying first, what it means for a human being to be free or to enjoy liberty, and second, what it means to be just and to do justice. Both of these concepts need in turn to be related to what it means to participate in human communities and to do so under conditions of free and open communication where a community of people can come to a critical understanding of the meaning of its own experience. All of these factors are mutually reinforcing if the normative and limiting conditions of a polycentric order are to be appropriately established.

An understanding of the meaning of freedom in the context of human societies is obviously not a freedom to do anything. Rather, freedom depends upon a reflective understanding of the human condition and what it means to be free while extending to others like opportunity to be free in the choices that they make. Such understanding is grounded upon generally accepted criteria of right and wrong. Freedom also depends both upon the essential autonomy of an individual to maintain his or her own integrity in the context of an open public realm where individuals are free to communicate with and inform one another about their own intentions and about problems that they share in common. If citizens are to participate in a democratic community, they must also reserve basic prerogatives unto themselves for determining the basic terms and conditions that apply to their own governance, how they can develop and exercise communicative competence with one another, and how they can make those essential decisions that citizens are expected to make both individually and collectively.

Both freedom and justice depend upon knowledge of what is feasible in consensual human relationships. But aspiring to be just requires a human being to confront the condition of human fallibility and the propensity to commit errors while recognizing that doing justice requires one to render judgment about others that may entail substantial deprivations for them. To be just and to do justice requires, then, that individuals be able to take the perspective of others and attempt to comprehend the explanations that they offer in justifying their own actions. This requires a substantial capacity to make interpersonal comparisons in rendering judgment about one's own actions and the actions of others. A serious offense against justice occurs where fallible creatures presume to know what is good for others and impose their judgments upon others. Human beings can aspire to justice only when they appreciate their own fallibility, are open to communication with others, attempt to understand the perspective of others, and appreciate the fundamental tensions that arise from the Faustian bargain that is necessarily inherent in all human societies.

Life in a community of open and free communication should enable human beings to begin to appreciate the place of both freedom and justice in the maintenance of reciprocal relationships that are of mutual benefit to those who shared in such a community of relationships. If people attain this level of understanding, they should be able to specify the terms and conditions of governance that might apply to a self-governing community. They would then have the proper criteria for maintaining effective patterns of relationships in a self-governing community where each individual is capable of developing mutually productive relationships with other members of the community (V. Ostrom 1991).

However, such a possibility is only within the realm of possibilities and is confronted with numerous potential threats. The human potential for learning and the generation of new knowledge always poses a potential threat to any human attainment. New knowledge gives rise to new possibilities, and new possibilities always evoke uncertainty in facing the future. Human beings are always testing limits in relation to prior attainments. Error and misunderstanding thrive in such conditions.

Given the potential for error and misunderstanding, it is relatively easy for human beings to find themselves confronting problems of institutional weakness and institutional failure where patterns of human interaction yield results that are at variance with the intentions or goals that motivate individual behavior. Boulding's "Pure Theory of Threat Systems" and Hobbes's parable of man in a state of nature both manifest tendencies toward patterns of interaction that leave each participant worse off even though each individual seeks his own good. Similarly, a competitive market economy evokes a pattern of interaction on the part of competing producers that tends to minimize profit while each seeks to maximize profit. The disparity between individual motives and results that are yielded by patterns of interdependent human relationships implies that a simple set of means-ends calculations provide an insufficient basis for understanding patterns of interaction in human communities. Solutions conceptualized on the basis of simple means-ends calculations are likely to yield their own pathologies grounded in errors that derive from the failure to account for strategic behavior in interdependent relationships (Olson 1965).

The basic inequality inherent in the exercise of governmental prerogatives always means that some have an inherent advantage in relation to others in dominating collective decisions. Differential access to the legitimate use of instruments of coercion means that some have access to resources that can be used to dominate decisions in relation to others. Incentives then exist on the part of those who gain special advantage in dominating decisions with reference to others to form more extended coalitions so as to surmount limiting conditions and gain general dominance over the exercise of governmental prerogatives. Incentives to extend patterns of dominance by forming coalitions to gain control and overcome all limiting conditions implies that a polycentric order can erode to a point where the dominant coalition exercises a monopoly over all decision structures. Such a pattern of organization has all the attributes of a unitary sovereign. Ostrogorski has demonstrated these tendencies in his book on *Democracy and the Organization of Political Parties* ([1902] 1964).

These potentials can be exacerbated when relationships among human beings come to be dominated by envy and an exaggerated demand for equality grounded in envy. As Tocqueville ([1835–1840] 1945) has demonstrated, individuals—in demanding the elimination of inequalities—depend upon increasing centralization of authority to do so. Such demands only increase the relative dominance of those who exercise the prerogatives of rulership over those who are ruled. As people become more equal under law, they run the risk of increasing the relative dominance of those who rule.

A shared understanding about the normative criteria that are appropriate to informing choice and evaluating performance is fundamental to the operation and maintenance of a polycentric order. Norms, however, are not enough. Individuals participating in such a system must also know the circumstances to which the norms apply. This implies a general knowledge about the nature of organization in human societies and what implications follow from relying upon different structures of institutional arrangements for organizing human relationships. When appropriate normative criteria and a warrantable knowledge of the relationship of structures to consequences exists, we might then think of human beings maintaining a structure of social relationships where diverse communities of interest are governed with reference to a concurrent exercise of self-governing capabilities.

Instrumental Conditions

If moral precepts and appropriate conceptions of human relationships are to be built into human societies, they must be embodied in an enforceable system of law and then be acted upon by individuals who have a shared understanding of their meaning and significance. This, however, poses a problem of how those who exercise the prerogatives of government in human societies are to be held accountable to law. Hobbes holds that those who exercise the ultimate prerogatives of government are the source of law and as a consequence are above the law and cannot be held accountable to law.

To hold those who exercise the prerogatives of government accountable to an enforceable rule of law requires that Hobbes's solution be foreclosed. If everyone is to be held accountable to law, no one can exercise unlimited authority and all authority must be subject to limits. Several conditions that are instrumental to the maintenance of a polycentric order can be specified.

First, if instrumentalities of government are themselves to be subject to rules of law, it is essential that members of such a society have means available for specifying the terms and conditions that apply to the conduct of government as an enforceable system of law. By definition, the terms and conditions that apply to the conduct of government are constitutional in nature. A constitution can be distinguished from ordinary law where a constitution applies to the conduct of government and ordinary law applies to the social relationships occurring among the members of a society.

These distinctions cannot be effectively maintained unless processes of constitutional decision-making can be distinguished from the processes of ordinary governmental decision-making. Where such distinctions can be maintained, a government is no longer competent to determine its own powers but is dependent upon processes of constitutional decision-making exercised by the larger community. A government then would be capable of enacting and modifying ordinary law but would not be competent to modify those rules that applied to its own conduct.

So long as a distinction can be made between constitutional law and ordinary law, it then becomes possible to build into a constitution a distribution of authority relative to the exercise of the prerogatives of government so that all authority is subject to limits and no single center of authority is allowed to exercise unlimited authority. The most fundamental division of authority pertains to the authority of individuals to act individually and collectively with correlative limits upon the exercise of authority by those who are assigned the extraordinary prerogatives of government. Thus, the prerogatives of individuals to freedom of speech, press, and association with other individuals are essential to the maintenance of a public realm of discourse and voluntary association that is free from dominance by governmental officials. In turn, the right to a due process of law implies enforceable obligations on the part of officials to discharge the prerogatives of government in a way that is consistent with standards of critical inquiry and justice.

Authority can further be divided among diverse and independent decision structures so that those who are responsible for formulating and enacting law can do so apart from those who are responsible for determining the application of law and for enforcing law. Where such prerogatives are separated, law can come to have a knowable and autonomous existence where those who determine its application can render independent judgments apart from those who enact and those who are responsible for the enforcement of law. A shared common understanding of the meaning of law is necessary if it is to apply to all individuals alike.

Limits among such decision structures can be maintained by the assignment of veto capabilities. Veto capabilities enable one set of decision-makers to limit or constrain other sets of decision-makers. The mutual exercise of veto capabilities specifies the parameters for establishing and maintaining the legal and political feasibility of any program or course of action. A loose equilibrium within the respective veto positions without recourse to any single dominant center of authority can be maintained where independence of action is feasible within constraints. Where vetoes are exercised with reference to the terms and conditions of constitutional law, the conduct of government itself would be subject to a rule of law.

Further provision for specifying the terms and conditions of government can be used to make provision for citizens to participate in the various processes of government. These might range from the election of public officials to direct participation in the judicial process by the use of citizens as jurors. Citizens functioning as jurors have a direct voice in determining the application and limits of law. Right to a jury trial implies that the enforcement of law depends upon shared understanding about the meaning of law that is concurred in by a representative panel of citizens. Grand juries provide further opportunity for citizens to investigate the discharge of public trust and evaluate the performance of public instrumentalities.

The viability of such arrangements for maintaining the enforceability of constitutional law also depends upon the consciousness with which the larger community of people in such a society are critically aware of the norms that apply to the conduct of government and the tensions that inevitably exist with regard to the maintenance of appropriate limits. Such a system can be maintained only so long as citizens make decisions that are consistent with relevant norms and the maintenance of appropriate limits. Citizens need, then, to know when to resist improper exercises of governmental authority. It is only under such conditions that we can be confident that lawful limits can be maintained in the exercise of governmental authority.

Once the possibility exists of establishing the terms and conditions of government as enforceable rules of constitutional law, that possibility can be reiterated with reference to diverse communities of interests. People can then gain access to multiple units of government that are capable of acting in relation to diverse communities of interest. So long as each unit of government can be constrained by the terms and conditions of a positive constitutional law grounded upon commonly held criteria of choice and a political science that stands critical scrutiny, it is then possible for human beings to aspire to the possibility of exercising self-governing capabilities where all are accountable to common standards of morality and rules of law. All authority is limited and no one exercises unlimited authority.

Interorganizational Relationships in a Polycentric Order

Thus far, this essay has advanced the argument that it is possible to create and maintain a political system that is devoid of a single center of authority from which law derives its coherence and rationality and a commonwealth derives its unity and order. This implies that human governance does not depend upon a single ultimate center of authority that has the last say in all matters that affect a commonwealth. Rather, multiple organizations have a differentiated and limited authority. The governance of society then depends upon the sharing of power among diverse decision structures or organizations. Government in the most general sense is an interorganizational system that requires an interorganizational level of analysis.

The unity of such a commonwealth depends upon common understanding and agreement shared by citizens about the normative and limiting conditions that apply to human governance. Such an understanding requires a substantial level of critical and reflective insight into the human condition. By first coming to understand oneself, it is possible for human beings to understand how others think and feel. By learning how to take the perspective of others and to view one's own position from the perspective of others, it is possible for human beings to develop norms to apply alike to the different individuals who form human communities.

Standards of morality must, however, always be applied with reference to an understanding of the circumstances that arise in interdependent human relationships. As David Hume has observed, we need to be cautious "of what frequently happens in political institutions, that the consequences of things are diametrically opposite to what we should expect on the first appearance" (*Essays*, "Of Taxes," 1758, 195). An appropriate knowledge of conditions and consequences would provide the basis for human beings to exercise an informed choice about alternative structural possibilities that might apply to the constitution of self-governing arrangements in different circumstances.

The basic condition for the organization and maintenance of interorganizational arrangements in a polycentric political order, thus, depends upon the existence of individuals who are themselves sufficiently reflective and critical to understand the human condition, the basic criteria of choice, and the instrumental conditions that apply to the organization of human conduct. They would presumably be able to distinguish right from wrong, lawful from unlawful, just from unjust, and legitimate from illegitimate in ordering relationships with other human beings including those who exercise the prerogatives of government. With an appropriate instrumental knowledge about the nature of human institutions, such individuals presumably would be knowledgeable about the criteria and limiting conditions for establishing the technical, economic, legal, and political feasibility of any collective undertaking in a particular society. Such knowledge would form the basis for structures that would be appropriate to the organization of any private or public enterprise. The realm of interorganizational relationships is always based upon the prior conditions that involve the constitution of particular organizations that are capable of taking collective decisions and coordinating the actions of individuals in collective undertakings.

The creation and maintenance of systems of interorganizational arrangements, then, depend upon the nature of the task to be accomplished (V. Ostrom and E. Ostrom 1977). A very wide range of relationships can be maintained on the basis of quid pro quo transactions where each is acting to advantage in exchanging something for something. Where alternative options are available on both the production and consumption sides of economic relationships, one can anticipate competitive dynamics that will limit the advantage of producers and increase the relative advantage of consumers. This principle applies whether consumption is privately organized by individuals and households or publicly organized through governmental instrumentalities. The pressure of competition moves toward an equilibrium that governs relationships among all participants within limited constraints.

The more difficult problem to confront at the interorganizational level of analysis is where several organized entities share in common the use of some joint resource from which no single organization can be excluded. We confront the typical public good or common-pool resource problem where the pursuit of independent strategies by each organized entity leads to institutional failure and what Garrett Hardin (1968) has aptly called *the tragedy of the commons*. In such circumstances, some separate organized entity will have an incentive to pursue a holdout strategy, take advantage of whatever opportunities are created by others, and fail to contribute its proportionate share to a joint solution. This structure of incentives among organized entities leads to what is sometimes referred to as Balkanization.

As we know from the theory of collective action, a way must be found to foreclose the holdout problem and search out a solution that will be of mutual advantage to the several different organizations that share a community of interest in the common-pool resource or latent public good. Since competitive relationships in a situation where free riding can occur have the tendency that leads to the erosion of the good shared in common, grounds exist for any one party to seek a judicial remedy in relation to those who impose costs upon others. Courts can compel holdouts to appear and, in equity proceedings, do their part in contributing to an equitable solution. The logic of collective action can then be used to devise some new form of collective organization that will foreclose the holdout problem and permit collective action on the part of the larger community of interest.

These strategies are consistent with the federal principles of organization and can be indefinitely extended so long as human beings have the potential for conducting inquiry with regard to grounds for establishing common understanding and agreement. Where such understanding and agreement exists about fundamental values that serve as criteria of choice and the instrumental conditions that are appropriate to the taking of collective action, it is then possible for human beings to bound all exercise of authority by appropriate normative and limiting conditions. Those who rule would do so under a rule of law where the terms and conditions of government are subject to an enforceable system of constitutional law.

Conclusion

A theory of constitutional choice, thus, lays the foundation for an interorganizational level of analysis. But the task will never be an easy one. Human beings always press limits in circumstances where all knowledge is bounded by ignorance and the future is necessarily plagued by uncertainty. Furthermore, patterns of organization to realize a joint or common good always depend upon access to instruments of coercion to maintain limits. Those who relish fruit from the tree of knowledge bear the burden of knowing the grounds for their own choices under the same terms and conditions that they would apply to others, if others were in their place. Sympathetic understanding grounded in critical dialogue affords the possibility that the use of evil to do good need not lead inevitably to human tragedy. It is this tenuous possibility that permits us to consider a system of relationships where interorganizational relationships are bounded by a multiorganizational milieu without having recourse to unlimited authority.

References

Arrow, Kenneth. 1951. *Social Choice and Individual Values.* New York: Wiley.
Boulding, Kenneth. 1963. "Towards a Pure Theory of Threat Systems." *American Economic Review* 53 (May): 424–34.
Greene, Vernon. 1978. "The Metaphysical Foundations of Constitutional Order." Ph.D. diss., Indiana University.
Hardin, Garrett. 1968. "The Tragedy of the Commons." *Science* 162: 1243–48.
Hobbes, Thomas. [1651] 1960. *Leviathan or the Matter, Forme and Power of a Commonwealth Ecclesiasticall and Civil.* Michael Oakeshott, ed. Oxford: Basil Blackwell.
Hume, David. 1758. *Essays and Treatises on Several Subjects.* New edition. London: A. Miller.
Olson, Mancur. 1965. The *Logic of Collective Action: Public Goods and the Theory of Groups.* Cambridge, MA: Harvard University Press.
Ostrogorski, Moisei. [1902] 1964. *Democracy and the Organization of Political Parties.* 2 vols. Edited and abridged by S. M. Lipset. Garden City, NY: Doubleday, Anchor Books.
Ostrom, Vincent. 1991. "Constitutional Considerations with Particular Reference to the Federal Systems." In *The Public Sector—Challenge for Coordination and Learning,* ed. Franz-Xaver Kaufmann, 141–50. Berlin and New York: Walter de Gruyter.
Ostrom, Vincent, and Elinor Ostrom. 1977. "Public Goods and Public Choices." In *Alternatives for Delivering Public Services: Toward Improved Performance,* ed. E. S. Savas, 7–49. Boulder, CO: Westview Press. Reprinted in Michael D. McGinnis, ed., *Polycentricity and Local Public Economies: Readings from the Workshop in Political Theory and Policy Analysis* (Ann Arbor: University of Michigan Press, 1999, 75–103).
Tocqueville, Alexis de. [1835–1840] 1945. *Democracy in America.* 2 vols. Phillips Bradley, ed. New York: Alfred A. Knopf.

4

Legal Pluralism, Polycentricity, and Faith-Based Organizations in Global Governance

Michael D. McGinnis

Looking Beyond "the State"

Vincent Ostrom fundamentally transformed my understanding of world politics. In graduate school I had been trained to think first of the *nation-state*, or *state* for short, to fixate on its geopolitical interests and its military or economic power relative to other states. According to the dictates of the still-dominant paradigm of international realism (Viotti and Kauppi 1998), global politics consists primarily of strategic interactions among sovereign states, each jealously protecting its own security from external threats and internal rivals. Conventionally, this pattern was taken to have been established by the Treaty of Westphalia (1648), which ended a long period of religious wars on the continent of Europe.

Vincent Ostrom did not accept this standard view. Instead, he vigorously contested the term *state*. He insisted that there were not many national governments that looked anything like the Hobbesian formulation of a "monocratic" system of power (V. Ostrom [1973] 2008a, 68). In particular, the United States of America, with its multiplicity of overlapping jurisdictions and the complex interlocking array of institutional checks and balances as enshrined in its Constitution (V. Ostrom [1971] 2008b), in no way resembles a Hobbesian state. If the most powerful military and economic entity on the planet today is not Hobbesian, then how can international relations (IR) realists say that all the important actors in world politics are Hobbesian states? Furthermore, some supposedly sovereign states (especially in the Global South) are barely able to govern their own capital cities. In his penultimate attack, Ostrom asked how a Westphalian system of sovereign states can be said to have been established by treaties (technically, the Treaties of Münster and Osnabrück jointly established the Peace of Westphalia) that included articles recognizing the legitimacy of the independent republics of the Netherlands and Switzerland, neither of which fit the definition of a state as used by international realists (V. Ostrom 1997, 240).

By refusing to acknowledge "the state" as the uniquely pivotal actor in a misnamed "Westphalian" system, Ostrom demonstrated that institutional analysts must recognize the full range of institutional arrangements that are actually being used by individuals and communities as they cope with shared problems and explore common opportunities. By neglecting to give equal consideration to unusual forms of governance that do not fit easily into our conceptual categories, institutional analysts run the risk of actually reducing the range of institutional diversity (V. Ostrom 1990a, 411). In this chapter, I apply this same lesson to the surprisingly diverse and vibrant roles of religious institutions in the constitution of political and social order at the global level. To do so, however, I must first summarize Ostrom's conceptualization of polycentric governance.

Epistemic Foundations for Institutional Diversity

Vincent Ostrom has published extensively on the epistemic foundations of patterns of order in human societies. To simplify his complex and subtle system of analysis, I focus here on the three most enduring influences on his work: Hobbes, Tocqueville, and the authors of *The Federalist*, and especially on the ways in which Ostrom weaves these three sources together into a seamless whole.

Ostrom insists that institutional analysis should begin with Hobbes's fundamental analytical technique of methodological individualism (V. Ostrom 1991, 31–41). Hobbes asks us to reason by means of extending our self-understanding to the commonalities shared by all humanity. Unfortunately, in his specific conclusions Hobbes had been led astray by his refusal to accept any partial solution to the problem of the radical insecurity of individual humans in the "state of nature." Because of the intrinsic human ability to communicate via language and thereby establish and sustain covenantal relationships, some communities should be able to escape from this trap without succumbing to the horrific structure of domination Hobbes advocates (V. Ostrom 1991, 53–68).

It was precisely these common factors that Tocqueville highlighted in *Democracy in America* ([1835] 1969). Of critical importance are social connections and personal experiences. The authors of *The Federalist* demonstrate one practical example by which a new form of governance was established by reflection and thought (V. Ostrom [1971] 2008b). The founders of this system knew full well what they were doing as they built an innovative set of institutions upon the foundations of what Alexander Hamilton had called the *general theory of limited constitution* (V. Ostrom 1991, 45). Checks and balances between different branches of government, and between national, state, and local levels of government were widely recognized as essential foundations for liberty as expressed in a federal system of governance.

Ostrom advanced an even more expansive vision of American federalism, by building upon Tocqueville's emphasis on the social and cultural foundations of democratic governance, and his conclusion attaching primary importance to the habits of heart and mind exhibited by people who can successfully govern themselves. Ostrom generalized Tocqueville's conclusions to argue that the establishment of democratic forms of governance should be possible in other cultural settings, provided supportive institutions can be identified and strengthened (V. Ostrom 1997, 271–302; see also McGinnis and Ostrom 1999). The U.S. Constitution is not a blueprint to be applied uncritically to vastly different circumstances. Instead, it serves as an exemplar of the process by which institutional arrangements should be crafted to fit relevant physical, social, and cultural circumstances. Finally, as Ostrom (1997) argued at length in one of his later books, Tocqueville raised serious concerns about potential dangers that tend to arise in all democratic societies. For Ostrom, the widespread use of the language of Hobbesian sovereignty poses an especially pernicious threat to the long-term sustainability of the self-governing capabilities of modern societies. Citizens must be educated in Tocqueville's science of association so they can continue to follow the example of creative artisanship in institutional design set by Hamilton, Madison, Jay, and all the other founders (and subsequent sustainers) of the American republic (V. Ostrom 1997, 271–302).

The complexities of polycentric governance emerge as a natural consequence of this pervasive ethos of self-governance, and polycentricity in turn provides a sustainable foundation for the continued practice of self-governance (McGinnis 1999a, 1999b, 2000). In contrast, for most theorists of IR, the primary consideration remains the establishment of order amid global anarchy. Hobbes was taken to have expressed the fundamental nature of the anarchic international system in his conceptual construction of the "state of nature." Tocqueville's *Democracy in America* has typically been deemed irrelevant to world affairs, even though his diagnosis of the fatal flaws in the *ancien régime* that contributed to the French Revolution (Tocqueville

[1856] 1955) continues to draw some attention. *The Federalist* rarely occurs anywhere in the IR literature, even though it stands as a classic statement of the assertion that political institutions may, in some circumstances, have substantial influence over state interests and their strategic choices.

Few of my international relations colleagues have appreciated the relevance of the first nine papers in *The Federalist* ([1787–1788] 1982), in which Hamilton and Jay applied the basic principles of international realism to the American continent. These advocates of the newly composed U.S. Constitution counseled their readers that, in the absence of a unified system of governance, the separate American states would, eventually, come to blows over some matter of importance, dealing with territorial boundaries, commerce, or popular passions (see V. Ostrom [1971] 2008b, 6–7). Beginning with Federalist 10, Madison and Hamilton laid out the institutional arrangements proposed to resolve that problem, as well as related problems then facing the new American nation. Thus, in this single book, international realism and political liberalism were united as policy problem and institutional response.

In addition, there was much more to Hobbes's analysis than his portrayal of the "state of nature" as the problem for which a sovereign *Leviathan* was the only practical solution. Indeed, in chapter 13, Hobbes ([1651] 1962, 101) specifically concluded that a "state of nature" among sovereign governments could never be as brutal as the chaotic state he imagined was waiting for individuals forced to live outside a commonwealth. Finally, Tocqueville's observations about the social foundations of democracy resonated well with contemporary processes of democratization, including the problems experienced by those seeking to export Western forms of democratic institutions to peoples from other cultures (V. Ostrom 1997, 239–45). After confronting the epistemic foundations of Ostrom's understanding of polycentric order, I have never been able to look at IR theory in quite the same way.

Classics of Legal Pluralism

Shifts in conceptual understandings rarely happen without prompting by an incessant source of tension. Vincent Ostrom is a master at this dynamic process of conceptual artisanship, as all of his colleagues can attest.

In my case, two books that he recommended were especially effective in pushing me toward a fuller appreciation of the complexities of global governance: *The Cheyenne Way* by Karl Llewellyn and E. A. Hoebel (1941) and *Law and Revolution* by Harold Berman (1983). Each is a powerful statement of *legal pluralism*, a theoretical perspective that served as an effective corrective to my graduate training, even though their particular topics, traditional practices of a Native American tribe and reorganization of the Catholic Church in eleventh-century Europe, seemed very remote from the burning issues of conflict in the contemporary world.

In *The Cheyenne Way*, a legal scholar and an anthropologist detail a complex system of informal law by which disputes are resolved according to unwritten but well-understood procedures. Llewellyn and Hoebel (1941) helped me realize the extent to which sustainable processes of dispute resolution depend critically on the continued presence of a shared community of understanding among the members of an active group. Furthermore, the system of informal jurisprudence developed by the Cheyenne turned out to be much more sophisticated than might be expected. Both themes reverberate throughout Ostrom's own work, an insistence on the pivotal importance of shared understandings and a deep appreciation of the irrepressible creativity of people throughout the world.

From this foundation I came to realize that no formal system of law can hope to survive unless it is supplemented by multiple informal mechanisms (Galanter 1981; Landes and Posner 1979; Moore 2001). For if all the disputes that arise in a society are automatically transformed into legal cases, then court systems would be overwhelmed. The many processes that fall under the label ADR (Alternative Dispute Resolution) turn out to be critical to the long-term viability of even the most formal systems of justice.

Ostrom's favorite example of ADR is equity jurisprudence, a relatively little-known practice that has the advantage of bringing together all of the principal stakeholders to discuss the underlying nature of their shared situation and to devise solutions that can, eventually, be imposed on all of them by mutual agreement. The resulting compromise is then treated as binding by the court system as a whole. In an equity proceeding, the affected parties meet together to talk through all aspects of the issue and try to arrive at a common response, one that takes into account all of their own concerns and interests (see E. Ostrom and V. Ostrom 2004; E. Ostrom 1965; Blomquist 2008). The basic idea behind equity jurisprudence struck me as quite similar to fundamental principles of mediation and international diplomacy, especially maxims articulated in the classic text *Getting to Yes* (Fisher and Ury 1981).

From Berman's *Law and Revolution*, I came to appreciate the mongrel nature of Western legal tradition, with *legal pluralism* as one of its defining characteristics. Berman detailed the ways in which strands from previously distinct cultures and traditions were imperfectly integrated into the less than coherent whole that we have come to know as "Western civilization." Berman traced the emergence of this distinctive blend of legal pluralism to the Papal

Revolution of 1075–1122, instigated by the reforms of Pope Gregory VII. Berman devoted separate chapters to the varieties of legal tradition already in place by that time, including canon law within the church, merchant and urban law, and the feudal, manorial, and royal laws. Vincent Ostrom (1997, 239–45) suggested that this same diversity of legal systems has continued in force until the present day, despite the academy's obsession with formal legal order at the national and international levels.

One aspect of Berman's analysis that I found especially intriguing was his discussion of the then-emerging system of informal rules and procedures that came to be known as merchant law. In many ways, this same system continues in effect today, albeit changed in significant ways in the intervening centuries. Many commercial contracts between firms located in different countries include specification of which body of laws will be considered applicable to the parties of that transaction, and especially to identify the process by which any subsequent disputes will be arbitrated (Benson 1989; Dezalay and Garth 1995). The members of an elite body of international lawyers support a lavish lifestyle by resolving, out of court and in an informal and nontransparent fashion, commercial disputes that arise between corporations based in different countries (Dezalay and Garth 1996). Without this system of informal dispute resolution, transnational commerce would be prohibitively expensive in terms of transaction costs. Also, national courts routinely defer to their judgments, because the parties had agreed to submit disputes to particular arbitration firms when they originally signed their contracts.

I began to appreciate a similar range of diversity in contemporary international law. For example, the contemporary discourse on human rights generalizes controversies that were long under contestation within the Catholic church (Lauren 2003). Also remarkable are the guild-like rules by which transnational professional associations govern themselves, including institutions of higher education, or the institutions of science. Functional regimes for the collective management of Antarctic resources or the Internet are examples of voluntary forms of self-regulation or commons management (McGinnis and Ostrom 2008).

Vincent Ostrom (1991, 240–43) argued that the uniquely complex system of governance being built in the European Union shares a close family resemblance to that of the Holy Roman Empire, with its loose collection of diverse political units, including cities with remarkable levels of autonomy and dynamism. Although rarely given much credit today for being a remote ancestor to the EU, the Holy Roman Empire was an especially eclectic blend of institutional arrangements in which it was standard practice, for example, for a free city to host the coronation of an elected emperor.

Ostrom's vision of a polycentric order within Western Europe resonated with observations by other prominent scholars. For example, in his influential study of the development of an international society based on Western conceptualizations of sovereignty, Hedley Bull (1977, 254) makes a fascinating reference to the potential emergence of what he terms a "neo-medieval order," characterized by "overlapping authority and multiple loyalty." This latter phrase closely resembles the "overlapping jurisdictions and multiple authorities" that define the basic logic of polycentric governance (V. Ostrom, Tiebout, and Warren 1961; McGinnis 1999a, 1999b, 2000).

Bull points in the direction of polycentricity, even though his own analysis falls short by remaining primarily state-centric. Sovereign states remain the primary inhabitants of Bull's international society, and these states are primarily responsible for constructing the institutions of war and international law to resolve their disputes.

Finding more effective ways to resolve conflicts of interest in a peaceful manner remains the central problem for international relations and indeed for all kinds of governance. A pluralistic arrangement of formal and informal means of dispute resolution is an essential component of polycentric governance, in which private, voluntary, and public forms of governance are closely intertwined, all the way from local communities to the global level.

Governance Networks and Missing Institutions

To sustain a viable system of self-governance, groups of all kinds must be encouraged and empowered to develop their own ways of resolving disputes and of working together to achieve whatever objectives they share in common. In their classic statement of the nature of *polycentricity*, V. Ostrom, Tiebout, and Warren (1961) articulated a vision of governance in which political authorities, each acting on the behalf of constituent groups of varying sizes and composition, could *provide* (select) goods and services desired by these groups either by *producing* them directly or by arranging for their production by private corporations or other entities. In addition, individual members of communities could themselves participate in the production of essential goods and services, in a process known as *co-production*. Attention must also be given to the mechanisms by which these processes were financed and especially to the rules that specified permissible actions by each type of organizational actor. The authors realized that coordination among all these actors would pose a challenge, but thought that the coordination costs were more than offset by the benefits. In this article, published more than four decades ago, Ostrom and his collaborators laid out all of the essential components for the policy networks or systems of network governance that later researchers came to realize play such an important role in so many areas of public policy (Goldsmith and Eggers 2004).

The foundational principle of polycentric governance is to make creative use of the complementary strengths of diverse forms of organization: complex networks of nested general public jurisdictions and overlapping arrays of specialized public, private, voluntary, and community organizations for the selection, implementation, and financing of policies at local, subnational, national, regional, and global levels. General political jurisdictions at the local, provincial/state, national, regional, and global levels can contribute by specializing on those public goods and services that are most efficiently produced or provided for at their own distinctive scale of aggregation. Yet these neatly stacked levels of a federal system also need to be complemented by making sure that citizens have ready access to specialized units of governments that cross standard jurisdictional boundaries. Hooghe and Marks (2001, 2003) call general-purpose and specialized jurisdictions Type I and Type II institutions, respectively, and they conclude both need to be in place for a governance system to be effective, especially in the long term.

In addition, a polycentric system of governance must reach out beyond purely political organizations to incorporate the unique contributions of voluntary associations, community-based organizations, and even private corporations. Hybrid organizations such as producer cooperatives, which cannot be located within any single sector of the public economy, must also be considered when appropriate. In sum, polycentric governance is both cross-sectional and multi-level.

One key insight of this network governance approach is that no one type of organization can achieve its full potential without the complementary support of organizations from other sectors (Lichbach 1996; E. Ostrom 2005). Just setting up a market in private goods is no guarantee of its efficiency, not if legal protection and supportive social norms remain absent. Nor can any political reformer fully achieve his or her objectives without taking into consideration the ways in which economic, social, and cultural processes will act to reinforce or to undermine these reforms.

Key implications of the logic of polycentric network governance include the following assertions:

1. Efficient markets require secure property rights, the production of other needed public goods, the availability of voluntary self-regulation, and sociocultural limits on commodification and exploitation.

2. Accountable governments require the involvement of an informed and vigilant citizenry embedded in dense networks of social capital, assisted by the presence of voluntary watchdogs and private sources of countervailing power.
3. To ensure the continued success of self-governance, voluntary associations need to be recognized as legitimate political actors and holders of property, provided they do not deviate too far from socially acceptable norms of behavior.
4. Sustainable communities require easy access to peaceful means of resolving conflicts, reasonable exit options, and at least a minimal economic rationality.

In practice, analysts or reformers attuned to this vision of networked or polycentric governance train themselves to look for *missing institutions*. For many economists, any observed inefficiency in public policy can be explained by identifying a missing market in some particular good or type of information. Institutional analysts look more broadly for gaps in the coverage provided by institutions from all sectors and all levels and types of governance.

For example, Vincent Ostrom drew my attention to an important missing piece in the overall structure of international law. In *The Federalist*, Hamilton asserted that the central government must be able to reach down to the individual level. If not, then only collective punishments could be enacted and there would be no way to assign responsibility to individuals or to hold each person accountable for his or her own deeds (V. Ostrom [1971] 2008b, 30–35). With the establishment of regional war crimes tribunals and especially the International Criminal Court (ICC), institutions of international law that were originally designed to specify the rights and obligations of sovereign states toward each other are increasingly being used to attribute responsibility to leaders as individuals. More generally, the institutions and principles of public international law are now routinely used by a wide array of interest groups, environmental activists, and human rights organizations. All this adds up to a rapidly evolving system of governance at the global level, albeit with important gaps remaining.

Recent years have seen considerable ferment in the area of international law as new institutions of global governance are being crafted. A discourse on potentially universal human rights has emerged through which some shared community of understanding of basic moral values may ultimately emerge (Lauren 2003). Ostrom saw this coming, too, in his portrayal of the Golden Rule, in all its many forms, as expressing a common moral standard shared by virtually all religious traditions (V. Ostrom 1991, 34–41; 1997, 180–84).

As we shall see in the next section, Ostrom has long emphasized that institutional analysts need to more fully understand the fundamental importance of religion in the constitution of order in human societies.

Recognizing Religion's Contributions to Governance

In both *Law and Revolution* and *The Cheyenne Way*, religious traditions provided an essential foundation upon which these diverse systems of dispute resolution were built. Throughout his written work, Vincent Ostrom stresses the critical importance of religion as a foundation for the epistemic order needed to sustain democratic self-governance (see especially V. Ostrom 1990b; 1991, 53–68; 1997, 196–200). His view goes way beyond Tocqueville's well-known appreciation for the importance of religion as a primary political institution in the American republic (Tocqueville [1835] 1969, 287–92).

Ostrom considers Hobbes's reliance on the natural punishment of God as the sole means of disciplining a sovereign's excesses (V. Ostrom 1990b, 169–70) to be much less compelling than the biblical image of Jacob wrestling with God (V. Ostrom 1990b, 187–88; 1997, 197–98). Without endorsing any particular religious interpretation, Ostrom argues that the right kind of religious belief can provide an essential ingredient in the creative artisanship of self-governance. Once we realize that no one person can know everything about the universe, or even be certain about the nature of God, each of us needs to listen attentively to the arguments and judgments of our fellow human beings, if we are to jointly govern ourselves.

For Ostrom, this realization constitutes the essential meaning of the Golden Rule (V. Ostrom 1991, 35–41; 1997, 180–84). In contrast, political ideologues who believe they can see the Truth produce monumental disasters, as exemplified in the French Revolution and in twentieth-century Marxist dictatorships (V. Ostrom 1997, 190–93). Our language necessarily shapes the way we see the world, and for Ostrom language and religion are deeply bound up with each other and with the constitution of order in human society.

Ostrom highlights the role of religion in shoring up fundamental epistemic order, but religious organizations themselves are also worthy of careful consideration by institutional analysts. Whether or not they are ultimately grounded in supernatural forces, religious organizations, as they exist here and now, are human artifacts crafted to facilitate the realization of shared goals by particular groups sharing a common understanding of the meaning and implications of their religious faith. As such, rational choice theory offers a productive way to study the organizational manifestations of religious beliefs and behaviors (Stark and Finke 2000).

Any application of rationality to questions of faith remains highly controversial. Even Vincent Ostrom (1997, 99) argues that some human values are simply not reducible to consideration in terms of utility. I prefer to phrase it differently, by saying that believers experience rewards when they follow the dictates of their faith, or, alternatively, suffer guilt when their own behavior falls short of their religious ideals. As such, their daily choices concerning the own expression of their faith convey intangible benefits or costs to them. Individual believers make choices based on both practical and religious dimensions of utility. Since these two need not always point in the same direction, individual believers are forced to make trade-offs between desired goals.

Utility functions can incorporate both tangible and intangible perceptions of benefit and cost (E. Ostrom 2005, 146–48), and religious belief provides a foundation for a more systematic analysis of at least some aspects of intrinsic utility. These perceptions need to be formed and nurtured, which helps explain why teaching doctrine and monitoring the behavior of their followers constitutes such a large proportion of the effort expended by religious leaders. Norms need to be promulgated by agents of an organization, and rules enforced by agents assigned that responsibility. For such an organization to be religious there need not be explicit reference to any particular supernatural being, but there must be a shared understanding that certain beliefs, norms, rules, or punishments relate to supernatural factors that can never be fully ascertained in the here and now.

In summary, then, a *faith-based organization* (or *FBO*) is an *organization* for which the intrinsic benefits or role expectations defined by its constituent *norms* or the tangible consequences defined by its constituent *rules* have some relationship to an intrinsically intangible dimension of religious faith.

Political Consequences of Religious Choice

All this is potentially relevant to politics because oftentimes the manifestations of an individual's faith extend beyond participation in worship to also engage in activities that have demonstrable effects, for good or ill, on others. To use the appropriate technical term, activities of faith-based organizations generate *externalities* to which other actors might respond. Those discomforted by the activities of religious organizations will naturally complain to their own public officials. These officials, in turn, can try to shape the incentives of the agents of faith-based organizations so as to enhance their positive effects and discourage continued generation of negative externalities (McGinnis 2006). Any manipulation of the transaction costs faced by believers operating in the political realm necessarily affects the shape of the organizations they construct to aid them in their efforts. However, as Adam Smith realized in *The Wealth of Nations* ([1776] 1976, 317–22), a certain degree of subtlety is required if the political manipulation of the motives of religious actors is to have any chance of success.

Prominent among positive externalities are benefits that disadvantaged groups receive from the assistance offered them by disinterested religious actors: charities, clinics, and other programs of public service. Public authorities may enter into contractual arrangements to encourage these activities, and to direct them toward desired beneficiaries. In response, congregations and faith communities of various traditions tend to establish separate service-based organizations to engage in these public services, and it is these organizations in partnership with public authorities that most observers refer to when they use the term faith-based organization (Berger 2003; Ebaugh et al. 2003). Despite the common perception of a cherished "wall of separation" between church and state in the United States (Davis 2001), religious and political organizations have long engaged with each other in networks of practical policy partnerships (Chaves 1998, 2004; Ebaugh et al. 2003; Monsma 1996; Smith and Sosin 2001; Wuthnow 2004). Many of the largest and most innovative international NGOs involved in development assistance or humanitarian relief are closely associated with particular denominations or broader religious traditions (Kniss and Campbell 1997; Nichols 1988; Benthall and Bellion-Jourdan 2003; McCleary 2004).

The term *faith-based organization* incorporates two sub-categories: (1) congregations and other faith-centered (or faith community) organizations and (2) faith-based service organizations. The former category includes organizations directly related to worship, however that core ingredient of religion is interpreted. The term congregation has been used by several researchers to denote primary faith communities of all religious tradition, especially in the United States, where this originally Christian form of organization has been adopted by those of other faiths (Chaves 2004; Ammerman 2005). Denominations are the classic form of secondary level organization among faith communities, but at higher (tertiary) levels of organization no single term seems appropriate (Demerath et al. 1998). Membership and full participation in a congregation or faith community organization can convey a powerful sense of meaning and belonging to individuals. Any form of community can have profound effects on an individual's sense of identity, yet there seems something uniquely complete or fulfilling about religious faith, according to the reports of believers (James [1902] 1997).

Congregations and other faith-centered organizations may closely resemble community-based organizations, but faith-based organizations engaged in the delivery of public services more closely fit the profile of third sector or civil society organizations. It is this latter type of organizations that act in close partnership with public agencies and private corporations in networks of service delivery.

This same type of activity takes place in more informal manifestations. For example, Islamic mosques frequently serve as centers for the delivery of community services of various kinds, especially the care of widows or orphans (Kuran 2001; Alterman, Hunter, and Philips 2005). Even though formal service organizations are rarely established, the impact on local communities can be substantial. Indeed, it is their attention to the actual needs of their surrounding communities that has made some Islamic groups especially attractive whenever open elections are held (Esposito 1992). Since governments in this part of the world rarely deliver many social services to their own population, further successes of Islamic-based political parties should be expected to occur as democratization spreads throughout this region (Benthall 2003; Roy 2000). More generally, Islamic law has become an increasingly important transnational legal system, even if its detailed interpretation varies widely in different countries (Marshall 2005).

A deep distaste for injustice inspires many believers to support the rights of poor or marginalized groups unable to protect themselves in the political arena. In times of violent struggle, faith leaders may act in the interests of peace, by bringing warring parties together and helping them reach reconciliation of their differences (Appleby 2000). Peace and justice-seeking activities are often organized around interfaith alliances in order to make their voice more influential in policy debates. In addition, certain faith communities, notably the Quakers and the Mennonites, define the realization of peace as a fundamental component of their life of worship. These and other historic peace churches play unique roles as relatively unbiased facilitators of peace in many parts of the world, and many individual believers and faith-based organizations are involved in diverse forms of diplomacy and peace-building (Johnston 2003; Johnston and Sampson 1994).

Faith-based organizations may also engage in political activism in defense of the interests and policy preferences of their own membership, in the form of interest group lobbying, voter mobilization, or working in alliance with political parties (Wald and Calhoun-Brown 2006). Under conditions of legal pluralism, such as in India (Larson 2001), for example, each major religious community may act to protect the legitimacy of its own system of personal law. In rare but sometimes spectacular cases, faith-based political activism takes violent form. Clearly, religious belief can be transmuted into support for a wide range of political goals and methods (Appleby 2000).

For some believers, the core concern is to spread their faith, no matter what the political ramifications may be. Christian evangelicals, for example, are convinced that their Lord commands them, in the Great Commission, to spread the Gospel to all peoples of the world (Barnett 2005a, 2005b). Over a span of several centuries, Christian missionaries have enjoyed remarkable successes in many parts of the developing world and, as a consequence, Christianity has evolved into a truly global religion (Jenkins 2003; McGinnis 2007). Yet overly aggressive proselytism can generate negative externalities and potentially intense political controversies.

Proselytism-driven politics can take different forms, depending on the configuration of relations among proselytizers, their targeted group, other religious organizations, and political authorities in both home and target countries (Grim and Finke 2006; McGinnis 2006). Connections between proselytism and other motives can be subtle and even intentionally hidden. For example, the *tentmaker* strategy encourages individuals to covertly proselytize while officially being in country to deliver aid, build a business, or teach (Barnett 2005a, 2005b). Such duplicity naturally deepens suspicion. Two recent cases are noteworthy. First, Indonesian officials complained about faith-based humanitarian aid organizations responding to the December 2004 tsunami by converting orphans under their care or including bibles in aid packages (Casey 2005). Second, in April 2006 the global news media catapulted to (temporary) celebrity status one Abdul Rahman, an Afghan who had converted years earlier "while working as a medical aid worker for an international Christian group helping Afghan refugees in the Pakistani city of Peshawar" (Cooney 2006).

In an especially complex configuration of political interests, evangelical Christian leaders worked with secular human rights activists and other groups to convince Congress to pass the International Religious Freedom Act of 1998, which requires the State Department to issue a detailed yearly report on all violations of religious rights in other countries throughout the world (Hertzke 2004). Since public officials in Russia, China, India, and many other countries deeply resent aggressive proselytism among their own peoples, similar controversies seem certain to arise more frequently in the future (Cozad 2005; Fore 2002; Gunn 2000; Marthoz and Saunders 2005; Potter 2003; Witte and Bourdeaux 1999).

Perhaps the most critical contribution of religion to governance is its role as a source of countervailing moral authority. In an influential critique of the widespread tendency among political analysts to misunderstand religion as a purely individual matter when religions are instead fundamentally communal in nature, Stephen Carter articulates the political implications of religion in a succinct and powerful manner.

> Religions are in effect independent centers of power, with bona fide claims on the allegiance of their members, claims that exist alongside, are not identical to, and will sometimes trump the claims to obedience that the state makes. . . . A religion, in this picture, is not simply a means for understanding one's self, or even of contemplating the nature of the universe, or existence, or of anything else. A religion is, at its heart, a way of denying the authority of the rest of the world; it is a way of saying to fellow human beings and to the state those fellow humans have erected, "No, I will *not* accede to your will." (Carter 1993, 35, 41; italics in original)

Precisely because of its deep roots outside the standard realm of politics, religion can serve as a uniquely efficacious constraint on the excessive partisanship so characteristic of many struggles for political power. When appropriately deployed, religion can reconcile former enemies and draw connections between peoples living in different political jurisdictions. In this way, religion can serve as an essential sinew of peace and good governance.

In sum, faith-based organizations make significant contributions to policy at the global level, specifically in the areas of humanitarian assistance, development aid, peace-building, human rights, and the promotion of democracy and justice. Although typically ignored by theorists of international relations, the import of these organizations becomes evident once one looks at global governance from a broader perspective. No matter what our own religious convictions may be, we, as institutional analysts, have a professional responsibility to recognize and appreciate the unique contributions made by all types of governance institutions. As scholars we should strive to help sustain the capacity of local, national, and global communities to devise effective institutional arrangements, including organizations originally instituted for primarily religious purposes.

Acknowledgments

The author wishes to thank Mark Sproule-Jones for his constructive comments and the Joan B. Kroc Institute for International Peace Studies, University of Notre Dame, for support of sabbatical research while this essay was written, as well as his home institutions of the Department of Political Science and Workshop in Political Theory and Policy Analysis, Indiana University. Of course, none of these institutions or individuals are responsible for the content of this essay.

References

Alterman, Jon B., with Shireen Hunter and Ann L. Philips. 2005. "The Idea and Practice of Philanthropy in the Muslim World." Center for Strategic and International Studies (CSIS) PPC Issue Paper no. 5.

Ammerman, Nancy T. 2005. *Pillars of Faith: American Congregations and Their Partners.* Berkeley: University of California Press.

Appleby, R. Scott. 2000. *The Ambivalence of the Sacred: Religion, Violence, and Reconciliation.* Lanham, MD: Rowman & Littlefield.

Barnett, Mike. 2005a. "Creative Access Platforms: What Are They and Do We Need Them?" *Evangelical Missions Quarterly* 41(1): 88–96.

———. 2005b. "Innovation in Mission Operations: Creative-Access Platforms." In *The Changing Face of World Missions: Engaging Contemporary Issues and Trends*, ed. Michael Pocock, Gailyn van Rheenen, and Douglas McConnell, 209–44. Grand Rapids, MI: Baker Academic.

Benson, Bruce L. 1989. "The Spontaneous Evolution of Commercial Law." *Southern Economic Journal* 55(3): 644–61.

Benthall, Jonathan. 2003. "Humanitarianism and Islam after 11 September." In *Humanitarian Action and the "Global War on Terror": A Review of Trends and Issues*, ed. Joanna Macrae and Adele Harmer, 37–69. London: Overseas Development Institute, Humanitarian Policy Group Report 14, July.

Benthall, Jonathan, and Jérôme Bellion-Jourdan. 2003. *The Charitable Crescent: Politics of Aid in the Muslim World.* London and New York: I. B. Tauris.

Berger, Julia. 2003. "Religious Non-Governmental Organizations: An Exploratory Analysis." *Voluntas: International Journal of Voluntary and Nonprofit Organizations* 14(1): 14–39.

Berman, Harold. 1983. *Law and Revolution: The Formation of the Western Legal Tradition.* Cambridge, MA: Harvard University Press.

Blomquist, William. 2008. "Crafting Water Constitutions in California." In *The Practice of Constitutional Development*, ed. Filippo Sabetti, Barbara Allen, and Mark Sproule-Jones. Lanham, MD: Lexington Books.

Bull, Hedley. 1977. *The Anarchical Society.* New York: Columbia University Press.

Carter, Stephen. 1993. *The Culture of Disbelief: How American Law and Politics Trivialize Religious Devotion.* New York: Basic Books.

Casey, Michael. 2005. "Tsunami Relief Efforts Mingle with Religion." *The Seattle Times*, January 14. http://seattletimes.nwsource.com/html/nationworld/2002150723_faith14.html.

Chaves, Mark. 1998. "The Religious Ethic and the Spirit of Nonprofit Entrepreneurship." In *Private Action and the Public Good*, ed. Walter W. Powell and Elisabeth S. Clemens, 47–65. New Haven, CT: Yale University Press.

———. 2004. *Congregations in America*. Cambridge, MA: Harvard University Press.

Cooney, Daniel. 2006. "Afghan Christian May Face Death Penalty for Conversion." Associated Press, March 20. Posted at multiple sites, including http://www.washingtontimes.com/world/20060320-123722-5185r.htm.

Cozad, Laurie. 2005. "The United States' Imposition of Religious Freedom: The International Religious Freedom Act and India." *India Review* 4(1): 59–83.

Davis, Derek H. 2001. "Separation, Integration, and Accommodation: Religion and State in America in a Nutshell." *Journal of Church and State* 43(1): 5–19.

Demerath, N. J. III, Peter Dobkin Hall, Terry Schmitt, and Rhys H. Williams, eds. 1998. *Sacred Companies: Organizational Aspects of Religion and Religious Aspects of Organizations*. New York: Oxford University Press.

Dezalay, Yves, and Bryant Garth. 1995. "Merchants of Law as Moral Entrepreneurs: Constructing International Justice from the Competition for Transnational Business Disputes." *Law & Society Review* 29(1): 27–64.

———. 1996. *Dealing in Virtue: International Commercial Arbitration and the Construction of a Transnational Legal Order*. Chicago: University of Chicago Press.

Ebaugh, Helen Rose, Paula F. Pipes, Janet Saltzman Chafetz, and Martha Daniels. 2003. "Where's the Religion? Distinguishing Faith-Based from Secular Social Service Agencies." *Journal for the Scientific Study of Religion* 42(3): 411–26.

Esposito, John L. 1992. *The Islamic Threat: Myth or Reality?* New York: Oxford University Press.

Fisher, Roger, and William Ury. 1981. *Getting to Yes*. Boston, MA: Houghton Mifflin.

Fore, Matthew L. 2002. "Shall Weigh Your God and You: Assessing the Imperialistic Implications of the International Religious Freedom Act in Muslim Countries." *Duke Law Journal* 52(2): 423–53.

Galanter, Marc. 1981. "Justice in Many Rooms: Courts, Private Ordering, and Indigenous Law." *Journal of Legal Pluralism* 19: 1–47.

Goldsmith, Stephen, and William D. Eggers. 2004. *Governing by Network: The New Shape of the Public Sector*. Washington, DC: Brookings Institution Press.

Grim, Brian J., and Roger Finke. 2006. "International Religion Indexes: Government Regulation, Government Favoritism, and Social Regulation of Religion." *Interdisciplinary Journal of Research on Religion* 2, article 1.

Gunn, T. Jeremy. 2000. "A Preliminary Response to Criticisms of the International Religious Freedom Act of 1998." *Brigham Young University Law Review* 2000(3): 841–65.

Hamilton, Alexander, John Jay, and James Madison. [1787–1788] 1982. *The Federalist*. New York: Bantam.

Hertzke, Allen D. 2004. *Freeing God's Children: The Unlikely Alliance for Global Human Rights*. Lanham, MD: Rowman & Littlefield.

Hobbes, Thomas. [1651] 1962. *Leviathan or the Matter, Forme and Power of a Commonwealth Ecclesiasticall and Civil.* Michael Oakeshott, ed. New York: Collier Books.

Hooghe, Liesbet, and Gary Marks. 2001. *Multi-Level Governance and European Integration.* Lanham, MD: Rowman & Littlefield.

———. 2003. "Unraveling the Central State, but How? Types of Multi-Level Governance." *American Political Science Review* 97(2): 233–43.

James, William. [1902] 1997. *The Varieties of Religious Experience: A Study in Human Nature.* New York: Simon & Schuster.

Jenkins, Philip. 2003. *The Next Christendom: The Coming of Global Christianity.* New York: Oxford University Press.

Johnston, Douglas, ed. 2003. *Faith-Based Diplomacy.* New York: Oxford University Press.

Johnston, Douglas, and Cynthia Sampson, eds. 1994. *Religion: The Missing Dimension of Statecraft.* New York: Oxford University Press.

Kniss, Fred, and David Todd Campbell. 1997. "The Effect of Religious Orientation on International Relief and Development Organizations." *Journal for the Scientific Study of Religion* 36(1): 93–103.

Kuran, Timur. 2001. "The Provision of Public Goods under Islamic Law: Origins, Impact, and Limitations of the *Waqf* System." *Law & Society Review* 35(4): 841–98.

Landes, William M., and Richard A. Posner. 1979. "Adjudication as a Private Good: Part I. The Market for Judicial Services." *Journal of Legal Studies* 8(2): 234–59.

Larson, Gerald James, ed. 2001. *Religion and Personal Law in Secular India: A Call to Judgment.* Bloomington: Indiana University Press.

Lauren, Paul Gordon. 2003. *The Evolution of International Human Rights: Visions Seen.* 2nd ed. Philadelphia: University of Pennsylvania Press.

Lichbach, Mark I. 1996. *The Cooperator's Dilemma.* Ann Arbor: University of Michigan Press.

Llewellyn, Karl N., and E. Adamson Hoebel. 1941. *The Cheyenne Way: Conflict and Case Law in Primitive Jurisprudence.* Norman: University of Oklahoma Press.

Marshall, Paul. 2005. *Radical Islam's Rules: The Worldwide Spread of Extreme Sharia Law.* Lanham, MD: Rowman & Littlefield.

Marthoz, Jean-Paul, and Joseph Saunders. 2005. "Religion and the Human Rights Movement." *Human Rights Watch World Report 2005*, 40–69.

McCleary, Rachel M. 2004. "Taking God Overseas: Christian Private Voluntary Organizations in International Relief and Development." Paper presented at the annual meeting of the International Studies Association, Montreal, Canada, March.

McGinnis, Michael D., ed. 1999a. *Polycentric Governance and Development: Readings from the Workshop in Political Theory and Policy Analysis.* Ann Arbor: University of Michigan Press.

———, ed. 1999b. *Polycentricity and Local Public Economies: Readings from the Workshop in Political Theory and Policy Analysis.* Ann Arbor: University of Michigan Press.

———, ed. 2000. *Polycentric Games and Institutions: Readings from the Workshop in Political Theory and Policy Analysis.* Ann Arbor: University of Michigan Press.

———. 2006. "Proselytism Games and Humanitarian Aid." Presented at the 2006 North American Meeting of the Peace Science Society (International), Columbus, OH, November 10–12.

———. 2007. "From Self-Reliant Churches to Self-Governing Communities: Comparing the Indigenisation of Christianity and Democracy in Sub-Saharan Africa." *Cambridge Review of International Affairs* 20(3): 401–16.

McGinnis, Michael D., and Elinor Ostrom. 2008. "Will Lessons from Small-Scale Social Dilemmas Scale Up?" In *New Issues and Paradigms in Research on Social Dilemmas,* ed. Anders Biel, Daniel Eek, Tommy Gärling, and Mathias Gustafsson, 189–211. Berlin: Springer.

McGinnis, Michael D., and Vincent Ostrom. 1999. "Democratic Transformations: From the Struggle for Democracy to Self-Governance?" Paper presented at the 2nd Workshop on the Workshop conference, Indiana University, Bloomington, June 10–12.

Monsma, S. 1996. *When Sacred and Secular Mix: Religious Nonprofit Organizations and Public Money.* Lanham, MD: Rowman & Littlefield.

Moore, Sally Falk. 2001. "Certainties Undone: Fifty Turbulent Years of Legal Anthropology, 1949–1999." *Journal of the Royal Anthropological Institute* (N.S.) 7: 95–116.

Nichols, J. Bruce. 1988. *The Uneasy Alliance: Religion, Refugee Work, and U.S. Foreign Policy.* New York: Oxford University Press.

Ostrom, Elinor. 1965. "Public Entrepreneurship: A Case Study in Ground Water Management." Ph.D. diss., University of California at Los Angeles.

———. 2005. *Understanding Institutional Diversity.* Princeton, NJ: Princeton University Press.

Ostrom, Elinor, and Vincent Ostrom. 2004. "The Quest for Meaning in Public Choice." *American Journal of Economics and Sociology* 63(1): 105–47.

Ostrom, Vincent. 1990a. "Problems of Cognition as a Challenge to Policy Analysts and Democratic Societies." *Journal of Theoretical Politics* 2(3): 243–62. Reprinted in Michael D. McGinnis, ed., *Polycentric Governance and Development: Readings from the Workshop in Political Theory and Policy Analysis* (Ann Arbor: University of Michigan Press, 1999, 394–415).

———. 1990b. "Religion and the Constitution of the American Political System." *Emory Law Journal* 39(1): 165–90.

———. 1991. *The Meaning of American Federalism: Constituting a Self-Governing Society.* San Francisco, CA: ICS Press.

———. 1997. *The Meaning of Democracy and the Vulnerability of Democracies.* Ann Arbor: University of Michigan Press.

———. [1973] 2008a. *The Intellectual Crisis in American Public Administration.* 3rd ed. Tuscaloosa: University of Alabama Press.

———. [1971] 2008b. *The Political Theory of a Compound Republic: Designing the American Experiment.* 3rd ed. Lanham, MD: Lexington Books.

Ostrom, Vincent, Charles M. Tiebout, and Robert Warren. 1961. "The Organization of Government in Metropolitan Areas: A Theoretical Inquiry." *American Political Science Review* 55(4): 831–42. Reprinted in Michael D. McGinnis, ed., *Polycentricity and Local Public Economies: Readings from the Workshop in Political Theory and Policy Analysis* (Ann Arbor: University of Michigan Press, 1999, 31–51).

Potter, Pitman B. 2003. "Belief in Control: Regulation of Religion in China." *China Quarterly* 174 (June): 317–37.

Roy, Sara. 2000. "The Transformation of Islamic NGOs in Palestine." *Middle East Report* 214 (Spring): 24–26.

Smith, Adam. [1776] 1976. *An Inquiry into the Nature and Causes of the Wealth of Nations.* Edwin Cannan, ed. Chicago: University of Chicago Press.

Smith, Steven Rathgeb, and Michael R. Sosin. 2001. "The Varieties of Faith-Related Agencies." *Public Administration Review* 61(6): 651–70.

Stark, Rodney, and Roger Finke. 2000. *Acts of Faith: Explaining the Human Side of Religion.* Berkeley: University of California Press.

Tocqueville, Alexis de. [1856] 1955. *The Old Régime and the French Revolution.* Trans. Stuart Gilbert. New York: Doubleday.

———. [1835] 1969. *Democracy in America.* Ed. J. P. Mayer, trans. George Lawrence. New York: Doubleday.

Viotti, Paul, and Mark Kauppi. 1998. *International Relations Theory: Realism, Liberalism, Globalism.* 3rd ed. New York: Prentice Hall.

Wald, Kenneth D., and Allison Calhoun-Brown. 2006. *Religion and Politics in the United States.* 5th ed. Lanham, MD: Rowman & Littlefield.

Witte, John, Jr., and Michael Bourdeaux, eds. 1999. *Proselytism and Orthodoxy in Russia: The New War for Souls.* Maryknoll, NY: Orbis.

Wuthnow, Robert. 2004. *Saving America? Faith-Based Services and the Future of Civil Society.* Princeton, NJ: Princeton University Press.

5

Challenges to Interreligious Liberative Collective Action between Muslims and Christians

Anas Malik

Establishing trust can be a significant social problem, and arises in part because ideas can play two roles. On the one hand, ideas can get taken seriously as being constitutive to a particular social context; in this version, ideas represent core inner beliefs shared by actors. On the other hand, ideas can be dismissed as mere ploys and deceptions, propagandic manipulations covering an underlying "boss rule" reality. In this version, cynical actors deploy ideas selectively as fig leaves for other interests. The person who takes ideas seriously risks being a sucker.

This dichotomy—ideas as authentic values vs. ideas as propagandic deceptions—is troubling from an institutional analysis and design perspective. It is troubling because ideas are frequently necessary underpinnings to a social order. When misused, ideas can have meaning gutted from them. The result in its extreme form is something like George Orwell's "doublespeak" attributed to *1984*. Language itself can lose meaning and thus all communication becomes suspect and untrustworthy. This dystopian impulse is a major threat to a successfully constituted civil order. It undermines the prospect that legitimate, deeply felt grievances can be aired and redressed through civil means.

Ideas are prominent in interreligious dialogue as well as interreligious collective efforts for ecological and human justice. Idealistic religious traditions should have a strong role in working together to speak truth to power and bring more justice to the world. A growing literature that I have termed the Interreligious Liberative Collective Action (ILCA) program addresses and encourages this. This literature has roots, cognates, and parallels in numerous traditions, including "liberation theology" in Latin America.

Religious politics are heavily imbued with ideas, ideology, and symbols; there is constant and frequent justification for particular policy choices and platforms based on a religious tradition's letter and spirit. In that idea-drenched context, one would imagine a greater problem in distinguishing when ideas ought to be taken seriously, and when they are simply deceptive machinations veiling other purposes. Writers such as Hans Küng, Paul Knitter, Farid Esack, and Edward Schillebeeckx have engaged in an institutional supply effort, trying to provide the institutional resources for successful collective action in religiously diverse contexts. But a formal analysis exposes an uninterrogated assumption: the challenge to successful CA is assumed to be a Harmony challenge, similar to the Harmony Game, rather than a challenge analogous to the Prisoner's Dilemma. This essay argues that the Prisoner's Dilemma metaphor captures an important, frequently recurring situation. This demands specific institutional mechanisms for successful ILCA, particularly one decision rule stating that the more powerful actor must take the biggest risk first. If Prisoner's Dilemma assumptions (and consequent incentives to defect, free-ride, or shirk) are not included in working on the institutional design problem, then genuine and successful ILCA is unlikely.

Strategic analysis requires making strong assumptions and reducing complexity. Several strategic form analogies from game theory, including Harmony, Coordination, and Prisoner's Dilemma, are described. The Küng-Knitter proposal has arguably been written as if the underlying strategic form were Harmony or Coordination. While this may sometimes be the case, Prisoner's Dilemma is arguably a frequently reasonable depiction. Under these assumptions, there is significant potential for individual rationality to produce collective irrationality. Mistrust, even in small amounts, can trigger defensive damage-prevention behavior and undermine collective action. Social cooperation is preferable to noncooperation, but can be thwarted under even weak Prisoner's Dilemma assumptions about individual motivations.

The focus here is primarily the Christian-Muslim boundary, often a sharply polarized divide. This is ironic given that as proselytizing traditions with universal ambition, they display recurrent "twinness," and perceptual mirror images (Bulliet 2004). Europe as "Christendom" was arguably defined in hostile contradistinction to "Islam," leading Tomaz Mastnak to ask whether there is a permanent crusade underlying "Europeanness" (Mastnak 2003). Given such a contentious historical legacy and its accompanying mistrust, it is appropriate to wonder about prospects for high-stakes collaboration. This study suggests that that interreligious civil society can yield significant cooperation increases, but failure to adequately design institutions can scuttle such efforts, or further exacerbate catastrophic conditions. When designing such institutions, religious norms can be a powerful tool, but the most effective designs will also pay attention to other pragmatic factors enumerated in the institutional design literature.

Interreligious Liberative Collective Action (ILCA) Proposals

Various voices in the clerical, activist, and academic arenas, along with statements from interreligious organizations, have stressed the need for different religious communities to collaborate in pursuing justice and collective well-being. I examine a prominent position taken by Hans Küng (1991) and modified and elaborated by Paul Knitter (1995).

Küng has argued that "one world needs one basic ethic" for survival given catastrophic ecological and social conditions (1991, cited in Knitter 1995, 68). Küng believes that an overlapping ethical consensus is possible and achievable through dialogue, eventually forming a "moral platform on which countries can form common action for common problems" (Knitter, 68). Such morality requires a religious foundation (Knitter, 70).

In *One Earth, Many Religions: Multifaith Dialogue and Global Responsibility*, Knitter (1995) argues that an orientation toward social justice and respect and care for the earth can be the basis for a genuinely pluralistic interreligious dialogue, or in his language, a "pluralistic, correlational, global responsible" model for dialogue. All nations, Knitter asserts, have or will recognize three ethical insights:

> 1) Human beings, as individuals and as communities, have a *global responsibility*—that is, a responsibility to promote the wellbeing and life of a threatened humanity and planet; 2) Such a responsibility cannot be *carried out separately* by individuals or individual communities. Disjointed, uncoordinated actions simply are not up to the job. Global responsibility must be communal responsibility; it must be a joint project; and 3) Such a joint, communal project is impossible—here Küng is right—without some kind of *communal agreement or consensus on ethical values*, visions and guidelines for action. We need global dialogue toward a "global ethics" in order to carry out our global responsibility. (1995, 70; emphasis in original)

This three-piece statement can be augmented to say that the global dialogue must be driven by more than ideas alone, and more than individual praxis and efforts to collaborate, but systematic thinking and tactical strategizing about effective routes to collective action.

Knitter appears to believe that the major threat to his advocacy comes from religious exclusivists, some inclusivists, and post-modernists. A focus on strategic forms, however, shows that there is a collective action hurdle that poses new questions about privilege, risk, trust, and preference. These can thwart the entire project even when there is a strongly shared broad ideological vision. How can well-meaning individuals who want to work together actually come together? Do they use existing forums, for example, through a resolution introduced to the World Parliament of Religions? Do they seek to create new organizations altogether? Or do they simply rely on anomic solidary groups that form and disband as occasions arise? The apparently "spontaneous" collective action—such as a mob riot amid social deprivation—also needs to overcome thorny collective action obstacles.

Knitter's greatest appeal lies in his proclamation that injustice must be ethically addressed and those who suffer have authentic grievances requiring redress. Injustice is suffering that need not or should not be, and can be found in human suffering through poverty and war, and earth-suffering through environmental destruction (Knitter 1995, 63). Religious persons cannot ignore this, and in fact must react to victimization and injustice with "the realistic, humble, and repentant recognition that religions themselves have played a significant and shameful role in fostering or sanctioning the exploitation of some people by others" (Knitter, 65).

Much associational activity happens within religious contexts. ILCA proponents appeal to a new interreligious associational impetus relying on citizenship based on shared values and concerns. This is an argument for religious civil society. It draws on the motivating and energizing forces that inhere in religions, adds substantial content, and directs it toward the most pressing catastrophes in our time—injustice against the earth and its people.

Exclusivism, Inclusivism, and Pluralism among Christians and Muslims: Selected Perspectives

Knitter advocates an interreligious dialogue that is both correlational (acknowledging the equal rights and possible universal validity of all religions) and globally responsible ("affirming a commitment to eco-human well-being as a ground for dialogue") (1995, 54). This raises critical questions: Does working with other faiths on a common value basis weaken or obscure one's own faith tradition? How do religious individuals approach and bridge such differences? What bases are there for working with people of other faiths? And how might collective action be interpreted from Muslim perspectives?

There are substantial difficulties in comparing across religious traditions while retaining appreciation for the pluralities within them. It is nevertheless striking that a general ethic promoting collaboration for the common good and a productive social order can be identified. The likely amenability to ILCA is influenced by how religious individuals from one faith tradition approach those who adhere to other faiths. It is superficial, though, to presume that the less validity one sees in other faiths, the more likely one is to treat them as competitor, diabolic, or untrustworthy collective action partners. Such simplistic correlations are belied by even cursorily and selectively summarizing different approaches among Muslims.

Christianity's approach to other faiths has been classified into three perspectives: exclusivist, inclusivist, and pluralist (Knitter 1995). Exclusivists are most associated with strict evangelical positions that see the Truth and being Saved as only possible through accepting Jesus as Christ. Inclusivists see possible salvation in other faiths but most fully only through Christ, or through being an "anonymous" Christian. An allied perspective is the view held by such figures as Louis Massignon and perhaps Charles de Foucauld, suggesting that God is working through Muslims. Pluralists genuinely accept the possibility that salvation may be achieved through other faiths. Some religious individuals fear that pluralism presumes equal validity among all, watering down each tradition and producing a gooey sameness. But this greater togetherness can lead to more thoroughly understanding difference and diversity, as Alfred Whitehead has suggested.

Soteriology (the concern with salvation) and the focus on suffering are (to many Muslim ears) particularly Christian ideas, although there are important corollaries in Muslim scripture and religious guidance, through such concepts as *najaa* or *falah*, and *khusraan* (being saved or success, utter loss), related closely to reward and punishment in *dunya* (lower world, this life) and *akhira* (the later condition, the Hereafter); a common supplication asks for the good in *dunya* and *akhira*, as well as protection from the Fire's punishment. Similarly, exclusivism, inclusivism, and pluralism are categories drawn from Christianity's evolution, but there are rough parallels to important current and traditional voices in Muslim scholarship. Here, I briefly consider a traditionalist perspective that is exclusivist; an inclusivist perspective based on Quranic translations by Marmaduke Pickthall, Muhammad Asad, and Yusuf Ali (and a reference to Abu Hamid Ghazali's quasi-inclusivism); a perennialist view; and a "progressive" Muslim perspective that purports to continually subject all positions to critical re-evaluation while prioritizing a common commitment to fighting injustice.

Powerful scriptural support for an exclusivist Muslim position exists. Surat Al-Imran, verse 85 reads, "And whoso seeketh as religion other than the Surrender (to Allah) it will not be accepted from him, and he will be a loser in the Hereafter" (Quran, 3:85, Pickthall translation, 1976). "The Surrender" in the Quranic Arabic is al-Islam—if this is taken as the proper name, Islam with a big I, then it supports exclusivist thinking. Nuh Keller, a staunch *madhabi* (adherent to the classical jurisprudential schools), also adopts an exclusivist view, citing Quran 3:85 (mentioned above), and stating:

> As for today, only Islam is valid or acceptable now that Allah has sent it to all men, for the Prophet (Allah bless him and give him peace) has said, "By Him in whose hand is the soul of Muhammad, any person of this Community, any Jew, or any Christian who hears of me and dies without believing in what I have been sent with will be an inhabitant of hell". . . (al-Baghawi: Sharh al-sunna 1.104). That Islam is the only remaining valid or acceptable religion is necessarily known as part of our religion, and to believe anything other than this is unbelief (kufr) that places a person outside of Islam, as Imam Nawawi notes: "Someone who does not believe that whoever follows another religion besides Islam is an unbeliever (like Christians), or doubts that such a person is an unbeliever, or considers their sect to be valid, is himself an unbeliever (kafir) even if he manifests Islam and believes in it" (Rawda al-talibin, 10.70). This is not only the position of the Shafii school of jurisprudence represented by Nawawi, but is also the recorded position of all three other Sunni schools: Hanafi (Ibn Abidin: Radd al-muhtar, 3.287), Maliki (al-Dardir: al-Sharh al-saghir, 4.435), and Hanbali (al-Bahuti: Kashshaf al-qina, 6.170). Those who know fiqh literature will note that each of these works is the foremost fatwa resource in its school. The scholars of Sacred Law are unanimous about the abrogation of all other religions by Islam because it is the position of Islam itself. It only remains for the sincere Muslim to submit to, in which connection Ibn al-`Arabi has said: "Beware lest you ever say anything that does not conform to the pure Sacred Law. Know that the highest stage of the perfected ones (rijal) is the Sacred Law of Muhammad (Allah bless him and give him peace). And know that the esoteric that contravenes the exoteric is a fraud." (al-Burhani: al-Hall al-sadid, 32) (Keller 1996)

Exclusivism does not necessarily mean automatic opposition or lack of common cause with liberation-seekers in other communities. Liberative dialogue is arguably embedded in the Quranic approach. The philosopher Shabbir

Akhtar has argued that liberation theology amounts to an "Islamization of Christianity" (referenced in Murad 1999). Zaid Shakir, a Muslim traditionalist scholar, points to various exhortations in Muslim scriptural and jurisprudential literature exhorting the community toward collective security arrangements, and presents a moral vision for peaceable, ethical collaborations with non-Muslims on ecological and social issues (Shakir 2006).

The inclusivist position generally acknowledges the possible validity that other religions have, but nevertheless reserves for one's own faith greatest or fullest salvation or most thorough receptacle for God's Grace. A quasi-inclusivist perspective may be taken from the following Quranic verse: "Who receiveth guidance, receiveth it for his own benefit: who goeth astray doth so to his own loss: No bearer of burdens can bear the burden of another: nor would We visit with Our Wrath until We had sent an apostle (to give warning)" (Quran, 17:15, Yusuf Ali translation).

One way to interpret this is that God does not punish a people until He sends them a messenger, or fair warning in other words. Islam's message, although "universal," might not have reached non-Muslims in genuine, undistorted form, and so they could not be said to truly have been sent a messenger. Thus, such people might be saved (akin to a well-known position taken by classical scholar Abu Hamid Ghazali). A separate position is that people can independently locate theistic truths by philosophy alone (akin to a Mutazilite rationalist position that depicts reason and revelation as alternative paths to Truth).

But this leaves some open questions. For one thing, detractors at the Prophet's time also spent much time distorting his message. Also, people have their preoccupations—suffering, injustice, and other human problems. For those who Muslims have oppressed, there are likely to be severe psychological obstacles to seeing "Islam's truth." The Quran clearly specifies that God does not burden a soul with more than what it can bear. Children are therefore not culpable, because they are insufficiently mature to discern the moral underpinnings and implications in their choices. Likewise, this applies to people who are in extenuating circumstances—extreme trials, mental illness, and the like.

Furthermore, Surah Baqarah states what Muhammad Asad (2003) has translated as follows:

> 2:62 VERILY, those who have attained to faith [in this divine writ], as well as those who follow the Jewish faith, and the Christians, and the Sabians—all who believe in God and the Last Day and do righteous deeds—shall have their reward with their Sustainer; and no fear need they have, and neither shall they grieve.

And in Asad's translation, Surah Maida states:

> 5:69 for, verily, those who have attained to faith [in this divine writ], as well as those who follow the Jewish faith, and the Sabians, and the Christians—all who believe in God and the Last Day and do righteous deeds—no fear need they have, and neither shall they grieve.

The Sabians are included too, and they are not "of the Book." This is another indication that other religions are potentially from Divine revelations. So a Muslim scholar committed to Quranic constraints does not have to do great intellectual gymnastics and contortions in order to locate a "book" in a religion. And this is in addition to the general belief among Muslims that messengers are sent to all peoples as warners and bearing good tidings. Surah al-Anbiyaa in the Quran (chap. 21, "The Prophets") records prophet after prophet sent to different peoples.

Those who continue to tolerate other faiths belong most closely to Knitter's second category, inclusivism. They see some salvation in other faiths, but the surest path and fullest truth is in their own. But certain Quranic verses seem to go beyond this, and appear to assure the reader that salvation can be achieved by all as long as they behave ethically while oriented toward God. Consider chapter 2, verses 110–12:

> 110. Establish worship and pay the poor-due and whatever of good ye send before (you) for your souls, ye will find it with Allah. Lo! Allah is Seer of what ye do.
> 111. And they say: None entereth Paradise unless he be a Jew or a Christian. These are their own desires. Say: Bring your proof (of what ye state) if ye are truthful.
> 112. Nay, but whosoever surrendereth his purpose to Allah while doing good, his reward is with his Lord; and there shall no fear come upon them neither shall they grieve. (Pickthall translation, 1976)

Verse 111 states an exclusivist position toward salvation. Verse 112 responds with what can be interpreted as a pluralist position. "Surrendering one's purpose to God" or "submitting to God" is literally what defines a Muslim (one who submits to God). So a Muslim exclusivist could still read this verse and see in it an argument for accepting Islam. But my understanding is that this is a broader statement applying to many contexts, including those that have no formal Muslims there at all.

The pluralist position takes a step beyond the inclusivist, and demands an ongoing honest self-examining dialogue that takes the probability that other religions have significant value very seriously. A distinct pluralist counterpart to the exclusivist position is the "perennialist" school, with prominent exponents such as Seyyed Hossein Nasr (Hahn, Auxier, and Stone 2001) and Frithjof Schuon (1984). Perennialists emphasize the sense that each religious tradition's central wisdom offers insight into divine reality through reaffirming the Divine Center, usually with virtue, prayer, and paths to transcendent truth. The great traditions are seen as contextual tools for approaching an essential unity, and each is depicted in a frequent metaphor as a wheel-spoke leading from rim to center. But most importantly, "intellect" is interpreted in a sense that includes the "heart's eye," an inner awareness and knowledge achieved through purity, humility, and righteousness, and providing insight into a deeper essential reality. Perennialists often understand themselves as Muslims. Muslims are taught that many prophets were sent, even though we are only given names for a few. These many prophets could surely have left different traditions in different places. Confucius, Buddha, and the Native American tradition Frithjof Schuon found in the Plains Indians—all these potentially had truth ingrained in them, even though it might be mixed with other contextual imports.

The Quran refers to the leader "ZulQarnain" or the "two-horned," who encountered a people that were naked, and rather then forcing them to follow his way, he let them be, and was not condemned for it in the Quran, but rather tacitly affirmed (Quran, chap. 18). All theists, then, might potentially have inherited a genuinely prophetic tradition. The burden on the Muslim observer was to better examine each tradition, and presume first that it had prophetic background unless that thesis could be disproved, rather than the more conventional approach, which presumed no prophetic background unless otherwise proved. God's guidance can thus potentially be seen in people's heritage everywhere.

There is even a way to incorporate ostensible nontheists under the pluralist umbrella. Belief in any value is to reject the purely relativistic Nietzchean position that there are no absolutes. Affirming an absolute value required a metaphysical faith in something greater and more lasting than oneself. In this view, the lasting, eternal thing, the object pursued by the temporally bounded fallible finite human, could be none other than God. This position is made easier intellectually by noting that most values that people pursue deeply are values that God's nature is supposed to embody—for example, Beauty, Truth, Justice, Mercy.

In the Muslim context, Esack (1997) takes a position that has a lineage and close relationship with Christian thinkers in the ILCA tradition. Like Knitter, Esack is conscious that some religious interpretation has served to perpetuate or bolster injustice. Farid Esack's *Qurán, Liberation, and Pluralism* seeks to develop a progressive Islamic theology that is oriented to the fight against injustice. He advocates a "South African qur'anic hermeneutic of religious pluralism for liberation" (Esack, 12). It is "progressive" in the sense that in reading scripture critically to better pursue "justice," he challenges orthodoxy and power by trying to critically reassess long-held positions in traditional scholarship, in such areas as women's rights and sexuality. Like Knitter, Esack also advocates interreligious collaboration and support for promoting the public good. One traditional public goods provider has been "government." But what Knitter and Esack argue is not for a government solution necessarily. Instead, their emphasis is on the transnational pressure group model for interreligious collaboration. It is a call for creating a global constituency for ethical, religiously grounded action against injustice.

Abdul Hakim Murad, a staunch Muslim traditionalist *madhab* adherent, acknowledges historical *fiqh* sources that implicitly support ILCA, but scathingly criticizes and denounces Esack's "progressive" methodology. The dive into pluralism is dangerous for the proponent in part because such negative reactions exist. Murad's response to Farid Esack is that Esack has become an imperialist tool in an insidious "religion-building." Appearing to be an imperialist lackey clearly delegitimizes one's value on the ground in a home territory where the sensitivity to invasive forces is high. Murad also fears that a post-modernist genie has been released from its bottle—today's extremism becomes tomorrow's innovation, and Islam self-destructs. To Murad, the Esackian approach opens the door to anarchy, potentially validating violent extremism and Wahabbi takfir, in addition to feminist and alternative-sexuality movements.

On the surface it would appear that Esack's progressive, pluralist approach might be the most amenable to ILCA projects. But Shakir (2006) clearly states a position advocating ILCA based on traditional sources, a call to collaborate for the common good that appeals to those with exclusivist views. As even this brief, selective, and introductory look at several Muslim positions on how to view those from other faith communities has suggested, whether one is an exclusivist, inclusivist, or pluralist, one can still accept that other faiths exist and motivate their adherents. This acceptance ethic—for which the Quran and Muslim tradition offer ample resources—provides support for ILCA, a personal doctrinal and theological basis for collaborating with people in other faith traditions in difficult efforts to fix injustices. A fuller look at the challenges to ILCA requires going beyond this theological-identification step into the strategic challenges that come with trying to act collectively. Game theory is a useful tool for shedding light on these challenges.

Modeling ILCA Using Strategic Forms from Game Theory

Farid Esack's public talks often include a bus metaphor—ILCA participants are on a bus going somewhere, and talking to each other on the way, headed to a common destination, but without necessarily all being exactly identical. This is an appealing picture: interreligious global coaction is akin to riders on a bus, on a journey together, and engaging in a conversation. But the collective action focus requires asking certain questions: Who pays for the gas and rents the bus? Who drives and who is the conductor? The answers to these questions are not obvious to all—each solution to this problem presents different costs, benefits, and power distributions to various participants. Thus, how interreligious discourse and action are organized is itself a political process. Addressing this challenge is a basic requirement for realizing the global ethic vision.

Game theory provides metaphors that distill strategic behavior given specific assumptions about incentives and choices facing actors. This can be problematic for religious contexts in which high moral principles are supposed to animate the believer beyond mundane and narrow interests. One might argue that religious individuals are extraordinarily self-motivated, ethically-driven characters who do not engage in mundane rational cost-benefit calculations and simply wish to do things "for others." The problem with such a position is that even such value-driven individuals will not want to be made "suckers" by others, for example if others claim credit for some achievement without genuinely paying the costs, or simply benefit from a public good without paying their fair share of the costs. Even if we elevate the assumed "serving others" orientation to the point where individuals are willing to pay costs even if others unfairly benefit, a thornier problem exists. Cynical, manipulative individuals may manipulate one's efforts, direct them to other, selfish objectives, and abuse trust relationships by defecting from agreements to gain some advantage. And that threat—captured well in the Prisoner's Dilemma game (elaborated below), driven not by one's own selfishness, but the fear that other parties might be tempted to behave selfishly—can debilitate social cooperation and collective action among actors from different religious traditions.

In ethnic politics, ideas can be manipulated for other purposes. Essentialist, instrumentalist, constructivist, and post-modernist views differ on the extent to which they can be manipulated (Varshney 2003). An essentialist reading would presume that certain guiding principles inhere within particular communities and do not easily change. An instrumentalist reading would suggest that elites deploy particular principles or symbols for other purposes. A constructivist reading would see these as an ongoing interaction that continually redefines the principles and with it identity. A post-modernist reading would see these terms as definable in different ways by different actors. Sayyid (1997) argues that Islam serves as a "master signifier." It contains multiple interpretations but nevertheless retains a coherence and unity in the way Muslims orient themselves. The implication is that both identity and principle can be simultaneous forces defining and linking the Muslim community.

Game Models

For illustrative and logical clarity, it is helpful to start with simplified models and survey their implications before adding more complexity to the picture. Assume that there are two social actors with two choices each—whether to cooperate or not with the other in a collective action. To allow some more concrete thinking, consider a hypothetical example in which one actor is a South African Muslim leader, and the other actor is a South African Christian leader, deciding on whether to work together to take action against the apartheid system in South Africa. Successful ILCA requires that both cooperate. If both choose to not cooperate (defect, in other words), then the ILCA will be unsuccessful. If only one cooperates while the other defects, ILCA will also be unsuccessful. Consider the depiction in table 5.1.

Each has the C option, to cooperate sincerely in a joint liberative effort. Each may also choose D, to defect, that is to not cooperate with such an effort. Assume further that each outcome carries with it an expected utility for each actor. For clarity, the analysis usually proceeds from Person A's perspective.

In other words, CC, CD, DC, and DD come with different expected utilities. I argue below that Knitter implies a model where the expected utility of CC exceeds all other outcomes. He further presumes that CC>CD=DC>DD. In other words, each actor sees the cooperative choice as the best possible action whatever the other one does, and therefore chooses to cooperate.

Table 5.1. Basic strategic form

		Person B (Christian leader)	
		Cooperate	Defect
Person A (Muslim leader)	Cooperate	C,C	C,D
	Defect	D,C	D,D

ILCA Proponents Presume Harmony and Coordination

Knitter's work implies that the strategic form games that closely model the situation for interreligious cooperation are the Harmony and Coordination games. The Harmony game is depicted in table 5.2 (drawn from Bueno de Mesquita 2006).

In this game, each actor prefers to always cooperate. By cooperating, one gains the maximal reward (4). By defecting, one might gain the reward (4) but might also be left with a (1). So the better choice is always to cooperate. In other words, from Person A's perspective, the game preferences are given by CC>CD>DC>DD. Imagine a situation where there are relatively few conflicting interests. The underlying harmony means that each prefers cooperation (Powner and Bennett 2006, 35). Applied to the South African case, the Muslim leader (assumed to be Person A) will always collaborate with the Christian leader in anti-apartheid efforts. Doing otherwise does not arise as a possibility because cooperation is the only option that always returns a "4" on the utility score.

Another possible model is the Coordination game, in which the worst thing is for some to cooperate and others to defect. Imagine drivers choosing whether to drive on the right or left side. Two solutions are possible, and neither is in itself more beneficial to one driver over another. What is important is that everyone has to stick with one solution. If "cooperation" means driving on the right side, then the ideal is that everyone cooperates. This minimizes traffic accidents and snarls. If everyone simultaneously defects and chooses to drive on the left side, then this is worse, because the road signs now point the wrong way—but at least cars are not driving straight at each other. If some try to cooperate while others defect, there will be cars driving both on the right side and the left side, with the worst possible result—many accidents and a frightening gridlock. This is represented in table 5.3.

Table 5.2. Harmony game

		Person B (Christian leader)	
		Cooperate	Defect
Person A (Muslim leader)	Cooperate	4,4	4,1
	Defect	1,4	1,1

Here, CC>DD>DC=CD. This might fit the interreligious model if we decide that the worst thing is for some to go along with a decision while others contradict them, so that the result is a great religious confusion, and religious actors are neutralized into irrelevance. It would be as if in South Africa under apartheid, some Christians and some Muslims sought to act against apartheid, but others acted to support it, and the two canceled each other out as a meaningful faith community impacting the country's future.

The Prisoner's Dilemma Game: An Alternative (and More Likely) Strategic Form

A Prisoner's Dilemma strategic depiction has been a major analytical tool for many collective action situations. Under Prisoner's Dilemma assumptions, DC>CC>DD>CD. Actors' interests may conflict in such a situation. By defecting, Person A gains something, while Person B loses something. Person A prefers this to choosing to cooperate and having the opposing actor defect. Person A sees the highest possible utility as coming from suckering out the other person by defecting while the other cooperates. Conversely, the worst outcome for Person A is to be the sucker by cooperating while Person B defects. If each actor knows that the other understands these strategic motivations, then each actor will choose to defect to avoid becoming the sucker. That individually rational choice, however, produces a collective irrationality: the actors end up in DD, which is worse than CC. If the two actors could somehow manage to overcome their fear that the other might defect, then a more preferable outcome would be obtained.

Continuing with the anti-apartheid struggle metaphor, the fear South African Muslims had was of being expelled should the struggle succeed.

Table 5.3. Coordination game

		Person B (Christian leader)	
		Cooperate	Defect
Person A (Muslim leader)	Cooperate	4,4	1,1
	Defect	1,1	3,3

In other words, they feared that successful collaboration with Christian groups would be bad for them patriotically in the long run. They feared that Christians might take advantage of this, much as Idi Amin kicked out South Asian-origin people from Uganda.

Christians, on the other hand, sought cooperation from Muslims to enhance the liberation struggle. But they also feared expulsion or expropriation under a black regime. The default position, inaction, was bad for both. It meant continued life under apartheid, with all its social ills and moral consequences. Both would prefer successful ongoing cooperation. Each feared the possibility that the Other would defect at some point, and use insider status on the revolutionary coalition to target the other's community, or important portions thereof. And that fear of being further targeted was estimated differently according to one's beliefs, perceptions, and expectations. The worst outcome, though, was to cooperate prophetically and then be targeted by a later defection. This is a purely hypothetical exercise for illustrative purposes; it is clear that in the real historical liberation struggle in South Africa, Muslims were disproportionately present and active contributors, explaining in large part the high legitimacy the small Muslim population enjoyed in the post-apartheid period.

The Prisoner's Dilemma game modeled below demonstrates this. The individual rationality each actor uses results in noncooperation, a collective irrationality. The dominant strategy (what an actor will prefer whichever choice the other makes) is to Defect, that is, DC>CC>DD>CD. The question for the interreligious dialogic interaction is whether this is a plausible strategic depiction, as described in table 5.4.

The PD game is more reasonable than Coordination or Harmony because it allows for the possibility that one actor will be tempted to take advantage at the other's expense. Anything less than total trust in the Other's motiva-

Table 5.4. Prisoner's Dilemma game

		Person B (Christian leader)	
		Cooperate	Defect
Person A (Muslim leader)	Cooperate	Successful collective action. Both help realize a better world. 3,3	Person A is the sucker. Person B gains some advantage—he has betrayed A, improved religion B's position. 1,4
	Defect	Person B is the sucker. Person A gains some advantage—he has betrayed B, and improved religion A's position. 4,1	No collective action; so world problems remain, as does the interreligious project's failure. 2,2

tions can potentially lead one to behave in a preemptive defensive fashion and defect first. This is a significant hurdle that Küng, Knitter, Esack, and other proponents have to cross in organizing diverse groups for collective action. The challenge faced is that the poor and oppressed and disenfranchised have little grounds to trust those from powerful communities, particularly when the powerful are blamed for victimizing, underdeveloping, and neoimperializing the poor.

It is possible that one actor may perceive the strategic situation as a Harmony game while the other perceives it as a Prisoner's Dilemma game. Some cynics who dismiss the ILCA prospects make the presumption that supporters are naïve optimists who minimize underlying conflicts. The "reality" in this critical view is that people's interests are in conflict, so the ones who end up realizing this sooner will end up defecting and thereby making suckers from the naïve Harmony envisioners, who always choose cooperation. ILCA proponents would like people to act as though they are in a Harmony game. But many people arguably see things as being closer to a PD game, whether or not they explicitly articulate this.

The Collective Action (CA) Problem: A Many-Person PD Game

Despite their emphasis on praxis and personal experiences in social movements, Knitter and Esack do not explicitly acknowledge a fundamental constraint to CA: the free-rider problem. Social cooperation requires overcoming the problem that some might defect from an agreement. "Free-riding" on the efforts made by others, or "shirking" one's duty in principal-agent relationships, are, like the dominant outcome in the Prisoner's Dilemma game, related problems for social cooperation.

In *The Logic of Collective Action*, the key insight that Mancur Olson (1965) popularized was that large groups have more difficulties in engaging in successful CA to obtain a nonexcludable good than small groups. The collective action paradox is that larger groups with shared interests are less able to act in concert to achieve the shared goals. The problem is that a potential participant knows that if the group is unsuccessful, then he will have paid the costs for nothing. If the group is successful, then he will benefit, but so will others who did not participate or pay the costs. Therefore, it makes individual sense to "free-ride," to sit out and hope others do the work. This is a powerful, counterintuitive insight. It explains why bankers' associations and doctors' associations are easier to form than borrowers' associations or patients' associations; why successful consumer action is often rarer than business collusion—even though there are more people who are consumers or borrowers or patients, it is harder for them to come together and act collectively.

Knitter emphasizes that joint action on a global scale is desperately needed. Such joint action will provide benefits to many people, but counts as a public good. In other words, once the good is made available (e.g., increased social justice, or peace), then people cannot be excluded from receiving the good's benefits. Because public goods are nonexcludable, providing them contains peculiar challenges. Coherent joint action needed to achieve this public good requires overcoming the "free-rider problem."

One does not usually view highly religious persons as those who would free-ride on the efforts of others. But that is only among the crudest, least subtle tendencies that free-riding represents. Although one might not want to free-ride oneself, the possibility that others could do so gives one pause. Moreover, a critical question for anyone engaged in trying to define a global responsibility ethic building on religious liberative sentiments is "whose justice? Whose liberation?" (Knitter 1995, 97–117). In such a context, with so much at stake, defection poses an even greater threat. Thus, while religious people might generally be granted a hopeful surplus in the personal morality department, there is also a greater temptation to defect or manipulate, because there are high stakes involved.

Or to take this even further, consider that there is the possibility that one actor might defect (an understandable possibility, given the impact that unequal power has in preventing perfect honesty among the weak, and promoting self-protecting behavior among the strong). The heroic trusting leap for genuinely investing oneself in a single global ethic requires presuming similar leaps from others. But what if one's own faith is diluted and others survive? Will they not become hegemonic? That's partly the fear expressed by Knitter's critics who argue that pluralism can be imperialistic, or be imperialism in disguise (because "pluralism" itself features public-private spaces and divisions in a context-specific mix, and this is then imposed on other places where it is experienced as a violation). This may be seen as a security dilemma, which in international relations can produce vicious conflict escalation cycles.

One apparent paradox is that smaller interests have their policy goals better represented because they have an easier time organizing. In contrast, larger latent interests are sometimes left unarticulated because it is difficult to figure out how to organize many individuals so that each contributes his fair share and the group acts collectively. A common solution to the free-rider problem in larger groups is for a powerful leader or hegemon to impose a solution and then extract contributions from individual group members. But hegemony can mean manipulation, "imperialism," or imposing an agenda and process that may not satisfy everyone.

The free-rider problem can be described as an n-person PD game. An individual's preferences may be summarized as DC>CC>DD>CD. The individual can choose to cooperate with the project. If others defect, the individual is left with wasted effort. Ideally, the individual would like to defect while everyone else cooperates. Because everyone feels the same way, all choose to defect. And this produces the collective irrationality that DD is chosen despite the fact that CC is preferable.

What if free-riding, or defecting in an n-person game, is more malevolent in outcome than simply saving a few resources? Consider a situation where the defector can gain a decisive advantage over others. An example is the security dilemma in international relations, in which states arm themselves to improve their security, end up scaring other states who fear hostile intent and react by counterincreases in armaments, and both are left with more firepower and continuing or worsened insecurity. Here, if all the actors were able to cooperate and cut their arms simultaneously, their security would not suffer. The challenge posed by disarmament, however, is that individual states have a motivation to try to retain some arms secretly and then deploy them when others' weaknesses are known, exposed, or increased. It does not help matters if only a few actors cooperate—unless everyone cooperates the whole experiment falls apart.

Religions have this potential and tendency too. Although some religious figures are inspiring tireless diplomats and collaborative paragons, it remains the case that religious appeals also motivate hostile boundary activations and help mobilize individuals for political violence. A dialogue table might be effectively portrayed as an attempt to lull Muslims into quietude and divert their energies and efforts while an imperialistic domination project continues unabated and unchecked. This is a concern given a global context featuring deep inequalities and asymmetries. Given such pitfalls, it follows that the individual faith bases supporting efforts to build collective governance are more likely to succeed when incentives to defect and free-ride are reduced through thoughtful institutional design.

Acknowledgments

The author gratefully acknowledges feedback from Paul Knitter, Marie Giblin, David Loy, Sheldon Gellar, and Salvador Espinosa, as well as the Midwest Muslim-Catholic Dialogue participants. Any errors and omissions remain the author's sole responsibility.

References

Ali, Yusuf. *The Holy Qur'an*. English translation. http://www.islamicity.com/QuranSearch (accessed December 3, 2007).
Asad, Muhammad. 2003. *The Message of the Qur'an*. Translated and explained by Muhammad Asad. Bitton, England: Book Foundation.
Bueno de Mesquita, Bruce. 2006. *Principles of International Politics: People's Power, Preferences, and Perceptions*. 3rd ed. Washington, DC: CQ Press.
Bulliet, Richard. 2004. *The Case for Islamo-Christian Civilization*. New York: Columbia University Press.
Esack, Farid. 1997. *Qurán, Liberation and Pluralism: An Islamic Perspective of Interreligious Solidarity against Oppression*. Oxford, England; Rockport, MA: Oneworld.
Hahn, Lewis Edwin, Randall E. Auxier, and Lucian W. Stone Jr., eds. 2001. *The Philosophy of Seyyed Hossein Nasr*. Chicago: Open Court.
Keller, Nuh Ha Mim. 1996. "On the Validity of All Religions in the Thought of ibn Al-'Arabi and Emir 'Abd al-Qadir: A Letter to 'Abd al-Matin." http://www.masud.co.uk/ISLAM/nuh/amat.htm (accessed December 3, 2007).

Knitter, Paul. 1995. *One Earth, Many Religions: Multifaith Dialogue and Global Responsibility.* Maryknoll, NY: Orbis Books.

Küng, Hans. 1991. *Global Responsibility: In Search of a New World Ethic.* New York: Crossroad.

Mastnak, Tomaz. 2003. "Europe and the Muslims: The Permanent Crusade." In *The New Crusades: Constructing the Muslim Enemy*, ed. Emran Qureshi and Michael A. Sells, 205–48. New York: Columbia University Press.

Murad, Abdul Hakim. 1999. "Book Review of Farid Esack's Quran, Liberation, and Pluralism." http://www.masud.co.uk/ISLAM/ahm/esack.htm (accessed October 17, 2005).

Olson, Mancur. 1965. *The Logic of Collective Action: Public Goods and the Theory of Groups.* Cambridge, MA: Harvard University Press.

Orwell, George. 1949. *Nineteen Eighty-Four (1984).* New York: Harcourt Brace Jovanovich.

Pickthall, Mohammad Marmaduke. 1976. *The Glorious Qur'an.* London: Routledge.

Powner, Leanne C., and D. Scott Bennett. 2006. *Applying the Strategic Perspective: Problems and Models.* 3rd ed. Washington, DC: CQ Press.

Sayyid, Bobby S. 1997. *A Fundamental Fear: Eurocentrism and the Emergence of Islamism (Postcolonial Encounter S.).* London: Zed Books.

Schuon, Frithjof. 1984. *The Transcendent Unity of Religions.* Wheaton, IL: Theosophical Publishing House.

Shakir, Zaid. 2006. *Looking Back to Look Ahead: Contemporary Studies in Classical Islamic Political Theory.* Audio Lectures Recording. Sterling, VA: Astrolabe Pictures.

Varshney, Ashutosh. 2003. *Ethnic Conflict and Civic Life: Hindus and Muslims in India.* 2nd ed. New Haven, CT: Yale University Press.

6

Democratization without Violence: Can Political Order be Achieved through Peaceful Means?

Filippo Sabetti

There now exists a huge and rich literature about democratization, said to begin with its "first wave" around the 1820s. Three generations of efforts in the form of comparative historical research have tackled the questions: "Do revolutions contribute to the democratization of social and political life? Or do they reinforce or establish tyranny, contradicting the libertarian and egalitarian hopes of their supporters?" (Skocpol 1984, 1). While it is possible to draw attention to the incompleteness of these analyses (Goldstone 1980), a general conclusion is that revolutions may succeed in transforming long-established monarchical states into mass-mobilizing national regimes, but they may also create more penetrating authoritarian regimes. So widespread has the creation of national political systems been through war, armed revolts, and revolutions that scholars have very rarely asked the question raised by Hamilton in Federalist 1 and that has preoccupied Vincent Ostrom for much of his professional life: "whether societies of men are really capable or not of establishing good government from reflection and choice, or whether they are forever destined to depend for their political constitutions on accident and force."

It is precisely during the first wave of democratization, after the Congress of Vienna, that the question that has animated much of Vincent Ostrom's work was raised throughout Europe, and especially among Italian patriots and scholars as the prospect of a single political regime generated considerable debate as to what kind of liberal, constitutional design was best suited to a population that had lived under separate and diverse political regimes for more than thirteen hundred years. Unlike Germany, no clash occurred in Italy between the liberal creed and the struggle for national independence (Woolf 1979, 359–60). If, in the end, the making of a united Italy followed the standard, forced, creation of states, this development still does not deny the importance of understanding (1) why things went this way in spite of the widespread recognition that it was more desirable to create a political order through reflection and choice and not through force, and (2) how proponents of the defeated peaceful alternative of constitutional choice responded to that challenge by insisting on the importance of creating a cognitive map for overcoming violence as the principal means for creating political order. The insistence that democratization can proceed without violence makes Carlo Cattaneo's analysis more than just an interesting historical addition to our knowledge of state formation, adding to (3) what this experience anticipated by nineteenth-century Italian scholar, Cattaneo, tells us about the foundations of political order.

The chapter begins by sketching the challenge of popular sovereignty that emerged following the Napoleonic wars and the Congress of Vienna. The chapter then turns to a discussion of how this challenge was understood and met among students and practitioners of politics in Italy. The chapter concludes with a brief discussion of the theoretical implications of that case for understanding the importance of cognitive maps in the choice between "seeing like a state" and "seeing like citizens" in the process of creating political order (Ostrom 2001; Scott 1998).

The Challenge of Self-Government

The reconstruction of Europe that followed the Congress of Vienna in 1815 restored absolutist and dynastic principles to their former preeminence. The restoration thwarted but could not entirely stunt the growing aspirations of people to rule themselves that had been given impetus by the American and the French revolutions, the rise of liberalism and nationalism, the spread of free trade among nations, as well as by the democratic direction of long-term social change. As a result, no sooner had the sovereignty of kings been reasserted than it ran up against the claim of popular sovereignty. This first wave of democratization was driven by liberalism as a transnational movement of ideas. A critical problem was how liberalism itself was to be understood and made operational.

In the course of the nineteenth century, liberalism came to stand for the replacement of absolutism by constitutional government, the rule of law, secularization or a complete break with the Catholic church, private property rights unrestricted by other forms of property, and electoral reform aimed at broadening political participation, if only on the basis of some restrictive capacity like education and property qualifications. In France and England, liberal ideas and practices grew within long established states, with the result that thinkers like Benjamin Constant, François Guizot, and John Stuart Mill sought either to redefine political power and sovereignty as representative government, or, as in the case of Tocqueville, to challenge the very entrenched view of the European state. By contrast, liberal ideas on the Italian peninsula combined with a quest for national unification to generate additional ways to achieve national as well as individual liberation and independence. In the past, liberal ideas had remained fundamentally regional, so that we can speak of Neapolitan as opposed to Sicilian or Piedmontese national aspirations. By 1848, the commingling of liberalism and nationalism helped to extend constitutional aspirations to the nation as a whole. But, at the same time, the strong local and regional roots of constitutionalism—in the words of Raymond Grew, "a rich constitutional culture" (1996, 221–31)—posed dilemmas in the risorgimento about the meaning of the past and how to face the future. The search for an appropriate constitutional knowledge grounded in human liberation offered a critical challenge concerning what useful knowledge ought to be applied for rethinking the conditions of life associated with the progress of civilization (*incivilimento*) and whether the world of action should have reference less to education and more to plotting and waging wars of liberation with the alluring rhetoric of statecraft. But this fundamental challenge was made all the more problematic by the democratic tendencies of the time (Mazzini [1847] 1891, 98). Liberalism, with its emphasis on constitutionalism, representative government, the rule of law and private property, had been reconciled with nationalist aspirations, but what constituted democratic governance and constitutionalism remained as yet unclear.

The last decade of the eighteenth century brought the word "democracy" into the public discourse of different speech communities, to the point of being favorably invoked and used by people as diverse as Paine, Robespierre, and the prelate who became Pius VII in 1801. Benjamin Constant's 1819 celebrated lecture on comparing ancient and modern liberty aimed to disconnect ancient from modern ideas, for the ancient notions of democracy had become too closely associated with terror and bureaucratic murder in the French revolution as the idea of a self-governing society had become understood as a self-policing society. Robespierre and the like were the most notorious modern imitators of ancient republics and of a self-policing society (see Holmes 1984). According to R. R. Palmer (1959, 18; see also Grew 1996, 222), "it was in Italy that the word 'democracy', in a favourable sense, was most commonly used in the years from 1796 and 1799" (but cf. Hazareesingh 1998; Rosanvallon 1995).

The French Revolution also gave the word "constitution" political currency throughout Europe. Likewise, this word gained

> a particular resonance in Italy where nineteenth-century constitutions were associated with the liberties of medieval communes; the historical and patriotic perspective of Muratori; the romantic figure of Paoli popularised by Rousseau; and the eighteenth-century projects for constitutions in Corsica, Tuscany and Lombardy, which were written by prominent Italians and widely discussed across the peninsula. (Grew 1996, 221)

Counterposing free government to absolutist government was not enough, for "free government" was loaded with a variety of local, regional, and countrywide meanings, ranging from the British constitutional monarchy to the failed French egalitarian democracy championed by Filippo Buonarroti (see also Di Scala and Mastellone 1998, 2–5). Practically every region of Italy could point to some form of "free government" or republican democracy in the past (Grew 1996, 221), with the result that in his own time, Mazzini could still write, "(t)he union of the democratic principle with representative government is an entirely modern fact, which throws out of court all precedents that might be appealed to; they have nothing but the *word* in common; the *thing* is radically different" (Mazzini [1847] 1891, 102; italics in original). What this complementarity—Mazzini called it a "thing"—stood for and how it could be achieved was not entirely clear.

A chief problem was that many self-declared democrats and constitutionalists in Italy, as elsewhere in Europe, tended to equate democracy either with an egalitarian Jacobin state or with a communitarian view of society that left little or no room to the individual practice of liberty (Palmer 1964, 302–305). For Mazzini, the object of constitutional democracy was clear—"let man commune with the greatest possible number of his fellows" (Mazzini, cited in Mastellone 2000, vii). The problem was that it remained unclear what kind of institutional arrangements could bring about and sustain such dialogical conception of democracy and realize, all at once, social and political equality as well as individual and national political liberation. It is true that, in his study of democracy in America, Tocqueville made equality of conditions the sociological definition of democracy and the great engine of revolution in modern society. But he did not clarify the political dimensions of *démocratie*—to the point that modern scholars are still debating what Tocqueville actually meant by "democracy in America" (e.g., Mill [1840] 1977; Schleifer [1980] 2000).

One issue, however, seemed clear enough: Neither the liberal nor the democratic movement, or some combination of the two understood as liberal democracy, offered a satisfactory resolution to the paradox of revolution that had emerged with the French Revolution and was reaffirmed in the 1820 and 1848 revolts. In the aftermath of successive failed revolts, and in spite of Mazzini's revolutionary fervor, one fact had become evident in Vienna as in other European cities: Just as national armies could not indefinitely shore up absolutist rule, so popular uprisings could not succeed without falling back into new forms of tyranny and subjection. For these reasons, and terminological ambiguity aside, Tocqueville was not exaggerating when he noted in 1835 that "the organization and establishment of democracy in Christendom is the great political problem of our times" ([1835] 1961, 1:337).

Alternative Responses to the Challenge

The problematics of revolution, reform, and change reverberating throughout Europe gripped the imagination of many intellectuals and challenged them to offer solutions. To those schooled in the statecraft of despotism—enlightened or not—the growing aspirations of different communities of people to rule themselves represented a paradigmatic challenge of major proportions. At the same time, these growing aspirations could easily go astray if people were unacquainted with, or did not understand how to reap the fruits of, the long-term democratic tendencies, *incivilimento*, taking place in society. Witness what had happened to the 1812 constitution of Sicily and to the liberal movement in Spain after 1820. The former had been doomed to failure, not only by the hostile international climate, but also by the very haste with which it had been introduced; the latter by its excessive rationalism or Jacobinism. Self-rule required new ways of thinking about old issues, as well as new ways of governance and a radical reordering of political ideas and practices that could not be easily achieved in a short time span. And here critical issues emerged that could be ignored only at great peril: Where could people turn for the likely sources of such ideas? Were prior conditions necessary for new habits of heart and mind to flourish? And if so, which ones? Could the paradox of revolt be overcome? Could constitutional government be obtained only with the consent of the monarch and with the support of the international system of states?

The debate gave rise to two broad currents of thought and action known as moderate liberalism and radical, or democratic, liberalism. Each current was intended to realize, promote, and advance what has been called "the liberal conception of European history" (Tilly 1975, 37). But the two differed on some fundamental aspects. The first derived from notions of representative government (often with restricted franchise, based on capacity). Hailed as "the grand discovery of modern times" (James Mill, quoted in Collini, Winch, and Burrow 1983, 102), this current drew support from the French and British experience and particularly from the work of François Guizot and John Stuart Mill (Craiutu 2003; Siedentop 1979). The other current rejected constitutional monarchy, went beyond representative government, and stressed self-governing—as opposed to state-governed—society. This current drew support from Tocqueville's analysis of democracy in America, but not from democratic notions derived from the ancient republics or the French Revolution as these notions had become tainted with terrorism.

The first movement of ideas is closely associated with the Piedmontese Prime Minister Cavour ([1850] 1971) and the creation of the Italian state; the other with the Milanese writer Carlo Cattaneo and the constitutional design that did not happen, the defeated federalist alternative. The net result was that, while the former lent support to the entrenched European view of the state, the latter lent support to a nonunitary, polycentric, political order. For this reason, Cavour and Cattaneo could agree on the basic features of *incivilimento* or progress in Europe, international free trade and even on how to resolve the Irish question, but they could not agree on what system of government was best suited to a free and united Italy.

The Paradigmatic Significance of Cattaneo

The paradigmatic significance of Cattaneo is that he tried to do for Italy what Tocqueville was trying to do for France. They both sought to orient people of their generation to orient themselves toward the challenge implied by the progress of civilization, the long-term trend toward equality, and the aspirations of people to govern themselves. Cattaneo's interest in the self-governing arrangements of American democracy developed independent of Tocqueville. Just around the time that Georg Wilhelm Friederich Hegel ([1830] 1975, 170) was suggesting to his students in Berlin that there was not much to learn from America, and when Tocqueville was still composing the first volume of his work, we find Cattaneo using the Nullification Controversy between South Carolina and President Andrew Jackson to reflect on the American political experiment (Cattaneo [1833] 1956d). What could Americans teach Europeans?

Both Cattaneo and Tocqueville concurred that the American political experiment could teach several things: (1) that human beings are not forever destined to depend for their political constitutions on accident and force and can indeed exercise reflection and choice in creating systems of government; (2) that such choices draw upon certain conceptions articulated as principles that are, in turn, used to specify structures or forms so that when acted upon, these conceptions and structures have effects that bear significantly upon the safety and happiness of a people, and upon other fundamental values important to their lives; (3) that it is possible to have local autonomy, and to fashion self-governing units, without reference to unitary conceptions of rule or to a central authority; (4) that rulers can also be ruled through a system of overlapping jurisdiction, checks and balances, juridical defense, and individual sovereignty; (5) that possibilities other than central government monopoly exist for solving public-sector problems; and (6) that, contrary to prevailing fears in Europe, the long-term trend toward equality and equality of conditions itself was not incompatible with the maintenance of liberal practices like representative institutions, individual liberties, local autonomy, private property, and even religion. Both thinkers viewed slavery with deep forebodings for both the oppressed and the oppressors as "no one offends the laws of humanity with impunity" (Cattaneo [1833] 1956d, 27).

Though their individual projects were animated by a common vision of what constituted a proper political order and by a strong interest in connecting political theory to political practice, the circumstances of their lives, including the specificities of their particular political problems, led Cattaneo and Tocqueville to pursue their respective inquiries differently.

Whereas Tocqueville used the American experience to present an alternative vision to that offered by the *philosophes* and the French statist experience, Cattaneo suggested that the alternative vision provided by America was consistent with the basic features of Italian and European ways of life and with what was universal, even if hidden from view, in the human condition. If in writing *Democracy in America*, Tocqueville sought to overturn the established French idea of the state, Cattaneo in his work sought answers to the fundamental problem facing people of his general and beyond: whether it was possible for national liberation and independence to be achieved peacefully, without destroying existing institutions of self-rule—namely, without following the model history of European nation-states or without being caged in by the paradox of revolution experienced in France.

Cattaneo, as well as other federalist patriots, drew particular inspiration and support for their national political program from developments taking place in Lombardy-Venetia. The evolutionary insight they derived provided the vantage point or basis for proceeding through reflection and choice rather than force or by accident. Justification for the eventual creation of a federal system for Italy, and ultimately for Europe, was grounded in the particularities specific to Italy and Europe, as well as in the more general foundations of self-governance that Cattaneo saw present, if often unobtrusively, in most societies.

"A Conspiracy in Open Daylight"

What developments were taking place in Lombardy-Venetia that inspired Cattaneo and other federalist patriots to develop their framework of ideas? There, under Austrian rule, a veritable agricultural, industrial, commercial, and educational revival was taking place that had all the characteristics of a risorgimento. In his now-classic work on economics and liberalism in Lombardy between 1814 and 1848, Kent R. Greenfield successfully captured the course of action that had the potential of achieving through reflection and choice the combined goal of independence and liberty:

> It is clear that in the inner circle of publicists who ventilated the public interests of Italy between 1815 and 1848 there was a common idea that even when cooperating with Austria they were working towards ends that were beyond the reach of Austrian policy, and also a common conviction that they were in conspiracy with the course of events, with the march of the "century"; in other words, that they had found a method of action which compelled even the national adversary to cooperate with them, in so far as that power was alert to its material interests. This was their "conspiracy in open daylight."
>
> They were right in their strategy: witness the confused and helpless opposition of Austria, whose rulers suspected but never fully comprehended their power. Metternich, with his germ theory of revolution, his persistent obsession that it grew solely out of a Jacobinical conspiracy which could be isolated and destroyed if the governments would only act in concert, proved incapable of meeting them on their own ground . . . liberal journalists [like Cattaneo] saw at least a partial fulfilment of their hopes. By 1848, largely through their efforts, an Italian public opinion had been formed that could never again be governed successfully by the principles and methods of the *ancien régime*, less because their material interests of the Italian community had been revolutionized than because the public had been indoctrinated with a new conception of those interests. ([1934] 1965, 286–87)

If such a conspiracy in broad daylight continued, unhindered to other parts of the peninsula, the time would come when it would be extremely difficult for any absolutist government or army of occupation to defeat it. But events connected with the revolts of 1848 and their aftermaths reduced the prospects of this strategy. Piedmont emerged from the revolts of 1848 as the only parliamentary, constitutional monarchy, with a standing army, capable of taking the lead on the military and diplomatic front while inspiring liberals throughout the peninsula to favor unification under its banners. After 1849, from his refuge in Switzerland, Cattaneo focused most of his attention and correspondence, and used all his power of persuasion and prestige, in trying to convince radical liberals and republican revolutionaries not to engage in secret conspiracies and revolutionary activities, as they would in the end skew outcomes in favor of a military solution that would bring a unitary system of government under the Savoy monarchy. This was the paradox of the Italian revolution, and it helps us to understand Cattaneo's insistence on the importance of creating a cognitive map for overcoming violence as the principal means for creating political order.

Little wonder that by 1848, Austrian authorities and Italian patriots alike did not know what to make of Cattaneo. To the Hapsburg authorities in Lombardy, already concerned with the spread of pan-Italian nationalism, Cattaneo appeared not at all reassuring, with his call for scientific progress, cultural regeneration, and communicative interaction among all the Italian communities. To Italian nationalists plotting to overthrow foreign and illiberal rule, his loyalty to the cause of national liberation and independence appeared hardly reassuring. His insistence that he was "a student of the art of peace and economy, and not of war and destruction" ([1838] 1965a, 92) made him, at best, a symbol of appeasement to foreign domination.

On the Importance of Creating a New Cognitive Map

Cattaneo found that, while academics continued to be largely concerned with the history of ideas, people beyond university porticoes and in work places, social circles, and on street corners were struggling to do political theory. These "obscure Socrates"—so Cattaneo called them—were posing new and unexpected questions about what goods and bads life offered, the monstrous inequality of conditions in which they lived, and what constituted the constitution of a good society. This was "truly philosophical material and true philosophy: man studies man and 'know thyself' [*nosce te ipsum*], as the ancient saying goes" ([1851] 1960b, 281–82). While official, university, culture still focused on arcane metaphysical disquisitions, revolutionary ideas discussed among common people were gaining popularity and arming revolts.

The experience of having lived through the crushed aspirations of the revolts of 1821, 1832, and 1848 confirmed for Cattaneo both the problem and the oncoming challenge—that the field for new ideas is neither entirely clear nor self-realizable even when these ideas appear victorious on the streets. It is encumbered with arms, bounded with chains, and laid with traps and gallows. People may have a well-developed sense of the ills of their society, and the injustices they have suffered; they can easily respond to calls for revolutionary action, to the barricades. But, Cattaneo continued, along the same lines as Tocqueville, this very fact may make them more prone to feats of arms and acts of heroism than apt to learn and to put more trust in the humdrum, less glamorous, practice of self-governance in their everyday life for they do not yet have explicit and firm ideas of what it means to be free. Surveying the European scene, he found reckless hopes on one side, and ruthless interests and senseless fears on the other ([1851] 1960b, 282).

Cattaneo's main preoccupation was that, in such a situation, it was relatively easy to mistake the temporal process of doing something, with simply the movement for national liberation and independence. He feared that the rush to action—with the inevitable reaction—would take precedence over learning and reflecting about what ideas to articulate as principles of self-governance. A widespread shared understanding of what liberty and self-governance meant was essential for a proper articulation of ideas as principles of governance. Without such an epistemic base, liberals of all sorts as well as republican revolutionaries would be tempted to mistake—and even engage in—struggles for sovereignty and power as struggles for freedom, as if what type of political order replaced the old made no difference in terms of what it meant to practice the art of free citizenship. National independence cannot be achieved at the expense of liberty. This, Cattaneo thought, would be a disaster of major proportions. Hardly had a few months passed after Cattaneo's reflections reached the finality of print than some of his radical friends did something to confirm the validity of Cattaneo's preoccupation.

On December 2, 1851, Napoleon Bonaparte staged a coup d'etat in France and eventually assumed the title of emperor as Napoleon III. Cattaneo's friends in France, who identified themselves with the radical-socialist factions in French politics and had a strong sympathy for the French revolutionary tradition, welcomed and supported the Bonapartist coup. They did so by insisting that all that the radical-socialists and democrats had lost was "our inadequate resources, our errors, misconceptions, and illusions; we faced a thick jungle that had to be cleared with a hatchet; should we bewail its sudden destruction by lightning?" (cited in Lovett 1979, 85–86). Louis Napoleon was now cast "in the role of an avenging angel whose flaming sword was dispelling the fog that had been generated in France by the sudden birth of the democratic republic and by its equally rapid demise" (Lovett, 86).

From Cattaneo's vantage point, this way of understanding French events epitomized what was wrong with those who put action ahead of the growth of democratic ideas and practices of freedom in society and the utility of institutional forms for the practice of self-government. In April 1852, in a letter to a political refugee long involved in clandestine activities in France, he did not mince words in what he saw as a critical problem for well-intentioned radicals: "You have a false doctrine; you wish to obtain liberty through means that lead to dictatorship and empire, which is another form of dictatorship" (letter to Tentolini, Cattaneo [1852] 1952c, 157). A few months later, responding to several queries from a Neapolitan revolutionary friend, Carlo Pisacane, Cattaneo sought to persuade him—unsuccessfully, it turned out, as Pisacane died heroically in an uprising with little or no prospect of success—of the danger of following a "false doctrine" (letter to Pisacane, Cattaneo [1852] 1952a, 167–70).

Cattaneo seldom failed to remind his interlocutors, or those willing to listen, that "France is indeed the country that popularized revolution, yet it is the European country where it is least possible to make one, if by revolution we mean a profound overthrow and renewal of interests and not just a superficial change of administrative rituals" ([1842] 1957a, 285). This was so, because

> [t]he French Revolution was unable to go beyond the centuries old tradition of, and its own faith in, the omnipotence of rulers. The king's representatives gave way to the nation's representatives but the fervor engendered by discipline made them abandon liberty. The people had the land but not the commune [i.e., self-government]. ([1864] 1965b, 419)

The problems of reforming, or decentering, the state in France posed an enormous challenge that could not be overcome by successive generations of people, including well-intentioned revolutionary bourgeoisie. As he put it, "the 'principle of ministerial omnipotence and omniscience' remained as a chief stumbling block to real change" ([1842] 1957a, 285).

Cattaneo's assessment is important in another way. Recent research on nineteenth-century France makes all the more questionable the attempt, particularly since Gramsci, to measure the middle class elsewhere against an idealized abstraction of the French (revolutionary) bourgeoisie. Assigning to any particular social class (or group, or region like Piedmont) the task of moving a country forward was, for Cattaneo, fraught with danger on several fronts: It dispensed people from properly considering what alternative constitutional designs were available to realize the common objectives of independence, liberation, and self-government; it led to the neglect of the role that individuals and groups from all social strata could play in realizing such common objectives (a point learned firsthand during the 1848 revolt); and it tended to ignore both the interactive process that applies to any form of collective undertaking and the exceedingly difficult task awaiting any single group trying to achieve and maintain a countrywide political and cultural hegemony.

We now know that a Sicilian liberal political economist, Francesco Ferrara, shared Cattaneo's views. Ferrara tried to convey them directly to Cavour in a memorandum in the summer of 1860. Cavour rejected Ferrara's memorandum on the assumption that what he, as prime minister of Piedmont, was working toward would not, in the end, replicate the French system of centralized government and administration. Cavour genuinely believed that his statecraft would have mostly beneficial effects, for his

> theory of the state [did] not imply either the tyranny of the capital over the rest of Italy or the creation of a bureaucratic caste that would subjugate all other bodies and would thus transform the position of the government into an artificial center of an empire toward which the traditions and habits of Italians and Italy's geographic configuration would always be against. (Cavour [1860] 1949, 220)

Cavour personally knew Tocqueville, whom he had met in Paris and London, and admired his work, for in Cavour's own words, it "throws more light than any other on the political questions of the future" (Cavour, cited in Jardin 1988, 228). All this to say that Cavour genuinely believed that he could do better than others, that he could succeed where others had failed. Cavour failed to realize that war, and forced creation of unity, have an inner logic of their own and that they have the power to drag even well-intentioned decision-makers into places they did not initially intend to go.

The problem of properly understanding the paradigmatic challenge of liberal democracy, of achieving both independence and liberty, was not just confined to France, to radical socialists like Giuseppe Ferrari, and liberal statesman like Cavour. It extended to republican revolutionaries like Mazzini as well. Cattaneo tried at some length to convince Mazzini—in a language that at times Mazzini must have assuredly found upsetting—that his "little undertakings [that is, uprisings] will be ineffective if the people do not rise *en masse*, and they are superfluous if the people truly rises" ([1850] 1952b, 45–46). Cattaneo urged Mazzini to spend all his efforts to affect a change in the people's heart and mind:

> I advocate the dissemination of writings that slowly but surely awaken mass consciousness about constitutional rules of governance (*diritto*), sentiments of freedom and self-mastery, contempt of princely concessions and transactions, respect of nations and mutual help, and peaceful resolution of questions of borders and commercial free trade. ([1850] 1952b, 45–46)

But Mazzini would not listen. He was impatient to await the fruit of what Cattaneo proposed, and continued his conspiracies.

The tendency to downplay the place of ideas and shared understanding in the world of action and even in the constitution of a political order appropriate to human liberation was not, however, confined to *engagé* intellectuals and political agitators. As Cattaneo discovered in 1860, when Garibaldi called him to Naples to act in a consultative capacity, it applied to sincere patriots as well. In the end, Garibaldi mistook Cattaneo's suggestions for a Neapolitan constituent assembly as a step in the creation of a political structure opposed to Italian unification; and Garibaldi was not at all displeased when Cattaneo respectfully withdrew from his entourage, declined to be an envoy in London and returned to his Swiss village.

News of the American Civil War must have added to Cattaneo's disappointment as the war appeared to discredit further the extension of federal principles to Italy and Europe—just as it did in the creation of the Canadian Confederation in 1867. Even the creation of the 1868 federal republic in Spain must not have been a source of optimism for Cattaneo as the republic contradicted an important premise in his mode of analysis: The Spanish federal republic had not emerged from below; its constitution was imposed in haste from the top down, without much reflection about Spain's own regionalist tradition and experience. What, then, sustained Cattaneo's positivity? He grounded his optimistic prognosis for the eventual acceptance of the cognitive map he proposed on two factors, one particular to Italy and the other more universal. Let us take each one in turn.

Historical Foundations for Self-Governance

Cattaneo considered Italy physically and historically a federal country.[1] Almost all his published work on Italy since the 1830s is devoted to elucidating the fact that Italy is a country of city and village republics. The blossoming of the practice of self-governance must start with an appreciation of the historical roots of constitutionalism at the local level. In 1858, he wrote a set of essays reiterating this conclusion against a prevailing argument that what Italy really needed was a strong, centralized system of government and administration to bring an end to weakness and rivalry. By emphasizing the importance of microconstitutional foundations for the blossoming of macroconstitutionalism, he was able to argue against the prevailing argument.

The city, he claimed, was the

> only organizing principle that allows us to make an evident and continuous exposition of thirty centuries of Italian histories. Without this organizing thread, the mind becomes disoriented in the labyrinth of conquests, factions, and civil wars, and in the frequent structuring and restructuring of states. ([1858] 1957e, 383)

Cattaneo began by going back to ancient times—to the civic culture of Magna Graecia in the south, and that of the Etruscan communities in the center and in the north. He identified and discussed nine different eras of civil evolution since those early times, and ended his analytical narrative with the city republics of the fourteenth century. He used this history, not to suggest a continuous, unbroken course of city development, but rather to emphasize certain features that made the city, or the local, both an historical community in Italy and an appropriate level of analysis. The set of essays on the city can thus be read at different levels: the city as a conceptual variable, as an historical community, and as a manifestation of the struggle for self-governance—not just as power struggles of the upper classes over time. He focused on the following dimensions:

- Civic consciousness. Even the Roman Empire, unlike other empires, began from a city, and retained, for a long time, many of its features. Communal society was and remains important for the shared understanding that enables people to become self-governing. This fact cannot be underestimated. Though at times this fact was crushed by internal or external forces, or denied by one lordship or another, as soon as the domination was relaxed, for whatever reason, the original elasticity reemerges and the municipal fabric of Italian cities blossomed again to regain its vibrancy. Sometimes it is the countryside that regenerates a destroyed city. Italy is a country of cities and towns such that no responsible legislator, entrepreneur, or analyst can fail to take notice

and respect local patriotism as it gives meaning to life and enlightens patterns of relationship.
- Municipal institutions. The constancy and permanence of municipal institutions is another fundamental fact. These institutions proved to be more durable than successive waves of conquest.
- Free cities. As self-governing communes, they were important for several reasons: the spread of individual liberties and freestanding individuals; the growth of law broadly understood to encompass commercial, maritime, as well as manorial or feudal law; the continuous exercise of the art of association within each commune and neighborhood and sometimes across different city boundaries. The basic principles of constitutional government were worked out in the free cities of Italy as well as Germany long before the Americans confronted the problems of constitutional choice. To illustrate this observation, Cattaneo was also fond of calling up the irrigation system in the Po River plain, which encompassed several provinces and territories. The creation and maintenance of such long-enduring institutions over many centuries, including circumstances where the Po River valley itself was the theater of war and conquest, attest to the constitutional knowledge and artisanship of successive generations of people and how microconstitutional experiments served as an important educative mechanism in the extension of the irrigation system throughout an entire area.
- Civic life contributed in a fundamental way to the growth of important centers of learning and more generally to the growth of a culture that privileged critical inquiry, disputation, problem-solving, and experimental science more generally.
- The similarities between north and south rapidly changed after the twelfth century. Cattaneo dates the rupture to the Norman conquest of the south in the eleventh century. Recent scholarship suggests that Cattaneo exaggerated the extent of the rupture in the civic culture of the south.
- The insufficiency of the free cities. For Cattaneo, what deprived Italian cities of the capacity to successfully manage local problems, reduce the risk of self-perpetuating oligarchies, and circumvent the prospects of foreign domination and conquest, was, in addition to the growth of absolutist monarchies, the absence of federative arrangements—that is, in Cattaneo's view, the unavailability of a polycentric, federalist perspective to political craftsmanship and problem solving. The availability of an explicit polycentric, federalist perspective by the nineteenth century meant that it was possible both to avoid past errors and, at

the same time, to extend principles of self-government from the individual, to the towns, and to the nation as a whole.

Uncovering More Universal Foundations for Self-Governance

Cattaneo's experience under foreign occupation made him especially sensitive to what to look for in the way of unobtrusive foundations for democratic self-governance. As he put it once,

> the culture and well-being of peoples do not depend so much on spectacular name changes from one regime to another, but rather on the steady application of certain principles that are passed on, unnoticed, through the working of *institutional arrangements often viewed of secondary importance.* ([1847] 1956b, 114–15; italics in original; see also [1837] 1956a)

He spent his apprenticeship year at the journal *Annali di Statistica* between 1831 and 1834, scanning domestic and foreign news and writing reports concerned largely with the diffusion of knowledge, commerce, and technology around the world. He wrote about many topics, including the opening of the Welland Canal in Upper Canada and the introduction of the telegraph in Bengal. These reports convey attentiveness to the rich diversity of human development across space and, at the same time, to an increasing common characteristic of people in different settings and circumstances struggling to become self-governing as they confronted problematic situations in their lives. Hence the range of news covered must have been puzzling to the Austrian censors as it went—to use one of his memorable phrases—"from the immortality of human ingenuity to the raisin trade" ([1833] 1964b, 47). In fact, his news notes take on renewed significance when read against the backdrop of his subsequent attempts to come to terms more directly with the relationship between human progress and liberty. In 1833, for example, he focused on events connected with former American slaves in Liberia, highlighting the need for former slaves to be "free possessors of themselves" so that, as freestanding individuals, they could reawaken, and put to use, their unused skills and the practice of associating together ([1833] 1964a). It was in the second half of 1830 that Cattaneo began to construct for himself a more systematic framework of analysis—a public science, he called it—concerned with foundations of democratic self-governance. Here I can only give a brief sketch.

First, there is a need to discern between institutions that are accidental and transitory and those without which a human society cannot stand. This is no small matter for philosophers who have often asked the wrong question: What would life be like without government? He argued that this question is based on the false presupposition that government refers only to the state, which explains the widespread tendency to treat the study of politics almost exclusively as either the study of power or the study of why some states are more powerful than others (Cattaneo [1842] 1957a). The way to identify which mechanisms are foundational to human existence is to focus on how human beings the world over deal with questions of complementarity, interdependence, and coordination. For Cattaneo, a common language as "the first element in social aggregation" is one such mechanism ([1837] 1948, 210–11). He argued that, without a state, human society can still stand. People had solved many problems of living together and acting in concert (*convivenza civile*) through all sorts of human associations, including communal societies and societies of neighbors—and these have existed beyond the family and kinship groups, prior to the consent of state legislators. For all his profound reservations about "the" government and "the" state and for his self-conscious use of terms, Cattaneo himself could not at times escape linguistic conventions in adopting terms like the state as synonyms for non-unitary political forms and political systems in general.

A second set of theoretical factors had to do with being open to the possibility—at times he called it a "generous persuasion"—to appreciate the constitutive dynamics of human beings in the world. We should stop treating individuals as blind instruments of a particular time or culture while at the same time remembering that they are not self-sufficiently alone or metaphysically independent of society. The pressing task is to construct a public science or political economy incorporating history, institutions, and culture and, at the same time, individuals as beings capable through their actions of destroying, derailing, or refashioning the heredity of the past and existing equilibria. His conception of the individual is, in fact, grounded in an ontology of the person that links being, becoming, and acting (or behaving) to form the constitutive dynamics of the person or, to use what Siedentop says about Tocqueville's somewhat similar conception, "virility" (Siedentop 1994, 141). This is another way of saying that Cattaneo sought to understand how individuals learn to be free; sovereign is the word he often used, while at the same time living in complementarity, interdependence, and coordination with others—the summary term he often used to characterize this was *convivenza civile*. Interested as he was about the origins of words and the use of language, Cattaneo seldom forgot that the root of civilization (*incivilimento*) is civis, the citizen. A common language is an important principle of aggregation, but it is not sufficient, even in a united Italy, to achieve self-governing patterns of human relationship and to prevent domination and exploitation.

Finally, the constitutive dynamics of human beings that manifest themselves in the world—which he liked to describe as the field of human liberty (*il campo della liberta' umana*)—must be studied in context, which is within the specificities of particular time and place. This field of human liberty takes individuals to be co-creators with God of the world they live in. This implied the recognition that much of the world in which humans live is artifactual. Cattaneo used the term "artificial" to refer to artifacts shaped by human knowledge like agriculture, commonwealths, and irrigation networks. The work of interconnected local institutions that, over many centuries, transformed the originally inhospitable Lombard Plain and created the social, economic, and political wealth that Lombardy has achieved, was the artifactual creation of successive generations of people, patient tillers of the soil as well as engineers and masters of canals—in brief, a display of human ingenuity as even the soil was not a gift of nature (Cattaneo [1845] 1956c, 5; see also [1844] 1957f, 419–30). But this artifactual world cannot be theorized about in vacuo, as this practice has already produced much disorientation in the history of philosophy. Nor can human and political artifacts be studied solely at the macro, national level, for the history of countries relatively free of foreign domination like Japan (at that time) reveals that "the independence of a state is no automatic assurance that its citizens are free" ([1860] 1957c, 61).

In his 1844 considerations on the principle of philosophy, Cattaneo sketched in more detail how to uncover the hidden foundations for self-governance in different societies ([1844] 1960a). He began by noting that every civilized nation embodies various organizing principles, each aspiring to permeate the state and make it its own. History and human events offer many examples of enduring contrasts among diverse organizing principles seeking to give direction and uniformity to societies. This heterogeneity of principles is no mere "ideology" but a concrete manifestation of the multiple dimensions that societies possess in their economic, juridical-institutional, cultural, and moral realms. There is more than one way to get particular things done. While a strong defender of private property rights, Cattaneo was respectful of other forms of possessing like common property, such as he found it in the Swiss Alps. As a way of illustrating the diversity, Cattaneo offered many examples of the multidimensional and complex world in which people have lived through time. He then introduces two important corollaries.

First, the tendency for some set of principles to dominate and direct the course of public affairs is seldom, if ever, realized. Before one set acquires dominance in the intellectual and public realm, including public opinion, other principles tend to emerge often unexpectedly, pushing the current of interests and opinion in many other directions. Second, the more civilized a people is, the more numerous are the organizing principles it contains. This open-ended epistemology is what made the European civilization "superior" or stand out when ranged alongside the other major world civilizations like those of imperial China, Hindu India, and the Aztec. But Cattaneo was quick to point out that stationary peoples and societies do not exist except in the abstract or in the minds of some theorists. He illustrates the point using the example of China that put him in sharp disagreement with the conclusions about China reached by, among others, Mill, Herder, Burkhardt, and Tocqueville. After comparing Italy and China, he turns specifically to the latter, focusing especially on its resource-based achievements requiring considerable human artisanship. He summarizes these accomplishments in this way:

> The person who considers China stationary will find it in continuous agitation if he looks closely to its history. He will see (people in) China introducing agriculture over a vast territory, embanking rivers, digging up canals, establishing settlements of cultivators along the thousand valleys of its two major rivers and innumerable cities, absorbing barbarous tribes from the mountains, embracing all its peoples in one civilization with the bond of a common language; fashioning laws, arts and writings; and China had achieved all this when Europe was pertinaciously barbarous and stagnating. Then we see China breaking up into several federated realms, and in this comparative liberty developing popular and assorted philosophies; then transforming itself now into one empire, now into two, as Marco Polo found. Twice, like in the case of Italy, barbarians conquered China; the first time it succeeded in expelling them; in other times, it softened their impact and aggregated the conquerors into its civilization. In the meantime, assiduous mental work was propagating on one side the Socratic philosophy of Confucius, and, on other sides, the abstract philosophy of Lao Tsue, and the theological metaphysics of Buddhism; more recently, the foments of a new revolution have come from the Bible [that is, Christianity]. ([1861] 1957d, 150–51)

Cattaneo continued, the China we know from history books is an artifactual creation made by successive generations of people—that is, all these activities reflect the development of knowledge and its application to solve concrete problems of human existence. In this sense, China is no different than Lombardy or other parts of the world. The history of humanity is more similar from country to country than we commonly believe; and the type of progress open to human beings varies as a function of the course of events specific to particular contexts, and not as a function of racial or natural predestination.

Movement and heterogeneity are then the life-giving forces of human society (Cattaneo [1846] 1957b). The antithesis between civilization and barbarism is here, and with it the future of individuals and people. Societal conditions provide the range of opportunities and possibilities for the all-important associational life, *convivenza civile*. For humans, the greater the variety of impulses that their wills can follow, the vaster is their range of liberty. By contrast, the more narrow and limited is the field of liberty and action, the more likely is for human capacity to reason to become confused with instinct, jeopardizing his freedom to act or not to act. Savage man is much more restricted in his sphere of action than is modern man, something that, Cattaneo continues, Rousseau did not consider when he ranked a primitive state above civilized existence. If in his own time, Cattaneo noted, Europe had become synonymous with civilization and Asia with barbarism, this was precisely because movement and heterogeneity were present in the first and were reduced to a minimum in the latter.

Heterogeneity, then, is both the result and a source of good institutional design. Cattaneo continued to use the term "state" but defined it as a set of fundamental rules that allow the many elements of social life to have an autonomous, self-governing existence while playing their part in society. The state is then, for Cattaneo, an immense interaction where property and commerce, what can be held and what can be disposed of, luxury and savings, the useful and the beautiful, operate every day to either conquer or defend portions of the public sphere that allow them to enhance their respective exigencies and compete with one another's way of life. And thus the supreme formula for good government and civilization is to create systems of governance whereby principles and ways of life do not override one another, where none is denied its own space. Just as important—for someone like Cattaneo who remembered his Montesquieu, valued the Enlightenment for drawing attention to how to put individual self-interest to serve the commonweal, and took pride in the long-enduring institutions surrounding the Po River—there was the need to educate and shape the interests of those controlling collective-choice mechanisms as to allow those officials to invest in maintaining and even crafting better rules for action.[2] This science of association can be extended with the application of federal principles of organization—in short, what he called federal law.

Federalism so understood promotes liberty as a plant with many roots. This is why against all odds, Cattaneo held firm to a positive view of life and to his vision of the possibility to achieve a good life, if only for others yet to come.

Conclusion

The case presented in this chapter supports the view found in the huge and rich literature about democratization, that armed revolts rarely if ever produce self-governing societies, contradicting the libertarian and egalitarian hopes of their supporters. The chapter goes beyond that literature when it suggests that transitions to liberal democracy can be better understood if we seek to understand motivations and expectations of actors as critical factors between initial conditions and constitutional outcomes. Many participants in the struggle for Italian unification—from Mazzini to Cavour—did know that a forced creation of unity could bring about the creation of a bureaucratic caste and transform the position of the new national government into an artificial center of empire that would work against the traditions and habits of Italians and Italy's geographic configuration. What Cattaneo highlighted is two-fold: First, those leaders failed to realize that a forced creation of unity has its inner logic of its own to drag even well-intentioned decision-makers into courses of action they did not initially intend to pursue; second, the importance for researchers to focus their attention on the cognitive maps used by actors as they pursue political action. A wrong cognitive map can lead to antithetical courses of action and even disastrous consequences. To students of Vincent Ostrom's work and game-theoretic analysis (Kitschelt 1993, 415, 425), Cattaneo's analysis throwing light on actors' beliefs, commitments, points of orientation, and reputation will have a familiar ring. Cattaneo and Ostrom shared the view that constitutional designs needed to be grounded in the different circumstances of different communities and ways of life.

No doubt, much more work remains to be done to account for when and why actors create particular cognitive maps that lead them to act beyond existing payoff matrices and viable courses of action (Kitschelt 1993). The case presented in the chapter supports this assessment and suggests that a gold mine of material may exist in the political history of Europe to enrich and broaden the insights of Vincent Ostrom and game-theoretic analysis—just as these insights can lead to a renewed appreciation of the work of earlier generations of scholars.

Acknowledgments

Research for this chapter is part of a larger project on civilization, progress, and democracy in the work of Carlo Cattaneo, supported by the Social Science and Humanities Research Council of Canada and by the Earhart Foundation, Ann Arbor, Michigan. For this work, I have many people to thank, beginning with Vincent Ostrom whose inspiration has been extraordinary and long-enduring, and including Barbara Allen, Elinor Ostrom, Mark Sproule-Jones, and Patty Lezotte.

Notes

1. This section draws heavily on chapter 3, "The Constitutional Design That Did Not Happen," of my book *The Search for Good Government: Understanding the Paradox of Italian Democracy* (2000).

2. Drawing in part on Cattaneo, Greenfield ([1934] 1965, chaps. 1–2) discusses several such rules for self-monitoring and adjustment that applied to renters, water police, and canal masters, among others.

References

Cattaneo, Carlo. [1837] 1948. "Del nesso fra la lingua valica e l'italiana." In *Scritti Letterari artistici linguistici e vari*, vol. 1, ed. A. Bertani, 209–37. Florence: Le Monnier.

———. [1852] 1952a. "A Carlo Pisacane a Genova, 4 agosto 1852." In *Epistolario*, vol. 2, ed. R. Caddeo, 167–70. Florence: Le Monnier.

———. [1850] 1952b. "A Giuseppe Mazzini, a Ginevra, 30 settembre 1850." In *Epistolario*, vol. 2, ed. R. Caddeo, 44–48. Florence: Le Monnier.

———. [1852] 1952c. "All'Ing. Luigi Tentolini, a Massagno, 24 aprile 1852." In *Epistolario*, vol. 2, ed. R. Caddeo, 156–58. Florence: Le Monnier.

———. [1837] 1956a. "Alcune ricerche sul progetto di un Monte delle Sete." In *Scritti Economici*, vol. 2, ed. A. Bertolino, 7–82. Florence: Le Monnier.

———. [1847] 1956b. "Di alcuni istituzioni agrarie dell'Alta Italia applicabili a sollievo dell'Irlanda." In *Scritti Economici*, vol. 3, ed. A. Bertolino, 68–145. Florence: Le Monnier.

———. [1845] 1956c. "Industria e morale." In *Scritti Economici*, vol. 1, ed. A. Bertolino, 3–30. Florence: Le Monnier.

———. [1833] 1956d. "Notizia sulla questione delle tariffe daziarie negli Stati Uniti d'America desunta da documenti ufficiali." In *Scritti Economici*, vol. 1, ed. A. Bertolino, 11–55. Florence: Le Monnier.

———. [1842] 1957a. "Di alcuni stati moderni." In *Scritti Storici e Geografici*, vol. 1, ed. G. Salvemini and E. Sestan, 255–301. Florence: Le Monnier.

———. [1846] 1957b. "Frammenti d'istoria universale." In *Scritti Storici e Geografici*, vol. 2, ed. G. Salvemini and E. Sestan, 97–122. Florence: Le Monnier.

———. [1860] 1957c. "Il Giappone antico e moderno." In *Scritti Storici e Geografici*, vol. 3, ed. G. Salvemini and E. Sestan, 61–81. Florence: Le Monnier.

———. [1861] 1957d. "La Cina antica e moderna." In *Scritti Storici e Geografici*, vol. 3, ed. G. Salvemini and E. Sestan, 130–65. Florence: Le Monnier.

———. [1858] 1957e. "La citta' considerate come principio ideale delle istorie italiane." In *Scritti Storici e Geografici*, vol. 2, ed. G. Salvemini and E. Sestan, 382–437. Florence: Le Monnier.

———. [1844] 1957f. "Notizie naturali e civili sulla Lombardia." In *Scritti Storici e Geografici*, vol. 1, ed. G. Salvemini and E. Sestan, 309–430. Florence: Le Monnier.

———. [1844] 1960a. "Considerazioni sul principio della filosofia." In *Scritti Filosofici*, vol. 1, ed. N. Bobbio, 143–70. Florence: Le Monnier.

———. [1851] 1960b. "Filosofia della rivoluzione." In *Scritti Filosofici*, vol. 1, ed. N. Bobbio, 272–86. Florence: Le Monnier.

———. [1833] 1964a. "Africa Liberia." In *Scritti Politici*, vol. 1, ed. M. Boneschi, 49–53. Florence: Le Monnier.

———. [1833] 1964b. "Sul commercio dell'uva passa dell'isole joniche cola Gran Bretagna." In *Scritti Politici*, vol. 1, ed. M. Boneschi, 46–49. Florence: Le Monnier.

———. [1838] 1965a. "Di vari scritti intorno alla strada ferrata da Milano a Venezia." In *Scritti Politici*, vol. 2, ed. M. Boneschi, 52–132. Florence: Le Monnier.

———. [1864] 1965b. "Sulla legge comunale e provinciale." In *Scritti Politici*, vol. 4, ed. M. Boneschi, 414–40. Florence: Le Monnier.

Cavour, Camillo di. [1850] 1971. "La *Storia del Piemonte* del Brofferio." In *Scritti Inediti e Rari 1828–1850*, ed. R. Romeo, 167–75. Santena: Fondazione 'Camillo Cavour'.

———. [1860] 1949. *Carteggi: La Liberazione del Mezzogiorno e la formazione del Regno d'Italia*, vol. 1. Bologna: Zanichelli.

Collini, Stefan, Donald Winch, and John Burrow. 1983. *That Noble Science of Politics: A Study in Nineteenth-Century Intellectual History*. Cambridge: Cambridge University Press.

Craiutu, Aurelian. 2003. *Liberalism under Siege: The Political Thought of the French Doctrinaires*. Lanham, MD: Lexington Books.

Di Scala, Spencer, and Salvo Mastellone. 1998. *European Political Thought 1815–1989*. Boulder, CO: Westview Press.

Goldstone, Jack A. 1980. "Theories of Revolution." *World Politics* 32 (April): 425–53.

Greenfield, Kent R. [1934] 1965. *Economics and Liberalism in the Risorgimento: A Study of Nationalism in Lombardy, 1814–1848*. Baltimore, MD: Johns Hopkins University Press.

Grew, Raymond. 1996. "The Paradoxes of Italy's Nineteenth-Century Political Culture." In *Revolution and the Meanings of Freedom in the Nineteenth Century*, ed. I. Woloch, 212–45. Stanford, CA: Stanford University Press.

Hazareesingh, Sudhir. 1998. *From Subject to Citizen: The Second Empire and the Emergence of Modern French Democracy.* Princeton, NJ: Princeton University Press.

Hegel, Georg Wilhelm Friederich. [1830] 1975. "The Natural Context or the Geographical Basis of World History." In *Lectures on the Philosophy of World History,* trans. by H. B. Nisbet with intro. by Duncan Forbes, 152–96. New York: Cambridge University Press

Holmes, Stephen. 1984. *Benjamin Constant and the Making of Modern Liberalism.* New Haven, CT: Yale University Press.

Jardin, Andre. 1988. *Tocqueville: A Biography.* 2nd ed. New York: Farrar and Strauss.

Kitschelt, Herbert. 1993. "Comparative Historical Research and Rational Choice Theory: The Case of Transitions to Democracy." *Theory and Society* 22 (June): 413–27.

Lovett, Clara M. 1979. *Giuseppe Ferrari and the Italian Revolution.* Chapel Hill: University of North Carolina Press.

Mastellone, Salvo. 2000. *La democrazia etica di Mazzini (1837–1847).* Rome: Archivio Guido Izzi.

Mazzini, Giuseppe. [1847] 1891. "Thoughts upon Democracy in Europe." In *Life and Writings of Joseph Mazzini,* vol. 4, 98–214. London: Smith, Elder & Co.

Mill, John Stuart. [1840] 1977. "De Tocqueville on Democracy in America [II]." In *Essays on Politics and Society.* Ed. J. M. Robson, 153–204. Toronto: University of Toronto Press.

Ostrom, Vincent. 2001. "The Challenge of Modernity: Seeing Like Citizens." *PEGS: The Good Society* 10(2): 40–41.

Palmer, R. R. 1959 and 1964. *The Age of the Democratic Revolution: A Political History of Europe and America, 1760–1800.* 2 vols. Princeton, NJ: Princeton University Press.

Rosanvallon, Pierre. 1995. "The History of the Word 'Democracy' in France." *Journal of Democracy* 6(4): 140–54.

Sabetti, Filippo. 2000. *The Search for Good Government: Understanding the Paradox of Italian Democracy.* Montreal: McGill-Queen's University Press.

Schleifer, James. [1980] 2000. *The Making of Tocqueville's "Democracy in America."* Indianapolis, IN: Liberty Fund.

Scott, James. 1998. *Seeing Like a State.* New Haven, CT: Yale University Press.

Siedentop, Larry. 1979. "Two Liberal Traditions." In *The Idea of Freedom: Essays in Honour of Isaiah Berlin,* ed. Alan Ryan, 153–74. Oxford: Oxford University Press.

———. 1994. *Tocqueville.* New York: Oxford University Press.

Skocpol, Theda. 1984. "Revolutions, Authoritarianism, and Democracy in Modern World History." Paper presented at the annual meetings of the American Political Science Association, Washington, DC, September 3.

Tilly, Charles, ed. 1975. *The Formation of National States in Western Europe.* Princeton, NJ: Princeton University Press.

Tocqueville, Alexis de. [1835] 1961. *Democracy in America*, vol 1. New York: Vintage Books.
Woolf, Stuart. 1979. *A History of Italy 1700–1860: The Social Constraints of Political Change.* London: Methuen & Co.

7

The Man Who Heated Up Economic Discussion with a Stove: Walter Eucken's Method of Institutional Design

Stephan Kuhnert

Should Walter Eucken, the founding father of the Freiburg school of economics, be seen as a precursor to what is now called modern institutionalism? This chapter does not make an attempt at giving a final answer. It questions whether the approaches are complementary and can be fruitfully combined. For both approaches, thinking in terms of institutions is a basic element to find solutions for all levels of governments and worlds of action. Eucken had his very specific approach to the analysis of institutional frameworks. Many of his policy recommendations, based on his analysis, were successfully applied.

Events are usually called miracles if no explanation can be provided for them. Germany's rapid recovery after 1945 is frequently referred to as an "economic miracle" although nowadays there is broad agreement that this "miracle" was a consequence of fundamental decisions about the institutional framework of the economic order that was deliberately designed to create room for spontaneous entrepreneurial action of all kinds. The design of that institutional framework was heavily influenced by the ideas of Walter Eucken and his followers. The focus of this chapter is a discussion of Eucken's methodological access to the design of institutions rather than his policy recommendations. I shall first give a short sketch of the historical meaning of Eucken and the Freiburg school, then discuss Eucken's approach to developing institutions, and finally outline some of the implications his insights may have for current efforts in institutional research and design.

The Institutional Design of a "Miracle"

Walter Eucken was probably the most influential academic economist in postwar Germany. Two of his works, *The Foundations of Economics* (*Grundlagen der Nationalökonomie*) ([1940] 1992) and *Grundsätze der Wirtschaftspolitik* ([1952] 1960), are central to his thinking. Although he made considerable contributions both to economic methodology as well as to the theory of economic policy, he never regarded himself as solely a methodologist. He had a strong will to see his institutional recommendations put into practice.

The teachings of his economic school of thought, the "Freiburg school," are still passed on to students of economics, although its influence has been weakened over the past decades. The translator of *The Foundations of Economics*, T. W. Hutchison, explains the fading presence of the Freiburg school in the public perception with the still-growing attention paid to neoclassical economists and their predominantly mathematical approaches to economics, especially in the United States.

More recently, the school's research program has attracted attention, due to the growing recognition that it has much in common with certain modern approaches in economics, particularly constitutional political economy and other subfields within the new institutional economics (Vanberg 1998, 172). The transatlantic exchange of ideas on the crafting of institutional frameworks for sustainable collective action and innovative entrepreneurial activity has led to a rediscovery of Eucken's ideas.

Walter Eucken was born in 1891, son of the philosopher and Nobel Laureate in literature Rudolf Eucken. He received his doctorate in economics at the University of Bonn in 1914 and completed his habilitation at the University of Berlin in 1921. In 1927, Eucken accepted a chair at the University of Freiburg, where he remained until his death in 1950. Although Eucken was opposed to the Nazi regime, he did not emigrate and in the 1930s founded, with his colleague Franz Böhm, the school of thought that was later referred to as Freiburg school of law and economics. Already in the late 1930s, Eucken and some fellows secretly developed a new economic order for postwar Germany. Also known under the name "Ordo-liberalism," the ideas of the Freiburg school constituted a major part of the theoretical foundations on which the "social market economy" was built. Eucken was the only non-emigrant German who took part in the 1947 conference at Mont Pelerin in Switzerland, initiated by F. A. Hayek, which resulted in the founding of the Mont Pelerin Society (Vanberg 1998, 172).

Eucken developed his own work as an explicit alternative to the program of the German historical school, which in Eucken's view had given up theoretical analysis and lost the ability to look at specific issues of economic policy within the context of the broader issue of the economic constitution as a whole. With his two major works, the *Grundlagen der Nationalökonomie* ([1940] 1992) and the *Grundsätze der Wirtschaftspolitik* ([1952] 1960), he wanted to provide an alternative to nontheoretical approaches to economic policy. His aim was to develop a systematically integrated approach to the theoretical study and the political shaping of a constitutional social-economic political order, or, to use the German terminology, a systematic approach to *Ordnungstheorie* and *Ordnungspolitik*.

Showing the Structure: Walter Eucken's Methodology for Penetrating the Complexity of Social Systems

As will be shown, Eucken developed a combination of methodological tools and a morphology to analyze economic systems. Eucken wanted to understand the general economic laws behind *observable* social phenomena, thus on the one hand avoiding distancing himself too much from reality, while on the other hand extracting the general principles and patterns behind the specific phenomena in question. He rejected the way in which some of his contemporaries made personified theoretical concepts like "capitalism" or "socialism" responsible for historical and economic developments. Eucken emphasized that such analyses fail to consider the specific institutional framework in a given historical situation and the reasons behind individual human decisions that are strongly influenced by that framework.

Integrating the Abstract and the Concrete: The Great Antinomy as the Most Fundamental Methodological Challenge

Eucken begins the outline of his concept by demonstrating how a sequence of simple questions can lead to the understanding of social phenomena:

> Like Descartes nearly three hundred years ago, I am standing in front of the stove which is heating my room. It is quite an ordinary stove, but to look at it prompts me to ask the most fundamental questions. What is the material out of which the stove is constructed, asks the scientist. This question alone gives rise to a host of others which lead back to atomic physics. Why does the stove give out a particular quantity of warmth? This leads us on to the theory of heat.

> *Our* questions are different. Why was the stove produced at all? Why was it set up in this particular room? These seem fairly simple questions. . . . But we know from everyday experience that many different kinds of specialized services co-operated in the making of this stove, from those of the man who installed it, back to those of the miners of the coal and ore, and to those of the metal worker who helped make the mining machinery. . . . How was the co-operation of all these services arranged so that they all contributed finally in the making of this stove? . . . How is this process with its far-reaching division of labor controlled in its entirety, so that everyone comes by the goods on which his existence depends? ([1940] 1992, 18; italics in original)

Eucken argues that a science can only remain alive by formulating direct questions about the real world ([1940] 1992, 25). From looking directly at the facts surrounding the stove, the scientist is led to ask about the interrelationships of everyday economic life. The economist resembles a traveler starting off on a journey from which he promises himself striking and spacious vistas. But already after the first step, Eucken predicts, he finds himself surrounded by a seemingly "impenetrable jungle."

The most fundamental challenge that any social scientist has to face on his way to penetrating the jungle is as follows:

1. He must see economic events as part of particular individual-historical situations if he is to do justice to the real world.
2. He must see them also as presenting general-theoretical problems if the relationships of the real world are not to escape him.

How these two views can be combined is, as Eucken emphasizes, the most fundamental methodological question. There are social scientists with a predominantly historical orientation who only heap facts upon facts without explaining their interrelationship. But, as Eucken states, material can only be collected and facts observed in a significant way if definite problems have first been formulated.

However, there are theorists who have no relation to reality at all. "There is today a very noticeable tendency in the abstract reasoner to keep his distance from the concrete object, and the equanimity with which he ignores historical conditions or leaves them to the historians is often quite astounding" (Eucken [1940] 1992, 59). Social scientists are confronted here by what Eucken calls the "Great Antinomy" of their subject, which they have to overcome if they are to understand social processes.

Ordnungstheorie: Grasping the Structure of Social Systems and Overcoming the Great Antinomy with Ideal Types and Real Types

Eucken assumes that "all economic actions rest on plans" ([1940] 1992, 118). The defining question for an economic system is "who has the competence of directing the use of resources," or "who has the right to plan"? In a centralized economy, since all economic actions follow as consequences of orders from the central authority, study must begin with the central planning agency. In the market economy, there are planning data from the point of view of the individual units.

Economic theory, in any economic system, has to answer the following four questions (Eucken [1940] 1992, 19–21):

1. Why and how are the available resources in land, labor, and finished and half-finished goods directed to different uses? How is the huge stream of consumers' goods divided up along different channels, and how does it finally disappear in different quantities and compositions into the individual households? (question of distribution)
2. Needs in the present, and in the future, are competing for satisfaction. How is the competition decided? (investing and saving)
3. What are the reasons behind the choice of certain (technical) production processes?
4. All production takes place in a special spatial setting, and from the places of production countless streams and counterstreams of goods move to and fro. How is production directed *spatially*?

All these questions are concerned with meeting the existing scarcity of goods through economic decision-making, which Eucken calls "planning." The individual economic unit is only a small part of the whole process of the social economy. Individual plans must always be "incomplete." It is a "partial" plan. The individual planner has to take account of the actions of other individuals and of their plans. Thus in the market economy, a new problem arises: the necessity of balancing the parts against one another and of coordinating the individual plans. Individual plans in the market economy are the main basis for coordinating the economic decisions of individuals. It usually appears that there is a divergence between the "planning" and the "factual" data.

Eucken suggests that if we are looking down on the world and its amazing "swarm of human beings," on the variety of employments, the different patterns of related activities, and on the streams of goods, the first question we should ask is, "What is the order or system underlying all this?"—as we could say nothing of significance about what was going on if the institutional framework remained unknown. In agriculture, manufacture, trade, and communications, whatever the country, there is always a particular partial system: labor relations are ordered in a certain way, and there is always a certain monetary system. All these parts fit together as sections of a whole system, that of the particular economic system in question (Eucken [1940] 1992, 81). Briefly formulated, the task of the scientific economist is to gain knowledge of the structure of actual economic systems. It is central to Eucken's thinking that he rejects "separate theories for different economic spheres, for example, production, distribution, consumption," because separate theories do not correspond with economic reality and cause us to lose sight of the unity of economic life. "There should be no independent theories in the economy, only one problem and one theory" ([1940] 1992, 26).

As the term *Ordnung* is the central concept in the research program of the Freiburg school, it is important to note that in the context of the program, it is related to the concept of the economic constitution, the "rules of the game" upon which economies or economic systems are based ([1940] 1992, 314). Eucken used *Ordnung* as an analytical concept that is meant to emphasize the systematic relation between the rules of the game, the economic constitution, and the order or patterns of economic activities that result under different kinds of rules or economic constitutions. It is not meant to imply any of the authoritarian connotations that the word *Ordnung*—or the English term *order*—has in other contexts. Eucken states that whether it is the economy of ancient Egypt or of Augustan Rome or of medieval France or modern Germany or anywhere else, every economic plan or economic action of every peasant, landlord, trader, or craftsman takes place within the framework of an economic order or system, and is only to be understood within this framework.

As Eucken ([1940] 1992, 308) insists, all economic activities take place within some economic order and can be adequately understood only in the context of that order. The main message is that economic orders must be understood in terms of their underlying economic constitution, which means *primarily* the formal legal-institutional framework but which *also* includes informal conventions and traditions that govern economic activities. According to Eucken, the large variety of specific economic orders that have existed in the past and that exist in the present can be understood as varied compositions of two basic principles—the decentralized coordination of economic activities within a framework of general rules of the game and the principle of subordination within a centralized administrative system ([1940] 1992, 118).

Market economy and the centrally directed economy—it is these pure forms that Eucken uses for his morphology. He assumes that "the number of pure formative elements to be found is limited" ([1940] 1992, 109). To study the formative elements thoroughly is to discover all those ideal types of economic forms from which actual economic systems (Eucken's *real types*) are composed. The pure forms or ideal types are to be used as "models" on the basis of which theoretical propositions can be worked out. "No other types of economic system, or even traces of others—besides these two—are to be found in economic reality past or present. It is hardly conceivable that others can be found" ([1940] 1992, 118). However, Eucken did not argue that ideal types are empirical statements about reality. In particular, he did not assume that economic systems as ideal types are statements on economic orders as real phenomena. Instead, the ideal types are epistemological categories that establish the ontological framework delineating the field of possible objects for economic theory, whereas the real types are complex descriptions and explanations of real economic orders that result from the inclusion of data of specific historical situations and frameworks (Herrmann-Pillath 1994, 53–54). *Ordnungstheorie* thus becomes an interdisciplinary analysis that includes psychological, evolutionary, and social factors.

Tending the Economic Garden with *Ordnungspolitik*

The Freiburg school can be said to comprise a theoretical paradigm (*Ordnungstheorie*) as well as a policy paradigm (*Ordnungspolitik*). The theoretical paradigm is based on the premise that an adequate analysis and explanation of economic phenomena has to account for the nature of the constitutional framework, or the rules of the game, under which they occur. The policy paradigm is based on the premise that economic policy should seek to improve the framework of rules, the economic constitution, such that a well-functioning and desirable economic order results, rather than seeking to bring about desired outcomes directly by specific interventions. Once the framework of rules is established, it requires careful "cultivation" for its maintenance and proper functioning. But this maintenance, the implementation of *Ordnungspolitik*, should only be like "tending a garden" (Böhm 1980, 115).

Eucken is convinced that the development of the economic order could not be left to itself. As Eucken demonstrates, the problem of finding a functioning humane economic order will not solve itself by letting economic systems grow up spontaneously. The Freiburg school took care to distinguish between the spontaneous working of markets (provided an appropriate legal-institutional framework is in place) and the issue of how the framework itself comes about. In other words, it clearly distinguished between the subconstitutional issue of how market competition works within given rules, and the constitutional issue of how the rules that make market-competition work are themselves established and enforced. "The launching of the social market economy was and had to be an explicitly constructivist act" (Hutchison 1981, 163). A "strong" government is needed to determine the form of the economic order, "strong" in the sense of being independent enough to resist the pressure of special interest groups.

The Freiburg school opposes the Marxian myth of the inevitability of historical development. Instead, it supports the freedom to choose an economic order, stressing that possible economic orders may exist alongside each other (Schmidtchen 1984, 58). However, man is not simply free: Freedom of choice exists, but only with respect to the way in which the pure forms of economic order can be combined, not with respect to the pure forms themselves.

Eucken's criterion for the choice of the best possible economic order is its contribution to solving the problem of direction. On the basis of a comparison of the performance of the two possible basic forms—centrally administered economy and market economy—Eucken recommends the choice of a system of polycentric planning and economic activity.

Finding a Common Language and Underlying Characteristic that Apply to All Human Beings: Vincent Ostrom on the Implications of Eucken's Approach

Eucken: It was possible to *resolve* the antinomy because an exact study of individual economies showed that economic systems with their almost unlimited variations and multiformity are made up of a limited number of pure forms, so that this multiformity can be reduced to uniform types. ([1940] 1992, 240; emphasis added)

Ostrom: Eucken *did not resolve* his own challenge. I doubt that any one of us shall succeed in doing so. ([1973] 2008, 169; emphasis added)

Perceiving Sweeping Vistas of Forests and Individual Trees

Vincent Ostrom notes that when Eucken discusses the work of economic historians, he "could as well have been discussing scholarship in public administration: abstract models and case studies with immense gaps between theory and practice" ([1973] 2008, 166). Some become so immersed in the detail that they simply heap facts upon facts, and others engage in abstract modeling with no regard to specific historical situations. The result yields a "great antinomy": theorists who increasingly distance themselves from economic reality and economic historians who paint idiosyncratic word pictures lacking a language of theoretical discourse. Much the same allegations, Ostrom states, might be made about policy analysis where increasingly abstract models of a state are used to conceptualize how a state rules over society. A fully specified model bounded by limiting assumptions is falsely presumed to have universal applications. Model thinking may serve the purposes of rigorous mathematical reasoning but neglects empirical "realities" and problematic human affairs. Many descriptive studies, by contrast, lack any theoretical abstraction and explanatory power.

There are social scientists who heap facts upon facts without having any consciously held intellectual tools to sort out facts and use them to assess what may be problematic in specifiable situations. These "are the people who see only particular trees. . . . Unfortunately, human endeavors often require more than seeing particular trees and their idiosyncrasies or sweeping vistas of forests" (Ostrom [1973] 2008, 167).

Finding Underlying Characteristics that Apply to All Human Beings

Ostrom agrees with Eucken in presuming that there are underlying characteristics that might apply to all who are coping with the problems of scarcity that recur in all human societies. Social scientists should thus be able to apply common methods whether studying life in an ancient or modern society, a less-developed or fully developed society, or a "capitalist" society. Eucken was suggesting that if we view patterns of order in human societies, we should be able to study the social forms or social structures by drawing upon the fundamental elements that are constitutive of the great diversity of structures in human societies. We need modes of inquiry that enable us to address many different levels and foci of analysis, but doing so with some basic appreciation for how studies might fit in relation to one another in configurations of relationships that are constitutive of human societies. Eucken demonstrates that we can, by analyzing and abstracting significant characteristics of the world we experience, develop "ideal types" that can be used as intellectual constructs. "In responding to Eucken's challenge, we need to sort out the basic elements that are inherent in theoretical reasoning and use these elements to develop a heuristic that will tell us what to look for" (Ostrom [1973] 2008, 167).

While Eucken regarded the Great Antinomy to be resolved by the tools of *Ordnungstheorie*, Ostrom only concedes that some important progress has been made toward its resolution. He predicts, however, that no one will ever actually succeed in solving the Great Antinomy. "Rather, Eucken's challenge reminds us that ways of thinking about social reality need as much critical attention as what is being observed" (Ostrom [1973] 2008, 169).

In Search of a Common Language Referring to Basic Elements

Eucken argues that the opportunity to shape the historical path through the choice of institutions is frequently underestimated because the language used in social discourse veils the potential for deliberate action. In particular, he repeatedly criticizes the personification of theoretical concepts like "capitalism," "socialism," or "less-developed country" to explain social phenomena. The concept of "capitalism" is frequently used to point to the effective responsible agent in modern economics. Such phenomena as the destruction of old handicrafts, the formation of cartels, the expansion of world trade, and the transformation of the social structure were looked upon as the actions of a real being, "capitalism." Eucken observes that most people are generally fond of thinking in such categories and of the particular emotional overtones that are added in. But in terms of economic theory, "those who like to describe . . . 'capitalism' in this manner . . . are falling back into the ways of thought of primitive magic" (Eucken [1940] 1992, 96). Individuals, not "-isms," shape the course of history through the choice of institutional design concepts and the individual capacity to organize a group of followers to implement the concept (Kuhnert 2000, 89; 2001, 20–22).

Ostrom reminds us that a scientific language requires reference to basic elements and relationships that are applicable to all forms of economic relationships. Different types of economies might be constituted in different ways. A common language referring to basic elements and relationships for dealing with different economic systems and levels of analysis would permit comparisons across differently structured economic orders. The use of a common framework would provide the context for an appropriate account of historical experience so that language might be formulated in a scientifically more meaningful way (Ostrom 1990, 256–57).

Ostrom refers to Eucken's criticism of vague verbal concepts that are used to personify the responsibility for certain social developments: Some economists talk abstractly about "the market," and political scientists about "the state." Bureaucracies are viewed as the key command apparatus that allows "states" to govern; development is viewed as a process of "modernization" that requires a centralized "state" and a "bureaucracy" to transform a "society" by means of "industrialization" and associated technological transfers. All of these factors are presumed to work to gross aggregates. Such ways of thinking, Ostrom warns us, "manifest a simple-mindedness of incredible proportions." He recommends that if we are "to gain some sense of reality, we need to remind ourselves of Eucken's stove heating his study and the extraordinary configurations of relationships that were necessary to yield that simple event" ([1973] 2008, 167).

References

Böhm, Franz. 1980. "Privatrechtsgesellschaft und Marktwirtschaft." In *Freiheit und Ordnung in der Marktwirtschaft*, ed. E.-J. Mestmäcker, 105–68. Baden-Baden: Nomos.

Eucken, Walter. [1940] 1992. *The Foundations of Economics* (*Grundlagen der Nationalökonomie*). Chicago: University of Chicago Press.

———. [1952] 1960. *Grundsätze der Wirtschaftspolitik*. Tübingen: Mohr.

Herrmann-Pillath, Carsten. 1994. "Methodological Aspects of Eucken's Work." *Journal of Economic Studies* 21(4): 46–60.

Hutchison, T. W. 1981. *The Politics and Philosophy of Economics*. Oxford: Basil Blackwell.

Kuhnert, Stephan. 2000. *Gesellschaftliche Innovation als unternehmerischer Prozeß*. Berlin: Duncker & Humblot.

———. 2001. "An Evolutionary Theory of Collective Action: Schumpeterian Entrepreneurship for the Common Good." *Constitutional Political Economy* 12: 13–29.

Ostrom, Vincent. 1990. "Problems of Cognition as a Challenge to Policy Analysts and Democratic Societies." *Journal of Theoretical Politics* 2(3): 243–62. Reprinted in Michael D. McGinnis, ed., *Polycentric Governance and Development: Readings from the Workshop in Political Theory and Policy Analysis* (Ann Arbor: University of Michigan Press, 1999, 394–415).

———. [1973] 2008. *The Intellectual Crisis in American Public Administration*. 3rd ed. Tuscaloosa: University of Alabama Press.

Schmidtchen, Dieter. 1984. "German 'Ordnungspolitik' as Institutional Choice." *Zeitschrift für die gesamte Staatswissenschaft* 140: 54–70.

Vanberg, Viktor. 1998. "Freiburg School of Law and Economics." In *The New Palgrave Dictionary of Economics and the Law*, ed. Peter Newman, 172–79. London: Macmillan.

PART III
Struggles for Polycentric Governance in Diverse Continents

8

Malawi's Lake Chiuta Fisheries: Intelligent Burden-Shedding to Foster Renewable Resources Stewardship

Jamie Thomson

Lake Chiuta is one of two remaining large Malawian lakes in reasonable "health" from a fisheries perspective. The other lake fisheries have been seriously degraded (fished out) in a country that formerly depended heavily on significant doses of fish protein in its children's diets as a key input for proper physical/mental maturation (Mkoka 2003).

This chapter relates how fishers on the Malawian side of Lake Chiuta drew on preexisting local institutional capital to organize themselves in the face of a potent threat to their livelihood. The threat took the form of an improved open water seine net that nonresident Malawian fishers introduced on Lake Chiuta. Resident fishers judged these nets unacceptable capture gear and took an unauthorized initiative to ban their use on the lake. They organized themselves to monitor compliance with their rule and, when they identified infractions, to enforce it by confiscating the nets that they had declared illegal.

This bottom-up initiative in fisheries stewardship is in itself promising. But even more promising was the Government of Malawi's (GOM's) subsequent decision to support fishers' efforts to police the lake by approving legislation that officially authorized and supported these self-help efforts. The GOM deputized fisher group officials as national law officers empowered to enforce their stewardship rules on their lake section.

The upshot was a mutually productive combination of local self-help and supportive enabling legislation within the context of a polycentric political system. The GOM crafted the legislation specifically to devolve responsibility for fisheries resource governance and management (RGM) from the GOM to resource users. This exercise in "burden-shedding" by an impoverished national government left Chiuta Malawian fishers—resource users—in better shape to ensure the sustainability of the fishery upon which their livelihoods depend while simultaneously reducing financial burdens on the cash-strapped GOM.

The chapter analyzes the self-help efforts undertaken by Lake Chiuta fishers in a polycentric system to protect their lake from overfishing. It also assesses the innovative efforts by GOM officials to (1) recognize fishers' revival of fisheries self-governance, (2) build on the local institutional capital that those same fishers were elaborating in the 1990s, and (3) creatively support those local institutional arrangements. They authorized fishers to make, monitor, and enforce rules on fisheries RGM, while freeing the GOM of two burdens (effective monitoring and enforcement) that clearly exceeded its capacity.

The GOM *continued to provide essential minimum backup support* activities (targeted dissemination of information about new national legislation on fisher empowerment, occasional dispute-resolution services, and minimal oversight—checks and balances—concerning fishers' rules for fisheries RGM), all of which reinforced the fishers' rule of law behavior.

Research for this chapter was conducted during one week in January 2004 on Lake Chiuta in eastern Malawi by a team consisting of the current author (team leader), another American, and two Malawian colleagues. The chapter draws on field research results and works noted in the list of references, especially those concerning Malawi Rift Valley fisheries.

Institutional Evolution in Malawian Fisheries Sector

In 1997, the GOM established a legal enabling framework for promising indigenous institutional arrangements in fisheries RGM. The Fisheries Conservation and Management Act (FCMA/1997) replaced the 1974 Fisheries Act:

> The most important feature of the new Act, one that distinguishes it from previous fisheries legislation, is that it makes specific provision for a shared or co-management regime through the conclusion of a legally binding agreement between the government and a recognized fishermen's body. All fishing areas that are not subject to a co-management agreement will continue to be managed by the Fisheries Department, in the way they have been in the past. (GOM/EAD 2002, vol. 2, section 3.3)

The Malawian Department of Fisheries (DOF), in common with most GOM agencies, currently suffers severe operating budget restrictions. The practical import of the FCMA is to *encourage self-help*. If fishermen do not govern and manage their "own" fishery stocks, primarily by regulating harvesting (through restrictions that they enforce on fishing gear, seasons, and places), and perhaps eventually by restricting access, they will likely see those stocks decline from overfishing. The "survival watchwords" that flow from this situation are, thus, *self-reliance* and *sustainable, sustained stewardship*.

Institutional Innovations

The Lake Chiuta fisheries case demonstrates in very pragmatic terms how, under certain technical and institutional conditions, Malawian fishers can make a critical contribution to sustaining a fishery and thereby to preserving their own livelihoods. Chiuta fishers have a clear grasp of their personal and family economic stake in this outcome. They rely on the DOF for minimal but critical assistance in this regard; fishers take responsibility for the bulk of co-governance and comanagement activities: rule making, monitoring, enforcement, resolution of trouble cases, adjusting rules to take account of changing realities, and mobilization of resources to "finance" their co-governance and comanagement activities.

Fishers do, however, expect ad hoc support from DOF personnel, particularly in terms of explaining to other GOM enforcement agencies that local fishers' associations are *officially* authorized to apply laws that they themselves make. DOF personnel on Lake Chiuta thus provide a very low-cost but exceedingly important service in shielding fisher associations from unwarranted (and *ultra vires*) intrusion in their affairs by, for example, the national police force. The latter, furthermore, when they appear in specific fishery trouble cases, seem to be making good-faith efforts to meet other citizens' demands for protection against "piracy"—the term owners of illegal nets use to characterize efforts by local fisher associations to enforce their association rules banning use of the *nkatcha* net. This gear is a modified open water seine net with lethal capture potential (for description see box 8.1); its systematic use pretty much guarantees overfishing and elimination of local fish stocks.

Fishers who rely entirely on the DOF to shoulder these renewable natural resource (RNR) governance and management burdens, unavoidable now that their fisheries have come under pressure and are menaced by depletion, will likely, in short order, find themselves looking for a new line of work. But the area near Lake Chiuta offers few economically viable alternatives to

> **Box 8.1. *Nkatcha* net fishing operations**
>
> Lake Chiuta's clear, shallow waters lend themselves to efficient use of the *nkatcha* open water seine net. *Nkatcha* net operations rely on services of a diver who, as a member of the fishing crew (other members of which are divided between the two boats required to work this seine net), directs capture operations. He dives until he identifies a school of fish. After surfacing, he directs his crewmates to deploy the net to completely encircle the school. One boat anchors the net while the crew of the other pays it out following the diver's instructions. Once the net is in place, the diver plunges to the bottom of the seine and, using ties attached to its lower edge, entirely seals the net around the school. If the *nkatcha* incorporates a sufficiently small mesh size, not even fingerlings escape the trap. This explains why this net's capture potential is so lethal and why, if a large number of crews consistently use it, even on a large lake, they can rapidly deplete a fishery. While fish supplies last, however, *nkatcha* fishers can sell their catch more cheaply than those who use less efficient capture gear, and so the former tend to earn more than the latter. *Nkatcha* nets create an additional source of friction: Use of these seines stirs up the muddy bottom of the lake, which annoys members of lakeside communities who use Chiuta for their water supply.

fishing. Indeed, the very bleakness of their economic situation is what makes fishery RGM compelling for fishers. This circumstance offers some hope that fishers *might* overcome similar challenges on a number of Malawi's other major water bodies. Yet this outcome is by no means certain, for reasons discussed below.

For Malawi's fisheries, the National Fisheries and Aquaculture Policy (NFAP), approved in 2001 (GOM/EAD 2002, vol. 2), is as relevant as the Fisheries Conservation and Management Act and its implementing rules. These rules build on a policy, of which:

> The general objectives aim at monitoring and controlling fishing activities to enhance the quality of life for fishing communities by increasing harvests within safe sustainable yields and to promote aquaculture as a source of income and to supplement fish supply from natural waters. (GOM/EAD 2002, vol. 2, section 3.2)

This policy legally recognizes significant institutional innovations (briefly noted in box 8.2 and in greater detail in boxes 8.3a and 8.3b). In particular, it:

> **Box 8.2. Beach and river village committees: evolution**
>
> Contemporary Malawian Beach Village Committees (BVCs) and River Village Committees (RVCs) build on an indigenous fisheries tradition of institutional innovation. During the colonial era (and perhaps before), enterprising individuals would "clear" a lakefront beach, meaning remove reeds, weeds, rocks, and other underwater hazards and impediments so that fishermen could land their dugouts in security and also fish beach seines in those areas without impediment.
>
> Those who created beaches charged fishers who used them a modest fee for access to the landing facility. BVCs, now recognized by GOM legislation as noted at several points *infra*, are authorized to control access to fisheries, to license gear, and to charge fishermen access fees.

- Authorizes artisan fishers to make their *own* rules *governing access* to their fisheries and *regulating harvesting practices*, for example, by establishing prohibitions on fishing gear, specification of dimensions of legal capture equipment, seasonal and place fishing restrictions.
- Recognizes officerholders of GOM-approved fisher organizations (e.g., Beach and River Village Committees [BVCs and RVCs]) as *law officers authorized by national legislation to enforce their own BVC and RVC regulations* (Wilson 2003, 54).
- Authorizes fishers to "formulate and review fisheries regulations" (Wilson 2003, 54: no. 6 (2) (g)). It should be noted in this regard that BVCs and RVCs are also required to enforce fishing regulations that have been approved and duly promulgated by the Malawian DOF. Among these are regulations pertaining to fish species and size, closed seasons, fish sanctuaries (closed areas, often spawning grounds), fishing gear size (e.g., mesh size, net length and height), type of fishing gear, stowage of same, and methods of fishing (Wilson, no. 6. (2) (d)).
- Authorizes fisher organizations to *retain fines imposed for infractions of their rules*.
- Authorizes fishers to create new levels of organization, for example, area (sub-lake) and lake-level fisher associations based on BVCs and RVCs found in those jurisdictions, to facilitate integrated governance and management of the fisheries within which they operate.

> **Box 8.3a. Chiuta BVC/RVC constitutional rules**
>
> These constitutional rules (CRs) reflect local initiatives and experiences in the Lake Chiuta area. Membership rules provide for true *user* groups; they do not include traditional authorities (TAs), for example, village headmen, group village headmen, senior chiefs, and the like as some of these demonstrated during the organizational phase, by accepting bribes from Lake Chilwa *nkatchai* net fishers, that they could not be relied upon to represent the interests of Lake Chiuta fishers and to support their efforts to create an institutional framework for a sustainable fishery on the lake.
>
> **CR1:** *Membership rules*: to become a member of a BVC or RVC, an individual must meet four criteria:
>
> **CR1a:** operate as a fisherman or fish trader, or be married to one or the other of the above;
>
> **CR1b:** citizen born in the Lake Chiuta area, or there resident for the past five years, known to be of good behavior and with an interest in the fishery [i.e., a primary *stakeholder*];
>
> **CR1c:** permanent resident [as specified under CR1b above];
>
> **CR1d:** 18 years of age (Wilson 2003, 23, section 6.2).

Lake Chiuta and Lake Malombe: Institutional Contrasts

Lake Size and Depth, and Their Implications for Capture Strategies

Chiuta is the smallest of Malawi's four major fishing lakes (in declining order of size, Malawi, Malombe, Chilwa, and Chiuta). It covers 200 km², of which 40 km² (20 percent) are situated within Mozambique, while the remaining 160 km² (80 percent) lie in Malawi. It has a mean depth of five meters (Wilson 2003, 10). It is uniformly shallow (fishing dugouts and other lake craft are *poled* rather than paddled, a sure indication that most areas of the lake are shallow) and remarkably clear (many lacustrine communities in fact use Chiuta as their major source of potable water).

Number of Communities on Lake

Lake Chiuta, on the Malawian side alone, counts thirty-one beaches, and probably an equivalent number of villages. On the Malawian side are eleven

Box 8.3b. Chiuta BVC/RVC and LCFA constitutional rules

CR2: *Officer recruitment rules*: Each BVC/RVC recruits the following eleven officers, who must all be members of the BVC or RVC within which they serve and, in addition, nominated by 2 percent of the members of the organization.

    CR2a: chairman and vice chairman
    CR2b: secretary and vice secretary
    CR2c: treasurer and vice treasurer
    CR2d: five council members

CR3: *Terms of service*: All officers serve voluntarily, but are entitled to reimbursement for expenses incurred while serving (Wilson 2003, 32, no. 16).

CR4: *Members' rights*:

    CR4a: members are entitled to use fishery resources in accord with BVC/RVC bylaws, rules, and regulations and with any relevant laws in force in Malawi.
    CR4b: members who have paid their fees and licenses (box 8.5) are entitled to vote at all regular and general meetings.
    CR4c: members are entitled to elect officers of their BVCs, RVCs, AFAs, and the LCFA.

CR5: *Authority to control access*: BVCs and RVCs are, by reason of the GOM "National Fisheries and Aquaculture Policy Supplement Chambo Restoration Policy," approved July 23, 2003, to have exclusive fishing zones and authority to regulate access to and fishing in these zones, in order to protect their fisheries (Wilson 2003, 9).

    CR5: *Amendment*: the LCFA constitution can be amended by two-thirds majority vote of the annual general meeting of the Fisheries Association.

CR6: *Rule-making/modification authority*: BVCs/RVCs can make and modify bylaws [presumably by majority vote] as they judge necessary for the governance and management of the Lake Chiuta fishery RNR. They are, likewise, entitled to appoint persons to monitor and enforce those rules, and to impose sanctions in cases of infraction.

CR7: *Enforcement*: BVC/RVC monitors and enforcers are authorized to *apply rules and sanctions to anyone fishing within the jurisdiction of their unit.*

CR8: *Disputes*: Traditional authorities are to hear appeals from any BVC/RVC decision.

For details of BVC/RVC, AFA, and the LCFA rules, see Wilson (2003, 24–33).

BVCs, but none on the Mozambican shore. That area was much depopulated during that country's civil war, and fishers there have still not been organized, or organized themselves. The DOF's 1998 "Frame Survey" (an annual census of fisher numbers, beaches, gear types, etc.) reveals that of 917 fishers recorded that year, only 86 (9.3 percent) worked as crew members. Most own the gear they fish, including the dugout canoes typical on the lake. This reflects the success of BVCs, Area Fisheries Associations (AFAs), and Lake Chiuta Fisheries Association (LCFA) in removing *nkatcha* fishers from the lake. The fishing gear that most Chiuta fishers use can be operated by a single person and does not require a crew to work it (Njaya, Donda, and Hara 1999, 6).

Technical Issues: Fish Species, Stocks, Gear Types, and Numbers

Lake Chiuta contains viable stocks of *chambo* (*Oreochromis* spp., particularly *O. shiranus*) (Wilson 2003, 10). Fishers also exploit other fish species. They use many types of gear in capturing Lake Chiuta fish, including fish traps, long (trot) lines, hand lines, gill nets, and (formerly) beach seine nets and open water *nkatcha* nets.

Market Access

Access to markets from Lake Chiuta is limited.[1] Malawian and Mozambican communities located near the lake on both the sides and in its immediate hinterland (Machinga, Ngokwe, Liwonde, Palaka, Phalombe) constitute the relevant *local* market. Access to more distant, but larger *urban* markets in both Malawi (Zomba, Blantyre) and Mozambique is more difficult, involving transportation and transaction costs over significant distances. Some of the fish caught in Chiuta and landed in Malawian villages are smoked for fishmongers who periodically visit the area to purchase fish at wholesale prices. Malawian Chiuta fishers report they prefer to sell to consumers in their immediate communities because the latter pay higher prices than traders do, and such sales avoid the transformation and transaction costs involved in selling fish in the closest urban markets.

Fisher Collective Efforts

Lake Chiuta constitutes the success story of two Malawian fisheries cases analyzed in the report that underlies this chapter (Thomson et al. 2004). Lake

Malombe BVCs are, despite efforts to the contrary, subject to greater control by traditional authorities than seems appropriate. By contrast, BVCs on Lake Chiuta are consistently bottom-up in origin, self-organizing, and largely fisher-driven in implementation. Lake Chiuta fishers consider their fisheries RGM activities to be successful, because fish stocks are recovering and fishers are bringing home more fish of larger sizes. As fishers work the resource on a daily basis and must be presumed to know something about the condition of fish stocks, their verdict is critical.[2] Fishers report Chiuta contains more fish, of larger sizes, than it did when they initially organized their fisheries RGM institutions.

Fishery Gear Enforcement Patterns and Fishery Health

The fishers' conclusion in terms of fishery health is singularly important because it confirms *that their investments of time and effort, and the risks and sacrifices accepted by members of these locally initiated, GOM-approved fisher groups are having their intended effects: The Chiuta fishery is in recovery.* This positive dynamic probably goes a long way toward convincing Malawian fishers on Lake Chiuta of the value of fishery RGM efforts. Lake Chiuta trouble cases—involving exclusively net seizures—reviewed in drafting the original report reveal that Malawian fishers resident on Chiuta continue to make efforts to ban use on the lake of the *nkatcha* open water seine net. BVCs on Lake Chiuta were reported in 2003 to have seized sixty-eight *nkatcha* nets from August 1999 to August 2003, or seventeen nets/year on average (1999 = eight; 2000 = nine; 2001 = three; 2002 = thirty-five; 2003 = thirteen).

Interestingly, these RGM co-policing efforts reflect broad participation by BVCs that constitute the LCFA. Some BVCs have confiscated many *nkatcha* nets. But this appears to reflect the fact that those BVCs are based on islands located in the middle of the lake, where community members can easily monitor a wide sweep of water, identify prohibited fishing activities, and then mount enforcement sorties. The participation of other BVCs, even at a lesser level of intensity, can be taken as a proxy measure of members' interest in ensuring that all fishers respect BVC rules. It seems fair to conclude, provisionally, that BVC members consider these (their own) rules legitimate and are prepared to back that evaluation with potentially dangerous action. Repeatedly, they have forcibly confiscated nets that the BVC regulations classify as illegal. By their own report, the resulting intensity of monitoring and enforcement, at least vis-à-vis the use of *nkatcha* nets on Lake Chiuta, is producing the intended effect: "bigger fish, heavier catches."

Lake Chiuta Case Problem Statement: RNR Demand Exceeds Supply

Technically, Lake Chiuta can be characterized as *exclusively* an artisan fishery. No modern fishing rigs ply the lake (*modern* fishing rigs, as the term is used here, designate machine-operated capture equipment [e.g., open water paired-trawler seines, etc.]; such rigs can only legally fish selected deep-water sections of Lake Malawi).

Economically, Chiuta is isolated, connected to comparatively distant urban markets via a network of laterite and blacktop roads, the first of which was constructed in 1985. Only then did this formerly subsistence fishery take on a partially commercial character (Wilson 2003, 10). These market access constraints serve, even at present, to moderate economic demand for fish taken in the lake. The fishery is economically important, that is, the DOF reported a total catch of two thousand tons of fish during the two decades from 1976 to 1996, or one hundred tons/year (Njaya, Donda, and Hara 1999, 3). This activity provides jobs and income to some (but not all) fishers, gear owners, fish processors and fish mongers, and others associated with the sector. Observers note that 90 percent of the Lake Chiuta catch is sold, first to wholesalers and then to retailers and consumers. Most (80–90 percent) fish traders are males (Njaya, Donda, and Hara [quoting Donda] 1999, 5).

Politically, Chiuta constitutes an intriguing case. It sits astride the international boundary between Malawi (160 km^2—80 percent of lake surface) and Mozambique (40 km^2—20 percent of lake surface) and presents considerable potential for international tensions (now present) over fishery RGM and difficult political challenges that, if not addressed successfully, will seriously undermine prospects for fishery sustainability. Fishers of both countries, be it noted, routinely ignore the international boundary on the lake.

Legally, Lake Chiuta constitutes a clear example of bottom-up, fisher-provided RGM (including policing), in which the Malawian DOF plays a limited but *crucial* supporting role. Rather than fisheries comanagement, Chiuta is more accurately designated a case of fisher self-governance and self-management, with modest but crucial elements of government support.

From the perspective of Chiuta resident fishers, the fundamental problem facing their communities is that of banning fish capture equipment so potent[3] that it can threaten the capacity of the Chiuta fisheries, as a complex RNR, to reproduce itself. At the head of their list of unacceptable gear is the highly efficient *nkatcha* open water seine net, invented some years earlier by a

Lake Malombe fisherman (for a description of how fishermen use the *nkatcha* net, see box 8.1).

The *nkatcha* net has since *metastasized*—the analogy to the process by which cancer spreads would appear none too strong in the eyes of Chiuta fishers—into other Malawian lakes (Chilwa, Chiuta, and Malawi). Lake Chilwa migrant fishers who could no longer make a living on their overfished home waters served as "*vectors* for the disease" when they took their *nkatcha* nets to other lakes, arriving on Lake Chiuta in the 1980s (Wilson 2003, 10).

If fishermen were allowed to use *nkatcha* nets in the clear waters of Lake Chiuta, they could very rapidly overharvest its fish stocks and threaten the sustainability of the fishery (cf. box 8.1). But Chiuta *resident* fishers were simply not prepared to allow the *nkatcha* menace to destroy their livelihood.[4] This consensus among Chiuta fishers led them to conceptualize, organize, and apply an effective ban on *anyone* using the open water *nkatcha* seine net (and eventually, even *nkatcha* beach seines) in their lake.

Lake Chiuta: Common-Pool or Common-Property Resource?

In pursuing this goal, Malawian Chiuta fishers have in effect treated Lake Chiuta as a *common-pool* resource and, largely through their own efforts in creating appropriate institutional arrangements, have converted it from a common-pool—open access—resource into a "quasi-" common-property resource. Use of the term "quasi" here highlights the fact that Lake Chiuta fishers make no attempt to control *access* to lake waters. Instead, they focus *their monitoring and enforcement attention* on regulating harvesting, particularly the kinds of fishing gear that are legally *acceptable* for use on Lake Chiuta, treated as a common property. Rather than trying to prevent others getting access to the lake, they focus on identifying and seizing illegal capture equipment. Experience with their own informally created, enforced, and respected technical stint has taught them that less "lethal" forms of fishing gear, even if abundant, will not materially harm the Chiuta fishery's capacity to reproduce stocks. Efforts to control access at this point would thus amount to unnecessary, and therefore wasted effort.

In shifting to a restricted form of common-property management, Chiuta resident fishers have come to govern and manage their home lake as a *global special district*. It *would appear* that this is a technically appropriate approach. Fish in Malawian lakes (principally ciclids, *Oreochromis* spp.) are mobile and not tied to a home ground (although they do have known spawning grounds, in swampy areas located at the southern end of the lake). This implies that one or a set of neighboring BVCs imposing a stint (restricting fish capture) *only* in the area under their control would probably not enrich their fisheries because new increments of fish would move away to less populated waters. Assume, however, that fishers do accept a stint on catching fish in their home waters and that this self-discipline (intensified fisheries RGM) fosters creation of new increments of fish stocks in those waters. Assume also that some of those growing stocks move away to other parts of the lake. If so, other fishers—while themselves refusing to *stint*—could *ride free* on sacrifices accepted by fishers in the first set of BVCs. They would in effect "free ride" by themselves, avoiding stinting behavior while scoring bigger catches from more abundant fish stocks found in neighboring or more distant waters. In consequence, it would appear that fishers *must*—because of what we assume to be the behavior of local fish stocks—manage the lake as an *undifferentiated*, unpartitioned, (quasi-) common-property resource. Typically, efforts to *govern and manage common-pool resources as common-property resources* involve efforts to define *authorized* users and then to *deny access* to *unauthorized* users. Chiuta Malawian fishers' efforts to govern and manage the lake as a common property fishery are, as noted, efficient because they have skipped the steps of defining unauthorized *users* and then trying to deny them access to lake waters, preferring to target their efforts instead to unauthorized *equipment*. In other words, *anybody* can fish as long as they respect the locally-defined rules of sustainability.

Note that further research of a technical nature on behavior of fish stocks in Malawi's major lakes—Chiuta, Chilwa, Malombe, and Malawi—might reject the assumption that fish regularly move to less crowded and thus richer habitat. Yet, it is also possible that Malawian fishers already know this to be the case, since they travel to fish in specific sites that they consider to be rich in fish. In any case, Lake Chiuta fishers *behave as though they think that fish move around in an opportunistic manner.* They developed and now monitor and enforce *lake-wide* rules that restrict capture gear. This behavior can be viewed as pragmatic evidence of fishers' belief that fish search out better habitat in an opportunistic manner.

This technical issue is a common, vexing problem. The larger the scale of the special district to be managed, the greater and more complex the challenge. Were it possible to *partition* lakes into smaller units, and could the fish that range across those aquatic environments be stabilized and compelled to respect partitioning limits, it would make it far easier to govern and manage them. Could fish populations be stabilized, user groups that *stinted* on their home territories (and also successfully excluded unauthorized users) could expect larger harvests over time. This should, in turn, make it easier to propagate sustained yield norms because the process would incorporate reasonable equity: Those who stint (accept short-term sacrifices in the amounts of fish they harvest) harvest more, and more reliably, over the longer term. With both free-riding by external actors and intragroup opportunism "assumed away," virtue would be its own reward.

Developing and Financing Fisheries Institutional Capital

In developing institutional arrangements to monitor and enforce rules restricting capture techniques, Chiuta fishers have drawn in the first instance on preexisting *local institutional capital*. They subsequently accepted two additional institutional innovations promoted by external actors. The old institutional capital now takes the form of BVCs and RVCs (see box 8.2).

The new institutional arrangements—the *Lake Chiuta Fisheries Association* and its two constituent *Area Fisheries Associations*—offer Chiuta fishers means to concert their actions for a more powerful overall effect. The phrase "offer . . . means" implies that these institutional innovations—in effect, *confederal* arrangements—are much a work in progress. The intriguing question is how Chiuta fishers will judge these arrangements in the final analysis. *In theory*, they represent constructive additions to the panoply of institutions that people have been developing over the last decade on Lake Chiuta. *In conception*, they afford Chiuta fishers the means to concert their actions, to explore—collectively—adjustments and refinements in their institutional arrangements, to mobilize significant financial resources and to resolve, at modest cost, trouble cases over fishing gear that continue to erupt from time to time on the lake. To exploit unmercifully the afore-noted cancer analogy, these institutional arrangements might be viewed as offering possibilities for *ongoing, collective chemotherapy* that could enable Chiuta fishers to remain vigilant, stay on top of and block spread of the *nkatcha net plague that formerly threatened Chiuta's fishery* (and, for that matter, other problems that might affect the future of their fishery). BVCs/RVCs, in coordination with the AFAs and LCFA, enjoy legal power to mobilize cash resources through sale of licenses, collection of membership fees, and the imposition of fines (see box 8.4). The LCFA and AFAs offer to fishermen, others involved in the fishing industry who are BVC/RVC members, and DOF officials institutional facilities within which they can engage in exchanges of information, for example, concerning rule changes, DOF extension messages, fishers' concerns, and so forth.

> **Box 8.4. Chiuta fisheries operational rules ("bylaws") and penalties for infringement**
>
> These operational rules (ORs), which Chiuta fishers developed initially over the course of 1995 in response to the threat they perceived "outsider" Lake Chilwa fishers were posing to their fishery, all tend to reduce capture potential and thus the effective level of demand for Lake Chiuta fish.
>
> **OR1:** prohibition of four kinds of nets: (a) *khoka la nkacha* (open water seine net); (b) *khoka la pansi* (beach seine nets) [fine for use: MK15,000–30,000; net to be returned once fine paid]; (c) mosquito nets, use of which is prohibited in both the lake itself and all its tributary rivers [infractions sanctioned by MK600 fine]; and (d) *mkwakwaza* (scoop nets), use of which is again prohibited in both the lake itself and all its tributary rivers [infractions sanctioned by fine of MK500];
>
> **OR2:** minimum mesh size in permitted nets (gill nets, minimum mesh 2.5 inches) and fish trap (*miano yamagalange*) openings (0.5 inches) [infractions punishable by fine of MK500];
>
> **OR3:** minimum legal length (6 inches) for important local species "chambo" (*Oreochromis sp.*), with the understanding that sub-legal length fish must be released; and
>
> **OR4:** corresponding prohibition on killing, trading, or holding *chambo* less than 6 inches in length.
>
> **OR5:** no poisoning of fish in any waters, particularly tributary rivers.
>
> **OR6:** every immigrant fisherman must register with the BVC, which governs the beach where he is based [fine for infractions: MK200].
>
> **OR7:** every immigrant fisherman must produce a transfer letter from his former BVC introducing him to his new one [infractions sanctioned by fine of MK200].
>
> **OR8:** any fisher or fish trader found guilty of stealing gear or fish to be expelled from beach where s/he is registered.
>
> **OR9:** illegal gear is subject to sanction without regard to its country of origin (Malawi or Mozambique).

Chiuta's current set of locally-generated and externally-induced institutions continue to evolve. It seems likely that *fishers will either consolidate them or allow individual institutions to wither and die depending on how useful they find them.* It also seems clear that the GOM lacks the capacity to finance these arrangements. They will either become self-financing, because fishers collectively judge them useful, or they will die peacefully of neglect because Chiuta fishers cannot find the time, energy, and financial resources necessary to maintain LCFA operations and those of the two AFAs and to add value through their operations. This issue, while far from being decided, has implications for the future of Chiuta's fishery. These are *not* all negative.[5] If resident fishers can finance these institutions, for example, through a modest additional tax piggybacked on the existing semiannual registration fee for boats and gear, or through a similar modest tax on the value of fish catches landed,[6] it should be feasible to finance (or, cofinance with DOF funds) participation by LCFA and AFA officers in relevant meetings. If Chiuta's fish harvests increase in value because the enforced stint permits fish to mature and reach a size where they command higher market prices, it should be feasible for Chiuta fishers to finance LCFA and AFA operations through license and registration fees, perhaps supplemented by a local tax on the value of catches.

One could speculate that the current widespread BVC/RVC failure to collect license fees is less a function of fishers' poverty and more a question of their uncertainty about whether association officials will use the money thus mobilized for the intended purposes and, if they do, whether their participation in LCFA and AFA meetings will in fact add value by further upgrading Chiuta fisheries RGM. The same calculations might partially explain the current lack of a functioning locally controlled fiscal system.

Financing with Fines: A Trap?

It should be noted here that the tendency of Lake Chiuta fishers to rely on fines imposed on those who violate local capture rules (e.g., by employing *nkatcha* nets or beach seines on the lake) *could turn into a significant point of institutional weakness.* The more effective is local monitoring and enforcement of locally generated rules regulating harvesting of fish in Lake Chiuta, the less attractive it becomes to try to *ride free* on other's sacrifices (sacrifices that take the form of willing, persistent compliance with local rules). Under such circumstances, the likelihood of being caught and fined for using illegal gear is so great that illegal fishing can become a money-losing proposition. This implies that if local co-policing continues to be as effective as it has heretofore been, incidents of illegal fishing will tail off toward nonexistence. The lucrative fines associated with such events will likewise dwindle. (For examples of fines for different infractions, see box 8.4.) Lake Chiuta BVCs will thus face a

> **Box 8.5. BVC/RVC regular revenue sources**
>
> OR6: 50MK membership fee, payable upon joining.
>
> OR7: 50MK fishing "levy" payable January 1 and July 1 of each year (effectively a semiannual fishing license).
>
> OR8: 150MK fish trading levy the first time a trader visits a BVC or RVC jurisdiction.
>
> OR9: 250MK ferry boat levy, payable annually to the BVC or RVC where the ferry (typically a plank boat) is based.
>
> OR10: Gillnet license fee, payable annually to the DOF on January 1 at the rate published by GOM in the official gazette. An agreed percentage of that amount is to be retroceded by DOF to the Lake Chiuta Area Fisheries Association by March 31, which in turn is to distribute that amount among its member BVCs/RVCs.
>
> *Source*: Wilson (2003, 34–35).

dilemma: Either they will have to relax their policing to encourage illegal fishing and so revive the possibility of imposing fines to finance LCFA and AFA activities, or they will have to strengthen the local resource mobilization system (fees for service, taxation of catches, etc.) authorized by existing enabling legislation (see box 8.5) or create a new resource mobilization system that will provide the funds required to finance Chiuta fishers' institutions.

A further issue in this regard, alluded to above, concerns the utility to Lake Chiuta fishers of their Area Fishers Associations. The need for the LCFA—potentially a lake-wide body—seems patent (at least to an outside observer). It provides a means to organize regular information exchanges among fishers and between fishers and DOF representatives. It also offers a framework to coordinate activities on the lake designed to conserve and enrich the fishery and the local fishery sector economy and associated jobs (fishers, gear owners, fishmongers, fish processors, transporters, and the like). Finally, it offers a potentially efficient means to articulate fisher perspectives, and possibly to facilitate dialogue with Mozambican fishers with an eye to resolving disputes over the operational rule banning use of *nkatcha* nets in Chiuta waters.

Indications exist that the AFAs and the LCFA were created in a somewhat top-down manner. That may not prove a fatal flaw insofar as the LCFA proves its utility in fishers' eyes and offers opportunities to adjust the institutional framework as they see fit (e.g., DOF agrees to finance participation of its representatives in these activities, which would marginally reduce the financial burden involved in organizing meetings). On the other hand, fishers believe that the AFAs were organized mainly to encourage traditional authorities (TAs) around the lake to support fisheries RGM by cutting them into a share of the "profits" represented by fines assessed for violation of gear regulations.

History of Interventions

First Interventions and Objectives. The DOF saw Lake Chiuta as a fishery self-regulated through the gear fishers habitually used. The DOF imposed no rules limiting access or regulating harvesting by Chiuta fishers. When the GTZ fisheries project decided to extend operations to Lake Chiuta, project personnel decided against adopting the *sitting fee* scheme that they had employed in their work on Lake Malombe (in which fisheries association members were paid to participate in association meetings) (cf. Thomson et al. 2004; Wilson 2003, 185). This decision, in conjunction with a strong commitment to ensure that BVCs really would be *user* groups composed primarily of fishers, appears to have had the desired effect. Chiuta fishers at present finance their own participation in important meetings, rather than depending on DOF or a project to provide them with sitting fees or transportation allowances. This self-help ethic appears both powerful and well anchored. It can occasion difficulties; for example, temptations to assess higher fines against wealthier net owners in order to obtain funds to finance meetings but, on balance, the benefits of this principle probably far outweigh its inconveniences. Chiuta fishers are neither *dependent* on the DOF or on projects to conduct their activities, nor do they seem artificially "*immobilized*" by lack of outside funding. As they have never become accustomed to the "union wage" of sitting fees, the thought of "striking" to get it seems—happily enough—not to have occurred to Lake Chiuta fishers.

Fisheries Department and Project Staff Deployed. The DOF has posted a single staff member to Lake Chiuta. This individual, Mr. Nixon K. Massi, is a DOF fisheries assistant (FA). His superiors visit the lake occasionally on supervision trips, but Massi appears left largely to his own devices. He has no operating budget (e.g., he does not receive a regular allotment of fuel to operate his outboard motor or motorbike). His success in promoting better fishery stewardship on Lake Chiuta is thus the more impressive. His role has consisted largely of encouraging fishers to conduct their own monitoring and enforcement (policing) operations. These activities involve confiscation of illegal *nkatcha* nets and occasionally, physical confrontations. Owners of illegal gear from time to time invoke police assistance in efforts to regain their nets without having to pay fines. In several of these situations, Mr. Massi has convinced both Malawian and Mozambican police that Lake Chiuta fishers are acting in full compliance with Malawi's laws regulating fisheries (this is in fact precisely accurate: cf. Wilson 2003, 35, "Lake Chiuta Fisheries Association By-Law Regulations," no. 1). *This has enhanced the authority of BVCs in the eyes of those who fish the lake, and has probably made it easier for them to co-police fishing operations.*

The one exception here concerns the role of some Mozambican fishers and traditional authorities in refusing to comply with the fishing regulations that Malawian fishers resident on Lake Chiuta have established. Mozambican traditional authorities reportedly encourage Mozambican fishers to engage armed guards to protect them from Malawian co-policing fishers while they use the banned *nkatcha* net on the lake. Thus far, no serious incidents (bloodshed or deaths) have arisen through altercations opposing Malawian fishers seeking to enforce their regulations and Mozambican fishers operating in violation of those regulations. Nonetheless, the potential for explosive incidents exists. Were such a confrontation to erupt, it could rapidly escalate into an international incident.

For this reason, the Malawian DOF and donor-financed projects associated with the DOF have sought to include the Mozambicans in conferences, workshops, and study tours designed to foster consensus on a set of formal (and working) rules that will elicit support and compliance from *all* fishers who use the lake. So far that goal has proven elusive, despite participation on several occasions in these dialogue activities by Chief Nsiya, a Mozambican senior traditional authority. As the special districts team was unable to interview Mozambicans engaged either in fishing or in supporting fishers who work Lake Chiuta, we are ill-placed to present the Mozambican perspective.[7]

Nonetheless, the unresolved problem of establishing a set of generally accepted rules that restrict fish-harvesting operations on Lake Chiuta may justly be considered a potential Achilles heel for the whole exercise. If Malawian fishers give up enforcing rules that limit capture gear and fishing times and places, Lake Chiuta will slip from its current status as a reasonably well-governed and managed quasi-common-property fishery to that of a fully open access fishery where *unregulated and unrestricted harvesting* is the only common rule. If the *working rules* that govern harvesting of fish in Chiuta were again to condone use of the *nkatcha* net on those waters, fishers using that gear could crash a fishery now in recovery.

Table 8.1. Lake Chiuta Area Fisheries Associations (AFAs)

Area fishery association names and members	
AFA Ngokwe (20 total members)	AFA Chikweo (20 total members)
9 BVCs and 1 RVC	4 BVCs
Rifune RVC	Small Chiuta Island BVC
Aduwa BVC	Njiriti BVC
Kalyolyo BVC	Mulambe BVC
Ali-Chikwawa BVC	Nafisi BVC
Njerwa BVC	
Matipwili BVC	
Moro BVC	
Misala BVC	
Big Chiuta BVC	
Mthubula BVC	

BVC = Beach Village Committee; RVC = River Village Committee

Community Fisheries Governance and Management Institutions for Co-Governance/Comanagement

Fishers on Lake Chiuta and a river that empties into the lake have organized a total of thirteen BVCs and one RVC, grouped into two AFAs within the overarching Lake Chiuta Fisheries Association. The two AFAs have taken their names from those of the traditional authorities—Chiefs Ngokwe and Chikweo—who respectively exercise jurisdiction over the AFA areas controlled by their constituent BVCs and RVC (see table 8.1).

BVCs/RVCs all organize along a single constitutional model, as specified ". . . in the First and Third Schedule of the Fisheries Conservation and Management Regulations (1999)" (Wilson 2003, 14: cf. pp. 53–56, for text of Malawi's 1997 Fisheries Conservation and Management Act (No. 25 of 1997) that contains these constitutional provisions).[8] For a summary of BVC/RVC constitutional rules, see boxes 8.3a and 8.3b.

> **Box 8.6. Chiuta BVC/RVC decision-making rules**
>
> **DR1:** BVC/RVC Committees (officers plus committee members) have authority, after consultation with members, to make and modify operational rules relevant to governance and management of Lake Chiuta resources within their BVC/RVC jurisdictions (see box 8.4).

BVC/RVC members are required to acquit themselves of certain fees and levies (see box 8.5) that are meant to provide each BVC/RVC with an operating budget, supplemented in part by revenue from fines assessed for violations of fisheries harvesting and other regulations pertaining to the sustainable use of Lake Chiuta's fish resources.

By comparison with Lake Malombe BVCs, Lake Chiuta fisher organizations are true user groups, with a membership heavily weighted toward and indeed dominated by fishers. Chiuta BVCs appear relatively homogeneous in composition, and seem to reach consensus with relative ease given members' shared professional interests in maintaining the lake fishery. Fishers in Chiuta BVCs, moreover, demonstrate a commitment to enforcement, exemplified by a willingness to take physical risks in confiscating illegal gear, against which the relative inertness of Lake Malombe BVCs pales by comparison. The heterogeneous nature of the latter—a combination of housewives, farmers, fishmongers, gear owners, and the odd fisherman crew member—probably goes a long way toward explaining their inability to take action, or even agree on a common program (for details on the BVC/RVC decision-making process, see box 8.6).

The Lake Chiuta BVCs also demonstrate a high level of *self-governance*. In these associations, fishers make the rules, and monitor, apply, and enforce them (cf. box 8.3b, CRs 6–7). They do rely on traditional authorities (TAs) for assistance in resolving disputes that they cannot handle locally (see box 8.3b, CR8), but in general, driven by a shared, intense interest in conserving the fishery, they take charge of their own affairs and make and implement their own decisions. Again, in sharp contrast, Lake Malombe BVCs appear dominated by traditional authorities, *flaccid* rather than *robust* as organizations and, from the perspective of fishery RGM, unproductive. Results of Lake Chiuta fishers' efforts at self-governance, in terms of operational rules that fishers themselves devised and now monitor and enforce, are detailed in box 8.4.

In conclusion, the fishers of Malawi's Lake Chiuta and the GOM's Department of Fisheries appear to have laid a solid foundation for continued, effective fisheries RGM on the lake (and potentially on other lakes in the country, assuming local fishers are prepared to accept the costs (and risks) of self-governance). That foundation addresses the critical issues of sustainable RGM, that is, vesting in resource users the authority to make, modify, monitor, and enforce rules governing access to and harvesting of fishery resources, mobilize resources, and resolve any disputes resulting from these activities.

The key innovation incorporated in the GOM strategy lies in its willingness to deputize BVC/RVC leaders as *national police officers* for purposes of enforcing their own rules in the lake area controlled by each association. By transferring to fishers the burdens of monitoring and enforcement, the GOM recognizes its own inability to provide real services in those areas, and vests in those with the greatest long-term interest in fisheries RGM a powerful tool to achieve that end. This, in turn, empowers fishers to act in ways that discourage conflict, by confiscating illegal fishing gear.

But, as noted, weak points exist in this set of institutional arrangements. The most serious weakness turns on Lake Chiuta relations between Malawian and Mozambican fishers, particularly as a powerful traditional Mozambican chief appears committed to encouraging "his" fishers to pursue a free-rider strategy that will make a mockery of Malawian Chiuta fishers' efforts to govern and manage their lake for sustainable use. If the chief is willing to encourage his ex-guerrilla partisans to protect Mozambican fishers using the banned *nkatcha* net on Lake Chiuta, he might generate conflicts that could potentially escalate into an international war between Malawi and Mozambique.

The genius of the GOM innovation of deputizing users to enforce the *national* laws that simply afford the force of formal law to users' own institutional arrangements lies both in the economy in state expenditures that it entails and, as important, in the on-the-job training it affords Malawian fishers interested in practicing the skills of self-governance. To place this opportunity in context, it should be noted that President Hastings Banda for years ran a very sterile polity in which *he* made the rules, the first of which was that *he* made the rules, with the logical second rule being that Malawians should avoid any efforts at self-governance.

Malawians are currently "in recovery" from this period of authoritarian imposition of avoidance of things political. The Chiuta fishers are making the most of the new opportunity and many in the new generation of Malawian politicians seem intent on supporting their RGM initiatives. If other fisher groups on other Malawian lakes and users of other types of renewable resources follow their lead, Malawians could offer a very positive example to a large number of other African countries. But that, of course, depends on politicians'—and GOM technicians'—"political will" to voluntarily abandon sources of rents by transferring governance authority to resource users.

Notes

1. Information in this paragraph appears in Njaya, Donda, and Hara (1999, 5, table 2).

2. This is even more so the case as the DOF has recently lacked funds to conduct scientifically-based monitoring of the evolution of Chiuta fisheries stocks. The DOF has long seen Lake Chiuta as adequately governed and managed, with fishing pressure held in check by resident fishers' reliance on less-productive (potent) varieties of fishing gear, for example, fish baskets (traps) with apertures large enough to enable fingerlings to escape, long lines baited with single or multiple hooks, and gill nets. None of these gear types approach the *nkatcha* net (see box 8.1) in capture potential. Chiuta fishers' predilection for gears that involve less-than-maximum feasible capture potential can be viewed as a form of collective *stint*, or deliberate policy of leaving more fish to reproduce themselves. This enlightened view of their long-term self-interest does not, however, guarantee that Lake Chiuta will remain a healthy fishery, despite fishers' current positive reports on the state of the resource (see comments, *supra*). If Chiuta fishers prove unable, either alone or in co-management actions with DOF officials, to curb *nkatcha* net incursions in the lake, either by resident Malawian or Mozambican fishers, or by Malawian migrant fishers, for example, from Lakes Chilwa and Malombe, this would represent a *very serious threat* to the Lake Chiuta fishery, one of Malawi's last two viable big lake fisheries (the other being Lake Malawi).

3. To reiterate, serious fisheries depletion in the Lake Chiuta case is not a hypothetical possibility or a lawyerly "tale of horrors." Malawian fishers only moved to assert firm control over "their" resource when migrant Lake Chilwa fishermen introduced the *nkatcha* net on Lake Chiuta and quickly harvested so many fish that they threatened to crash the fisheries. Chiuta fishers are countering what they viewed as a *clear and present danger*, not some abstract, possible future threat to their livelihood.

4. A potent factor that helped galvanize fishers permanently residing on Lake Chiuta in the face of the 1995 "invasion" by *nkatcha*-net-wielding migrant fishers from neighboring Lake Chilwa was the latter's success in putting their greater earnings from the fishery to work in enticing local women as lovers and spouses (Njaya, Donda, and Hara 1999, 7).

5. John Wilson, long-time observer and practitioner involved with evolution of fisheries institutions in Malawi, notes that fishermen recently *paid government DOF officials* to attend a meeting (personal communication, January 2004).

6. Malian fishers in the village of Fatola on the Senegal River formerly financed their own social security system with such a tax. The system collapsed when the

Manantali Dam further up the river was placed in operation and so significantly modified the natural river regime that weeds took over the entire riverbed, making it impossible for fishers to use their existing nets to catch fish (cf. Fatola fisheries case, in Thomson et al. 2004, Mali case studies there reported).

7. We can speculate that Chief Nsiya and Mozambican fishers on the lake feel that they did not have sufficient opportunity to craft Lake Chiuta fisheries rules and are thus unwilling to support them. While other speculative explanations are possible, it serves no purpose to present them without supporting data.

8. Wilson notes that the GOM might have adopted an approach providing for individual registration by BVCs and RVCs of their constitutions, but points out that it was considered more appropriate to register constitutions of all subordinate organizations through their overlapping Area Fisheries and Lake Fisheries Associations. From the GOM perspective, this offers two advantages: a reduction in the workload entailed in registering each primary fisher organization individually, and uniformity across fisher associations, for example, a common constitution and, at least initially, common bylaws (Wilson 2003, 15).

This approach may smack of rule imposition—except that, in the Lake Chiuta case, the uniform constitutional and operational rules were inspired by institutional arrangements (sets of rules) that Chiuta local fisher associations had themselves developed. Furthermore, the approach adopted does foster development of a uniform set of regulations (constitutional, decision-making, and operational rules) for the Lake Chiuta fishery (and, similarly, for other Malawian fisheries). This, in turn, facilitates treatment of each fishery—by its BVC/RVC members, by DOF FAs and other officers, as well as by GOM police officials—as a unified common-property resource. This is clearly a judgment call, in terms of possible infringement of the principle of "bottom-up fisheries management." It is important to recognize, however, the palpable advantage of local-level uniformity in rules during a period (1995 to present) when devolution of central government fisheries governance and management authority is underway (cf. Njaya, Donda, and Hara 1999, 2; Wilson 2003, 14). This promotes clarity in enforcement—everybody plays by the same set of rules—which implies that monitors, enforcers, and judges can reasonably assume that all fishers know the content of those rules (in this regard, see box 8.4).

References

Bell, Richard. 1998. "Community-Based Fisheries Management, Lake Malombe, Malawi." World Bank/WBI's CBNRM Initiative. http://srdis.ciesin.columbia.edu/cases/malawi-002.html.

Bell, Richard, and S. J. Donda. 1993. *Community Fisheries Management Programme: Lake Malombe and the Upper Shire River*. Final Report, vols. 1 and 2. Mangochi: Government of Malawi, Department of Fisheries and the Malawi-Germany Fisheries and Aquaculture Development Project (MAGFAD).

Bezai, Mattson, and James T. Thomson. 2004. BVC M'Tambo, Lake Malombo. Interview notes, Tuesday, January 20.

Chabal, Patrick, and Jean-Pascal Daloz. 1999. *Africa Works: Disorder as Political Instrument*. Oxford: James Currey.

Chima, James, and Ramzy Kanaan. 2004. BVC Matipwili and BVC Moro, Lake Chiuta. Interview Notes, Saturday, January 24.

Chima, James, Ramzy Kanaan, Mattson Bezai, and James Thomson. 2004. BVC Ntanga, Lake Malombo. Interview Notes, Monday, January 21.

Chima, James, Ramzy Kanaan, and N. K. Massi. 2004a. BVC Njerwa, Lake Chiuta. Interview Notes, Friday, January 23.

———. 2004b. BVC Misala, Lake Chiuta. Interview Notes, Friday, January 23.

Chima, James, Ramzy Kanaan, and J. J. Nyirongo. 2004. BVC Mwarija, Lake Malombe, Interview Notes, Monday, January 19.

Chima, James, Ramzy Kanaan, Stephen Phiri, and James Thomson. 2004. Interview, District Fisheries Officer Patrick Phiri, Monday, January 19.

GOM/DOF-GTZ (Government of Malawi, Department of Fisheries, and Deutsche Gesellschaft für Technische Zusammenarbeit GmbH). 2001. "Socio Economic Survey No. 5: Beach Village Committees at Lake Malombe." Elvira Ganter in cooperation with Mr. Chithagala, Mr. Kasuzweni, Ms. Mazuwa, Mr. Thidza, Mr. Thindwa, Mr. Kachilonda, and Ms. Mueller. National Aquatic Resource Management Programme (NARMAP). Lusaka/Zambia and Mangochi/Malawi, October.

———. N.d. "Guidelines for the Formation and Training of Beach Village Committees; Final Draft." National Aquatic Resource Management Programme (NARMAP). Mangochi, Lilongwe, Monkey Bay, Malawi.

GOM/EAD (Government of Malawi, Environmental Affairs Department). 2002. "Natural Resources Management Policies, Laws and Institutional Framework in Malawi." Vol. 2, "A Resource Book for Community Level Managers," April.

GOM/MNREA/DOF (Government of Malawi, Ministry of Natural Resources and Environmental Affairs, Department of Fisheries). 1997. "Fisheries Conservation and Management Act" (no. 25 of 1997).

———. 1999. "Fisheries Conservation and Management Regulations."

———. 2000. "Annual Frame Survey, September 1999." O. L. F. Weyl, M. Banda, G. Sodzabanja, L. H. Mwenekibombwe, O. C. Mponda, and W. Namoto. Fisheries Research Unit, P.O. Box 27, Monkey Bay. Fisheries Bulletin No. 42, Department of Fisheries, P.O. Box 593, Lilongwe, Malawi.

Hara, M. M., S. J. Donda, and F. Njaya. n.d. "An Evaluation of the Lake Malombe Co-Management Program." Proceedings of the International Workshop on Fisheries Co-Management.

Hardin, Garrett. 1968. "The Tragedy of the Commons." *Science* 162: 1243–48.

Hirschman, Albert O. 1970. *Exit, Voice and Loyalty: Responses to Decline in Firms, Organizations, and States*. Cambridge, MA: Harvard University Press.

Kanaan, Ramzy, and N. K. Massi. 2004. BVC Njerwa, Lake Chiuta. Interview Notes, Saturday, January 24.
Mkoka, Charles. 2003. "Chambo and Chips Missing on Malawi Menus." IslamOnline. net, October 29. http://www.islamonline.net/servlet/Satellite?c=Article_C&cid =1157365877988&pagename=Zone-English-HealthScience%2FHSELayout.
Njaya, F. J., S. J. Donda, and M. M. Hara. 1999. "Fisheries Co-Management Study: Case of Lake Chiuta, Malawi." Paper presented at the International Workshop on Fisheries Co-management, Panang, Malaysia, August 23–28.
No author, no date. "Brief Background of Lake Malombe PFMP [Participatory Fisheries Management Programme]."
Ostrom, Elinor. 1990. *Governing the Commons: The Evolution of Institutions for Collective Action.* New York: Cambridge University Press.
Thomson, James. 1994. "Legal Recognition of Community Capacity for Self-Governance: A Key to Improving Renewable Resource Management in the Sahel." Sahel Decentralization Policy Report, vol. III. Prepared for the Office of Sahel and West Africa Affairs, Africa Bureau, Agency for International Development. Decentralization: Finance and Management Project. Burlington, VT: Associates in Rural Development, Inc.
Thomson, James, Matson Bezai, Rebecca Butterfield, James Chima, Chéibane Coulibaly, et al. 2004. "Mali, Botswana, Namibia, and Malawi: Institutional Aspects of Renewable Natural Resources Governance and Management through Special Districts; Final Report." Prepared for the U.S. Agency for International Development under the Biodiversity and Sustainable Forestry (BIOFOR) IQC Contract no. LAG–I–00–99–00013–00, Task Order no. 3, June.
Thomson, James, and Stephen Phiri (Village Headman and Research Assistant). 2004. Interview notes, Mangochi, Malawi, Monday, January 19.
USAID (United States Agency for International Development). n.d. "Nature, Wealth and Power; Emerging Best Practice for Revitalizing Rural Africa." Document prepared in collaboration with CIFOR, WINROCK, WRI, and IRG.
Wilson, John. 2003. "Participatory Fisheries Management: The Development of Constitutions for the Beach Village Committees and Fisheries Associations of Lakes Chilwa and Chiuta and Mpoto Lagoon." Prepared for the COMPASS project under Development Alternatives, Inc., USAID Contract no. 690–C–00–99–00116–00, Activity no. 612–0248.
———. 2004. Personal communication.

9

From the *Cheyenne Way* to the *Chilean Way* (of Political Reconciliation and Impunity): A Retrospective on Political Architecture, Political Culture, and Institutional Design

Brian Loveman

Political science in the 1960s and 1970s sought to legitimize itself as science with an emphasis on postulating of hypotheses followed by empirical verification; "testing" alternative explanations with a variety of statistical models used as modes of measurement. To a great extent, that trend has become a permanent part of the discipline, across the subfields, with the exception of normative theory and the history of political ideas, and also with the exception of the relatively recent "constructivist" paradigm and the "cultural turn."

With this objective, the introduction to political science required students to understand (1) the methodological assumptions of the variants of logical positivism; (2) the variety of methods with which political inquiry could be carried out, for example, survey research, analysis of congressional voting records, secondary analysis of existing data collections, and so on; and (3) measurement issues, including the variety of social statistics available for assessing the "fit" of findings to hypotheses. All of these were taught in the political science department at Indiana University in the late 1960s and early 1970s, with increasing emphasis on the *science* part of political science, understood almost mechanically.

But that was not how Vincent Ostrom introduced us to politics and political science. First, he challenged us to think about the evolutionary organization of human societies based on human beings as the "basic units." That meant we should think about imperfect, fallible, volitional, cussed, and mortal organisms that could learn, but also could learn poorly and forget; that could design institutions, like artisans, but could also design shabbily, or with the deliberate intent of harming or dominating others. He asked us to think about language, all sorts of language, and its relation to cultural and institutional adaptation. We also learned that since institutions were artifacts, there could be no hard empirical generalizations equivalent to the law of gravity for human societies; that we could look for regularities, look for efforts to create order through law and other sorts of cultural rules.

Long before the current "cultural turn" of the social sciences, we learned about the cultural embeddedness of what we sought to understand, and the dangers of any sort of mechanical application of scientific models to the study of human society. Life might be, as another Indiana political science graduate and colleague of mine puts it, "a series of multivariate probability distributions" and we may sometimes "find ourselves on one or another tail"—but Ostrom taught us that those distributions were not only complex but also dynamic.

We also learned that we could discover regularities in human institutions significant enough to bother with: For example, concentration of authority and power, particularly without mechanisms for accountability and feedback, would tend to produce predictably unfortunate outcomes. In short, we were introduced to political science by considering its possibilities and constraints in relation to the nature of human organisms, human culture, institutional design, and institutional failure. The full meaning of that, and its application to my future research was not altogether clear to me at the time, but it has provided a foundation for a lifetime of insights, a career-long inspiration to discovery of patterned regularity and its implications in a variety of settings.

Discovering Patterns of Conflict and Conflict Resolution

The influence of this sort of approach has reasserted itself markedly during the last ten years for me in a joint research program in which I have engaged with a Chilean psychologist, Elizabeth Lira, who is well known for her contributions to development of therapies for torture victims. Beginning in 1996, we have studied together the patterns of conflict, civil war, political rupture, and reconciliation in Chile since the early nineteenth century, and we have sought, to lesser degree, to extend those findings to the rest of Latin America.

We asked a question about the 1978 amnesty decree by the Chilean military dictatorship (1973–1990) granting juridical impunity "to all persons who, whether as authors, accomplices, or 'obstructors of justice' (*encubridores*) have commited crimes during the state of siege, from September 11, 1973 and March 10, 1978, so long as they are not currently under indictment or sentenced to prison; likewise to all persons currently sentenced by military tribunals, since September 11, 1973. . . ." Why would a military dictatorship, in the name of political reconciliation, grant amnesty to many of its adversaries (whom it still persecuted)? And why did the military junta feel compelled to provide its own officials, civilian and military, an "auto-amnesty" when there was no likelihood in the near future that anyone could be prosecuted for the crimes, including massive violations of human rights, that they had committed?

From the *Cheyenne Way* to the *Chilean Way* (*La vía chilena*)

The answers to these questions are complicated by a history of civil wars, political conflicts, severe polarization, and then political "reconciliation." They involve the role of Catholic theology and the Church in Chile, persistent twentieth-century ideological contestation, bilateral relations with the United States, and international human rights regimes. Asking these kinds of questions came from the way of thinking about politics and human society to which Vincent Ostrom introduced graduate students in the late 1960s and early 1970s.

One of the ten books we have done together is *Arquitectura política y seguridad interior del Estado 1811–1990* (*Political Architecture and Internal Security of the State, 1811–1990*) (2002a). Though done in Spanish, most any student of Vincent Ostrom would recognize immediately the inspiration for our focus on *political architecture*—the problems and consequences of institutional design. Another is: *Las suaves cenizas del olvido: Vía Chilena de reconciliación política 1814–1932* (*The Soft Ashes of Oblivion: The Chilean Way to Political Reconciliation, 1814–1932*) (2000c). Chileans all think that "the Chilean Way" is an allusion to Salvador Allende's "Chilean Way to Socialism" (1970–1973). But Elizabeth Lira and I know that it refers to the "Chilean Way" in the same sense that Llewellyn and Hoebel (1941) referred to the "Cheyenne Way"—in a relatively little known but essential study melding legal, institutional, and cultural research. (By chance, this was the first book I was assigned in my first graduate seminar with Professor Ostrom in 1968.)

The Cheyenne Way

In their "theory of investigation," the authors of *The Cheyenne Way* insist on the need to discover:

1. the norms and rules that are felt proper for channeling and controlling behavior, that is, the "right ways";
2. practice, that is, "what really happens"; and
3. the "trouble case"—instances of hitch, dispute, grievance, trouble—what was the trouble and what was done about it?

They suggest that the three lines of inquiry are related; nor can any of them be understood without the others (1941, 21). Their theory and methods are more complex than this, but for our purposes, these questions are sufficient. However, for our study of the Chilean military amnesty decree of 1978, we asked the questions in reverse order: First, we found instances of amnesty laws and decrees; then we researched the historical circumstances, that is, the origin, history, and outcome of conflicts that led to "crimes" requiring amnesty or pardons; finally, we analyzed the discursive and normative rationale for the amnesties conceded since independence, reviewing congressional debates, newspapers, literature, memoirs, and other sources.

From this long-term study we discovered (1) a pattern of *policies for reconciliation* after civil war and political conflict, (2) a pattern of *political reconfiguration after each major conflict* that had characterized the country since the early nineteenth century, and (3) terms of discourse and rationale for action with remarkable continuity regarding the desirability or undesirability of amnesties, pardons, accountability, impunity, justice, punishment, and "forgetting" as political strategies.

At the core of this "Chilean Way" was an unresolved tension between accountability and impunity, between justice (punishment) and political stability, between "truth" (both in the sense of criminal investigation and in the sense of the historical record) and "forgetting" (both in terms of juridical impunity and in terms of social and historical accountability)—even in the writing of official textbooks.

When in the past, before the 1978 amnesty decree, had amnesties been used in Chile? Surprisingly, no one had asked that question systematically, and even more surprisingly it took us almost two years to research the answer fully, and discover the "Chilean Way"—and variations on it that have contributed to political transition from dictatorship to more democratic government in Chile and around much of Latin America in the last ten years.

Table 9.1. Modalities of political reconciliation

Policies

(1) commutation of prison sentences, pardons, and amnesties (*conmutaciones de penas, indultos, amnistías*) for "political crimes" and for crimes committed by military, police, and government officials during the period leading up to, during, and to the "end" of the political trauma

(2) return of political exiles, with or without restitution of government posts, with or without pensions or other forms of reparation

(3) concession by general law or special laws (*leyes de gracia*) of pensions, subventions, or one-time payments to military and police personnel, and family members, on both sides of the conflict

(4) special laws for named individuals passed with the explicit purpose of reparation for injuries during the conflict

(5) miscellaneous symbolic measures (monuments, public acknowledgments, inviting family members to participate in government or public ceremonies, social invitations to high-visibility events)

Political reconfiguration

(6) creation of new political coalitions in which some of the "losers" in the conflict are included

(7) redefinition of key actors (political parties, church leaders, military elites, entrepreneurs (later, workers' organizations)) in the conflict of doctrinal positions and programs, to permit governability

(8) reincorporation of "losers" into cabinet posts, foreign service, military, congress, bureaucracy, university, teaching positions in secondary and primary schools

(9) constitutional, electoral, and legal reforms to ratify and formalize the reestablished "union of the Chilean family"[a]

---

[a] Thus, new constitutions in 1828, 1833, 1825, and 1980; key electoral and legal reforms after political conflicts in 1837, 1851, 1859, 1860–1861, and the early 1870s; and efforts to address the social question with decrees (1924) and a new labor code (1931) to overcome the political rupture that disrupted constitutional continuity (1924–1932).

Table 9.1 summarizes the general patterns we found over almost two centuries. These are simply examples of "patterned regularities" discovered in the course of answering our questions about the 1978 amnesty decree.

La vía chilena (The Chilean Way)

In the nineteenth century, there developed a recognizable "Chilean way" of "political reconciliation" as a response to major political conflicts and internal wars. Gradually evolving from the time of independence into the 1920s, this *vía chilena* included discursive, institutional, and policy responses to civil war and political violence in order to achieve political reconciliation. From 1924 to 1932, this *vía chilena* was called into question, but reaffirmed. From the 1930s to the 1970s, the modalities of political reconciliation that subordinated concerns for justice to "looking forward rather than backward" became routinized aspects of everyday politics. From 1932, these modalities (see table 9.1) postponed another major breakdown of the political system until 1973. Indeed, in the view of those who carried out the military coup in 1973, they had responded to "a long-standing siege" of *la patria* by international Marxism, a struggle between antagonistic forces with irreconcilable discourses and social utopias.

By 1932, the elements of the *vía chilena de reconciliación política* had become so routinized and ritualized that they formed core elements of Chilean politics. For better, *and* for worse, they buffered the country against political rupture from 1932 to1973, making Chile the only Latin American country during that period to experience no illegal turnover in government and no unconstitutional presidential succession. According to this version of Chilean history, the final, but inevitable, battle had been postponed since the early 1930s until 1973 (Heinecke Scott 1992).[1]

A less dramatic interpretation would locate the political rupture of 1973 on the list of internal conflicts and civil wars in Chile from the early 1820s, and especially the civil wars of 1829–1830, 1851, 1859, 1891, and the severe political crisis (including several successful military coups) of 1924–1932. Such an interpretation would not label what occurred from 1973 to 1989 as the "final battle." It would also anticipate future such crises unless the cycle of political rupture and political reconciliation that has characterized Chilean politics since 1818 is broken.

Debates in Chile over political reconciliation in the 1980s and 1990s unconsciously echoed the newspapers, congressional debates, political parties, church leaders, and military officers of the nineteenth and early twentieth centuries. The modes (and limits) of political reconciliation of the 1980s and 1990s also mirror, in important ways, the *vía chilena de reconciliación política* constructed in the nineteenth century.

Political Violence, Civil War, and Reconciliation

An essential frame for viewing nineteenth-century Chilean politics is the sequence of political ruptures and reconciliations that occurred in establishing and modifying the political regime institutionalized in the 1833 Constitution: 1823; 1826–1831; 1850–1851; 1857–1861; 1890–1891. Each of these political ruptures involved civil war, not only in the sense of internal wars, but in the sense of divisions within families, social groups, the Church, and military institutions. These conflicts were literally fratricidal—biologically and socially (as occurred again in 1973). Each, whatever the underlying class and even racial implications, involved conflicts over constitutional norms, election laws, presidential-legislative relations, judicial autonomy, cabinet selection, and presidential succession. Though embedded in particular socioeconomic circumstances (the last two in deep economic recessions and labor disputes in northern mining centers), regionalism, resentment against the Santiago elite, and disputes within and among government and opposition factions, each major political rupture was justified by reference to supposed violations of the constitution and electoral irregularities (whether in registering voters, the actual voting, government intervention and manipulation of the elections, or corruption and violence during the electoral process). In each case, the opposition claimed that the president (or the government and congress) had acted illegally, suppressed the political opposition and media, and "intervened" in elections to assure victory for government-supported candidates—or that the government intended to do all these things in upcoming elections in order to gain/maintain control of the congress. In the last three instances, the threat that such electoral intervention would occur in upcoming congressional and presidential elections was an important precipitant of revolt. Always, there were charges of "dictatorship" and "tyranny." And whichever side emerged victorious in these political ruptures, the winning side claimed that victory meant *restoration of constitutional rule*—even if it was followed by significant constitutional and political reforms. Chileans spilled blood in the name of legitimacy and constitutionalism, whatever other motives underlay the conflicts.[2]

Finally, all contenders for control of the state (and its growing resources and patronage opportunities) claimed that their actions were taken to "save the patria" (*salvar la patria*) from the "crimes" and "abuses" of their adversaries. Soldiers, militia, and civilians died on all sides for *la patria*. No one fought against *la patria*. But the contending factions, parties, and interests did have different visions of, and dreams for, *la patria*. Antagonistic dreams for *la patria* justified for those in power various modes of political repression: preventive detention of political opponents, extrajudicial executions (assassination), abuse of prisoners, torture, internal "exile" (*relegación*), political exile, confiscation of property, and sundry other forms of political persecution. For those opposing the incumbent government, claims of tyranny and despotism, unlawful acts, and other political abuses justified street demonstrations, attacks on government property, efforts to subvert military and police forces, urban insurrection and, ultimately, internal war in efforts to oust the government. These conflicts left thousands of dead, thousands more injured, extensive damage and loss of property, families divided, and bitter social polarization. After each conflict there were calls for *reconciliation*.

How did Chilean political leaders reconstruct the political system and provide for governability after 1826–1830, 1836–1841, 1850–1851, 1856–1859, and 1890–1891? How did they "treat" political trauma? How did these experiences carry over to the two major twentieth-century political ruptures—1924–1932 and 1973–1989—and to intervening violent confrontations (e.g., the massacres at Ranquil, 1934, and the Caja de Seguro Obrero, 1938)?[3]

Crafting the *vía chilena de reconciliación política*: Impunity, Memory, and Governability

A schematic historical reconstruction of these events reveals that recurrent debates over how to construct and reconstruct a supposed "unified Chilean family," that is, a shared identity within a legitimate Chilean nation-state and political system, occurred after each major nineteenth-century conflict and again after the 1924–1932 political rupture that framed Chilean politics until 1970–1973. These debates, and the seemingly consistent Chilean approach to political reconciliation from the 1820s until World War I, shed light on the dilemmas facing Chile in the 1990s as a result of the most recent and most prolonged internal "war" in Chile's history: 1973–1990.[4]

Underlying all these historical efforts at political reconciliation after political cataclysm and political trauma was the concern by Chilean political elites with formal restoration of a shared legitimacy and with the practical matter of governability (usually translated in the nineteenth century as *paz social* and *orden*). Social construction of, and appeals to, nationalism—encapsulated in the sacred invocation of *la patria* and *la familia chilena*—were the symbolic foundations for iterated national "reconciliations." Both consciously and by seemingly autonomous application of culturally devised and inherited habits, they gradually developed a recognizable approach to political reconciliation, based partly on (1) premises of shared Ibero-Catholic culture and values, with little tolerance for religious or cultural pluralism; (2) adaptations of Spanish colonial traditions, especially the use of (a) amnesties, pardons, and reparations; (b) concession of pensions, jobs, and other economic opportunities; (c) legalistic formalities (*resquicios legales*) including the often-cited principle "I obey but cannot comply" (*se acata pero no se cumple*); and (3) pragmatism and elite political repacting.[5] The premises of this model are inherently incompatible when applied simultaneously, but do not come into conflict directly when applied alternately and unevenly. The typical modalities of the *via chilena* are arrayed in table 9.1.

In every case from 1818 to the early twentieth century, political reconciliation in Chile also included efforts to suppress and reconstruct social memory to facilitate impunity (from the perspective of victims) and political absolution (from the perspective of perpetrators) for "political crimes" committed during the political cataclysm. This "social memory"/ "official story" aspect of political reconciliation was long term, expressed in rewriting of government-approved history texts, in public ceremonies, and in numerous subtle acts of symbolic "reconciliation."[6] Reparation, as part of political reconciliation, routinely included reincorporation of "losers" into presidential cabinets, the legislature, and judiciary, and of ousted functionaries (*exonerados*) to positions within the military, universities, public schools, and government bureaucracies. By the 1860s and 1870s, for example, the most "revolutionary" liberals, even the leaders of the 1851 and 1859 civil wars, occupied ministerial positions, made Chilean foreign policy, controlled university and secondary school faculties, and exercised leadership in congress. Chilean presidents, presidential candidates, congressmen, and policy-makers from the 1860s to the 1880s had been persecuted by the governments of the 1840s and 1850s, jailed, exiled, and amnestied. Lesser political dissidents, former army personnel, and bureaucrats (and their families) received pensions or other benefits as a result of political reparation. This process was gradual and careful regarding inclusion and exclusion of beneficiaries, and demonstrated both the skilled pragmatism and the petty vengefulness of Chile's political elite. Stitch by stitch, the political fabric's torn parts were patched and rewoven. As with any repair job, unseen weaknesses and perceptible (for the careful observers) flaws remained, but the fabric was again usable and presentable in public.

Chilean political elites in the nineteenth century thus crafted an implicit set of procedures for political reconciliation after political cataclysm. There was never a formal political accord on the meaning of reconciliation or the political-psychological requirements for its achievement. But such an accord accreted as part of elite political culture. These implicit procedures were not uncontested *in their particulars*, nor applied uniformly, but the essential elements of the *vía Chilena* for political reconciliation are apparent in the late 1820s and recur after 1836–1841, 1851/1859, and 1891–1896.[7]

In every case, even the general amnesty proclaimed by President Joaquín Pérez in 1861 to cover all "political crimes" from 1851 to 1861, reconciliation policies were piecemeal, with debates over coverage (who would be included and excluded from the amnesties, pensions, etc.).[8] Incremental negotiation of "reconciliation policies" in private meetings and in the congress precluded immediate omnibus "laws of reconciliation." For example, the political trauma of the 1823–1830 civil wars, the repression of the liberals after the Battle of Lircay (1830) and adoption of the 1833 constitution, and the political conflicts of the 1830s elicited fragmented and partial reconciliatory legislation into the 1860s. Only in 1842 could the congress agree on restoration of honors and reparation for the leaders of the Southern cone independence movements, Bernardo O'Higgins and José de San Martín! In 1844, congress agreed to erect a statue to O'Higgins, to place his portrait in the *Sala de Gobierno*, and send a delegation representing each house of the legislature and the armed forces on a warship to Peru to bring his ashes back for interment in Santiago.[9] It was almost three decades after independence before opposing factions from the independence era could agree that the "Chilean George Washington" was a shared symbol for *la familia chilena* above, and despite the factionalism, family feuds, bloodshed, exiles, and bitter memories from 1814 to 1823.

With contextual variations, similar reconciliation policies and processes followed the ruptures of 1828–1830, 1836–1841, and the civil wars in 1851 and 1859.[10] The spirit of this evolving *vía chilena de reconciliación* is well captured in Francisco Encina's description of the general amnesty promulgated by President José Joaquín Pérez, October 18, 1861, to overcome the hatreds and wounds of the 1859 civil war and associated political repression:

> President Pérez had assumed the Presidency in the name of concord between the political bands, separated by violent hatred that came from long ago and had culminated in the repressive measures that made the revolution of 1859 inevitable. The first measure of his political program was *an ample amnesty that, if possible would erase even the memory of these past convulsions.* (Encina 1950, 199; emphasis added)

Chile's political class did not believe that such "forgetting" (*olvido*) was literally possible, but its members insisted, periodically, on the necessity for legal, political, and symbolic "starting over." This was not reconciliation of persons at an emotional or psychological level, nor of parties and movements at an ideological or programmatic level. Such reconciliation was neither possible nor expected. Political reconciliation meant that certain issues were not discussed, or if discussed, that policies on "sensitive" matters did not exceed certain limits that endangered the newly reconstructed *concordia*. Such reconciliation required moderation, prudence, and common sense (*cordura*). It required pretense and public masks. It meant *fictive harmony* and pragmatic toleration of differences, an end to violent conflict, reaccommodation to the "rule of law" (whatever that law was at the moment), and governability. Above all else, political reconciliation was the art of the possible, political pragmatism at its best—and worst. For reconciliation to translate into governability, it required effective leadership by the president and key cabinet members; it also required thick skins, long-term political perspectives, and a sense of humor.

1861 and 1990: "Political Transition" and Official Memory

Any understanding of the dilemmas, processes, and methods of political reconciliation in Chile after 1990 must begin with reconstruction and iteration of social memory (and memory loss) regarding other analogous moments in Chile's past—as we have outlined above. Chileans in the 1980s and 1990s virtually automatically (if only partially consciously) drew upon this *vía chilena* to reinvent a possible political reconciliation in the 1990s.[11]

Nineteenth-century Chilean political elites recognized how difficult it was to "erase the memory" (*borrarse hasta el recuerdo*) of political violence, hatred, and abuses. They invented and adapted methods for *political* reconciliation that were less exacting than those for application of personal, moral, religious, and strict legal (criminal law) principles. After independence in 1818, there were rarely demands for confession, recantation, or penitence, only for abiding by the "rules of the game" imposed-negotiated by the victors.[12] Those benefited by amnesties and pardons were free to engage in legal political activities and to struggle for political reform. They could also seek to (re)define social memory. The "real truth" (the *verdadera verdad*) could be disputed, but only to the extent that such activities did not threaten governability, the victors' version of the political system (the 1833 Constitution, and the parliamentary spin on the 1833 Constitution that evolved by the 1870s and was reaffirmed after 1891), or reprisals against the victors.

Clarifying this historically crafted *vía chilena* for overcoming political trauma and political cataclysm makes evident that the demands made by many groups after 1989 for "truth," prosecution of "victimizers" (heroes for some), and "social justice" far exceed the pragmatism of the historical pattern. In contrast, reincorporation of the "losers" into the political system, renewed efforts at political reform, and diverse forms of reparation for victims (subversives or terrorists, for some) are consistent with the historical emphasis on relegitimating political order and assuring governability. Since the 1820s, political "subversives," political exiles, political prisoners, and anti-regime revolutionary leaders routinely returned to public life and public office in Chile during periods of political reconciliation. Statues to honor their contributions to *la patria* adorn Santiago and provincial capitals.

Resistance to Reconciliation and Impunity: Creating and Contesting the "Official Story"

Resistance to reconciliation has also been a recurrent aspect of Chilean history, both by victors and vanquished. Debates over whom to benefit with pensions, *leyes de gracia*, and reincorporation into the public administration after 1990 are also consistent with previous experience. Both victors and "losers" in incidents of internal war and political violence harbor resentments and hatreds that are expressed in lingering legislative and administrative subtleties. In these respects, the events after 1990 have followed the *vía chilena de reconciliación* fairly closely (but with important departures, see below), to the regret of many victims and opponents of the military regime, *but also to the regret of many of the regime's supporters*. This is particularly evident in the determined effort of some Chileans to create an official history to document the crimes of the dictatorship (with the added twist of recourse to international norms for prosecution of ex-government officials as well as military and police officers). Such an "official history" serves as legitimation for private and collective social memories that contest the view of the military and their civilian allies: that the policies of the military regime, including any human rights abuses, were necessary to "save the patria" and that the legacy is a brilliant *misión cumplida*.[13]

Moreover, the extent to which some military and police in the military regime have been tried and punished for human rights violations goes far beyond (though not enough to satisfy human rights and victims' organizations) the traditional pattern. After seventeen years since transition from military to elected civilian government, some important elements of the Chilean *vía de reconciliación política* have been pushed beyond their previous limits. Both the National Truth and Reconciliation Commission (1990–1991) and the National Commission on Political Imprisonment and Torture (2003–2005), which are discussed below, somewhat extended the meaning of political reconciliation beyond the historical pattern—notwithstanding recurrent efforts to negotiate a "*punto final*" (final settlement) from 1990 to 1991 until 2001 and proposals in September 2005 for pardons for military and police who had violated human rights during the dictatorship.[14]

Along with its pragmatism and the concession of juridical impunity, the Chilean *vía de reconciliación política* also exhibits a persistent and parallel tendency to resist social and historical impunity. In addition to the array of private and opposition media efforts to reveal the not-so-secret methods of repression, government investigations, administrative hearings, impeachment proceedings, and trials seek to establish an "official truth" to counteract the seeming impunity of the powerful. This undercurrent in Chilean politics is pervasive; it resurfaces periodically, a legacy from colonial times, the first years of independence, and the struggles of the liberals against the Portalian regime in the nineteenth century.

One important mode for establishing public accountability has been the constitutional procedures of *acusación constitucional* against incumbents and ex-government officials, including ex-presidents. The debates occasioned by the *acusación constitucional* procedure are frequently fierce, full of savage imagery, graphic denunciation, and moral discourse. The attacks on incumbent officials and even on ex-presidents (denounced as brutal dictators, responsible for crimes against the constitution and humanity) are merciless. Defenders of the incumbent government, or of the previous regime, also offer impassioned arguments and historical justifications for the actions that critics now deem unconstitutional and criminal.

Above all else, "truth seeking" and efforts to construct an official historical story are *political and politicized*. They reflect the current "correlation of forces" of diverse social and political interests, but also the need to reconfigure the political map—and to provide relative social peace after periods of extreme violence and polarization. Ad hoc commissions and constitutional procedures (like the *acusación constitucional* in Chile) are inherently constrained by temporary political considerations at the same time that they claim to work according to universal religious, moral, and legal principles. They attempt to reconcile the immediate (and sometimes not so immediate) past with hopes for a better future—while enmeshed in the constraints and tensions of the present.

In reading the debates over most of these *acusaciones*, it becomes clear that not only the fate of individuals is at stake but the nature of official memory as filtered by the political and ideological antagonisms of the moment.

Both history and the future are debated, what "really happened" and what ought to be. Each of the *acusación constitucional* proceedings offers dramatic examples of resistance to impunity and demands for accountability—a plea for an alternative future based on revelation of the "truth" about the present or the past. Most also offer vigorous defenses of repression and persecution when necessary to "save" *la patria*.[15]

The Ibáñez Government (1927–1931) and the "Commission to Investigate the Acts of the Dictatorship" (August–December 1931)

Carlos Ibáñez governed Chile as president from 1927 to 1931 after ousting an interim president and orchestrating elections in which he won more than 90 percent of the vote. In 1930, Ibáñez, in collaboration with representatives of most of the political parties, organized a congressional "election" in which there was only one candidate in each electoral district—allowing, by Chilean law at the time, all these congressmen and senators to be "elected" without elections.[16] For all practical purposes, Ibáñez governed as dictator; political opponents were arrested, harshly interrogated and tortured, sent into exile, and sometimes killed. The government censored the press, arrested labor and community leaders who dissented in public, deported political opponents, and sent many persons into internal exile (*relegación*), including those sent to prison camps on Isla Más Afuera, Isla de Pascua, Chiloé, and further south.[17] A secret police force infiltrated community and labor meetings, followed and monitored the activities of prominent politicians and minor dissidents, and transcribed telephone conversations on tapped phone lines. In short, Ibáñez established a police state, though not as thoroughgoing or as systematically repressive as would occur in Spain and Italy—models for some of his supporters.

After four years in office, the Ibáñez government fell victim to the great depression and to strikes by student and professional organizations that brought the capital to a standstill. Even governing with congressionally granted dictatorial authority (*facultades extraordinarias*) since January of 1931, he could not pacify the opposition without deploying the army—which he refused to do. He left for exile in Buenos Aires, delegating the executive authority to the president of the Senate.[18]

With the fall of Ibáñez and the return of hundreds of exiles, demands surfaced for a complete investigation into the operations of the dictatorship. Opponents called for "the truth," and punishment "for the crimes of the dictatorship" (see Loveman and Lira 2000a).

A week after Ibáñez left Santiago for Buenos Aires, the minister of interior and future (late 1931 to June 4, 1932) president, Juan E. Montero, decreed creation of a commission to investigate the operations of the previous government.[19] On its own, the commission changed its name from "Comisión para Investigar la Gestión Gubernativa" (Commission to Investigate Government Activities) to "Comisión Investigadora de los Actos de la Dictadura" (Commission to Investigate the Acts of the Dictatorship).[20] The 1931 commission compiled twenty-one volumes of documents, including police and military records, transcribed telephone tapping, detailed reports on surveillance of opponents, censorship of newspapers, and testimonies of the victims of illegal detention, arrest, torture, and exile. It also investigated cases of alleged "'disappearances" (*fondeos*) and deaths (mostly in public political protests against the government) and documented corruption in the public administration. At the same time, it delivered information it considered relevant to congress for *acusación* proceedings against Ibáñez, both as president and as minister of interior, and against various of his cabinet ministers.

At first, the 1931 Commission received widespread and favorable press coverage. Then, the treatment became less favorable in some of the partisan press as some of the commissioners called into question the legitimacy of the congress itself (constituted without elections in 1930) and became a thorn in the side of President Montero.

The commission explicitly defined its work as an effort to discover the truth, send criminal cases to the courts, send information that would warrant *acusaciones constitucionales* against Ibáñez and his ministers to the congress, and provide evidence to the courts that would allow punishment of officials guilty of crimes during the dictatorship. It resisted "forgetting the past" and impunity. However, political conditions made the commission's activities increasingly inconvenient. Moreover, in 1931 and 1932, congress approved numerous amnesties in efforts to pacify the country and restore governability.[21]

In November 1931, members of the commission resigned in protest at the Senate's failure to approve the *acusaciones* against some of the ex-ministers of the Ibáñez government. The government initially refused to accept the resignations. At the end of December, the commission insisted on resigning; the government thanked its members for their efforts and decreed its dissolution.

The commission did not finish its work nor issue a final report. Twenty-one volumes of material in a Santiago archive document its essentially unsuccessful efforts to impede impunity. Most Chileans do not know the commission ever existed. Meanwhile, Ibáñez had written to the people to defend his patriotic leadership in difficult times. He rejected the campaigns of slander and falsehoods against him, denounced the *acusación constitucional* brought against him, and reminded the public that members of congress who had gladly collaborated with his government, giving him "extraordinary authority" to confront the economic crisis, now rose in congress to denounce him. He had done everything "for *la patria.*"[22] Ibáñez eventually returned to Chile, the beneficiary of several of the amnesties decreed by the interim governments. He became an inveterate plotter and participant in failed coups. In 1952, Chileans, tired of "politics," elected Carlos Ibáñez as president by a wide margin. He came to office with a broom as a symbol: he promised to sweep clean the corruption of the political parties and the politicians.[23]

La Vía Chilena Continues

From 1932 to 1969, the Chilean modalities for political reconciliation became integral ingredients of everyday politics. To avoid political breakdown, to restore governability in moments of crisis, pardons, amnesties, and other methods of political pacification conceded juridical impunity to government officials, military and police personnel, party and labor leaders, and miscreants of all sorts. Amnesties and self-amnesties became routine, ever more frequent, ever more institutionalized for political matters, for failed coups, for bureaucratic malfeasance, for violations of the electoral law, for failure to comply with the obligatory military service law, and for common crimes. The State Internal Security laws and labor laws made participation in "illegal strikes" serious crimes—and a common rationale for pardons and amnesties to resolve immediate political conflicts. All governments from 1932 to 1973 used pardons and amnesties in this fashion; eventual impunity, or relative impunity (pardons, reduced prison sentences, and expunging criminal records), became routine. This did not mean that no one went to prison, that no one went to exile, or that no one suffered. But for "political crimes," including illegal strikes and electoral violence, those who survived the initial repression, or avoided being the unlucky chance victims of the street clashes, were likely eventually to gain juridical impunity.[24]

As in the past, impunity reigned but was also resisted, both for moral and pragmatic reasons, as evidenced in the congressional debates and in the press (see Loveman and Lira 2000b). In the 1950s, there was almost no respite from amnesty debates in the legislature. Those debates, in which Salvador Allende, Raúl Rettig, Eduardo Frei, and many of the leaders in the 1960s and 1970s participated, were a forum for the antagonistic discourses that framed Chilean politics of the era.

The 1973 Coup

In 1973, Chile experienced its most brutal political rupture in the twentieth century. The amnesties, pardons, and other institutional constraints could no longer postpone the cataclysmic confrontation announced repeatedly from 1926 to 1970.

But this was the first political crisis in Chile seen on television globally via satellite. It occurred in a historical era framed by the sequelae of World War II, the Holocaust, the Universal Declaration of Human Rights, the Cold War (which was never *cold* in the Third World) and the Cuban Revolution. And of course there was no debate over whether wars had actually occurred in 1828–1830, 1850–1851, 1858–1859, and 1891, nor whether there had been an authoritarian regime in power from 1927 to 1931.

For the 1973–1990 period, while the rhetoric of war was adopted by all the contending factions, only the military, their close civilian supporters, and small factions of the revolutionary left claim that a "real war" existed in Chile. No matter. Whether the war was "real" or a juridical fiction, the dead had still died; the vanquished suffered in prison and in exile. The victors created a new political regime and formalized it with a new constitution (1980). They characterized their deeds as a glorious *misión cumplida*, a salvation of *la patria*. They echoed Diego Portales, Joaquín Prieto, Manuel Montt, the victors in 1891, and Carlos Ibáñez, self-proclaimed savior of *la patria* in 1931. The vanquished, as in the past, resisted this effort with an alternative history, in art, the theater, literature, the press, congressional debates, and in the politics and policies of reconciliation. And with the end of the military dictatorship, like the *pipiolos* (the liberal opposition from the 1830s to the 1860s) and the ex-Balmacedistas, the defeated supporters of the Allende government coalition sought government jobs, restitution of pension benefits, reparations, and an opportunity to again compete for political power. They also sought to establish "the truth" about the crimes committed, the abuses perpetrated, and to impede impunity for those who had governed the country from 1973 to 1990.

The Rettig Commission, 1990–1991

After almost seventeen years of dictatorship and massive, systematic violation of human rights, Chile returned to elected civilian government in 1990. President Patricio Aylwin named a commission, headed by longtime Radical Party politician Raúl Rettig. The decree creating the commission limited the scope of its investigation to only the most serious crimes, such as disappearances of people who had been arrested, executions, torture leading to death when committed by agents of the government or people in its service, and those kidnappings and attempts on peoples' lives committed by private citizens for political purposes.

According to lawyer, human rights activist, and commission member José Zalaquett, the Rettig Commission[25] faced the following dilemma: "How can a country overcome a legacy of dictatorial rule and massive human rights violations if the new government is subject to significant institutional and political constraints? How, in those circumstances, can the equally necessary but often conflicting objectives of justice and social peace be harmonized? What are the moral tenets which should guide the politician's actions in such ambiguous situations?"[26] Zalaquett also pointed to the political circumstances in Chile and Latin America more generally as transitions occurred from military to civilian rule: "The sobering lesson they taught was that the political stakes involved in settling accounts with the past are extraordinarily high, that a fully satisfactory outcome can hardly be expected, and that the social tensions brought about by the legacy of human rights violations linger on for a long time."[27]

What Zalaquett and other members of the commission did not consider was that Chile had faced this dilemma in the past, if admittedly not in the context of such a long-lasting, brutal dictatorship nor with such a massive and systematic record of human rights violations. They did not review previous "truth commissions" nor the historical pattern of amnesties and pardons. They defined their main mission as establishing the "truth" regarding the particular human rights violations in question, almost in the sense of a criminal investigation, and then suggesting possible forms of reparation. Zalaquett himself gradually came to favor what he called "truth and justice with mercy" (essentially pardons, applying the statute of limitations where appropriate, and accepting the application of the military's 1978 amnesty decree for most cases).[28]

General Pinochet referred to the commission as a "sewer" and declared that there was nothing to ask pardon for, that the armed forces had saved the country from terrorism and international communism and should be proud of the mission they had successfully carried out. Leaders of all the armed forces and national police (*Carabineros*) denounced the commission report as did the Supreme Court—which the commission had criticized for its laxity in defending constitutional rights and liberties—during the dictatorship. On the other side of the political spectrum, the Communist Party newspaper, *El Siglo*, headlined: "Crimes without Punishment?" while the Agrupación de Familiares de Detenidos-Desaparecidos (Association of Family Members of the Detained and Disappeared") lamented that the commission had not considered the cases of thousands of torture victims and exiles (see Loveman 2001, 315–17).

Overall, the Rettig Commission achieved limited but important success in investigating some of the human rights violations, documenting them, and providing a foundation for what would become a rather extensive politics of reparation over the next seventeen years.[29] In some ways, it conformed to the traditional Chilean pattern: it could not fully reveal its findings; it could not guarantee punishment of the civilians and military personnel who had violated human rights and the Chilean constitution; it could not overcome the apparent guarantee of impunity contained in the amnesty decreed by the military government in 1978. It seemed, at the time, that like the Senate *acusación constitucional* in 1891 and the 1931 Commission that had investigated the activities of the Ibáñez dictatorship, the Rettig Commission would be a bridge from public outrage to political reconciliation based on the 1978 amnesty and political reconfiguration. And, as in 1931, the constitution imposed after a military coup (1925, then 1980) would remain in place to frame national politics.

In the short term, the Rettig Commission report was buried in semi-oblivion when assassins killed Senator Jaime Guzmán, a principal author of the 1980 constitution and founder of the UDI party, the principal civilian prop of the dictatorship. The report passed from front-page news as the headlines focused on the war on terrorism and violent crime. Periodically, the human rights issues resurfaced, but everyday politics and the Pinochet supporters' resistance to constitutional reform took priority for the *Concertación* leadership that still feared the possibility of a military coup that might overturn the transition to civilian government.[30]

Acusación Constitucional 1998

Notwithstanding the painfully slow pace of implementation of the *Concertación* political and constitutional reforms, an unrelenting struggle to impede impunity for human rights violations and continuous court challenges to the validity of the 1978 amnesty decree proceeded. In March 1998, Pinochet stepped down as army commander and assumed his senatorial seat as a lifetime senator (*vitalicio*) as stipulated in the 1980 constitution. For human rights activists, victims, family members, and the political left, Pinochet's investiture in the Senate was an intolerable reminder of his (and the military government's) impunity for crimes against humanity. In response, a group of

Concertación legislators presented an *acusación constitucional* against Pinochet for "gravely compromising the honor and security of the nation"—one of the reasons specified in the constitution as a cause for *acusación*.

In accord with the constitution, if the Chamber of Deputies approved the *acusación* and the Senate ratified it, Pinochet would lose his congressional immunity (*fuero*), exposing him to civil and criminal prosecution in numerous pending cases. Fearful that such an outcome would destabilize the political system, the Eduardo Frei Ruiz-Tagle government (1994–2000) opposed the approval of the *acusación*, despite its sponsorship by parties of the coalition. In the end, the Chamber of Deputies rejected the charges. Rejection of the *acusación* had its precedent in the *acusación* against ex-president Manuel Montt in 1868.

More shocking events would dent the impunity of Augusto Pinochet Ugarte. He was detained and arrested in London, October 16, 1998, on a warrant from a Spanish judge for extradition to Spain. His subsequent trial by the British legal system made clear that the historical battle between justice and impunity, truth versus forgetting the past in the name of governability had been somewhat restructured: Enter international human rights law, the claim to universal jurisdiction, and the rejection of statutes of limitations in the case of crimes against humanity. The Pinochet case would become emblematic for international human rights law and also be a turning point in the routine application of the *vía chilena de reconciliación política*.[31] After Pinochet's return to Chile, he would be constantly barraged with criminal cases and have his immunity taken away, but he was never tried.

The Valech Commission (*Comisión Nacional sobre Prisión Política y Tortura*)

Despite the gradual erosion of Pinochet's public standing and place in history, civilian rule continued within the constraints of the 1980 constitution. No major constitutional reforms occurred from 1990 to 2001. Elections occurred as scheduled and the Concertación coalition controlled the government. The political right maintained its veto power in the Senate and resisted changes in the electoral law that might erode this veto.

When Ricardo Lagos assumed office as the first socialist president since Salvador Allende (1970–1973), he promoted a quiet judicialization of the human rights issue. Lagos created a special group (the Mesa de Diálogo) to incorporate the armed forces directly into the debates on human rights issues. After receiving the report from the Mesa, President Lagos urged Chileans to allow justice to take its course.³² Special judges investigated the cases; a slow, grinding, and, for the military and the political right, *annoying* process maintained alive the possibility that some cases would be prosecuted and that the 1978 amnesty might not be applied. No "*punto final*" could be negotiated, though halfhearted proposals of one sort or another surfaced from time to time, as they had between 1990 and 2001.

In November 2003, President Lagos established a commission headed by Monseñor Sergio Valech to find appropriate means to include torture victims as beneficiaries of reparation policies. Torture victims, except those killed, had been excluded from the Rettig Commission charge and recommendations, though some had received health care, including mental health services, under a program called PRAIS.³³ The commission took testimony from more than 36,000 persons who claimed that they, or family members who had died, had been tortured during the military government. The commission reported that they could verify more than 28,000 of these claims and acknowledged that they had no way to know how many more torture victims there might be. Nevertheless, the repeated assertions by military officers and the dictatorship's civilian allies that torture had been the result of "individual excesses" rather than a systematic policy of state terrorism were discarded.

Both the Rettig Commission and, now, the Valech Commission³⁴ had contributed to the increasingly negative image of the Pinochet regime among Chile's new generation. Aided by international human rights organizations, diffusion of information on the Internet, and an increasingly globalized human rights movement, the *vía chilena de reconciliación política* had been transformed but not altogether overcome. Simultaneously, the battle in Chile of "truth," "justice," and reparations against oblivion (*olvido*) and impunity had become emblematic of the global struggle between the norms of universal human rights and the policies of sovereign governments to fight a war against subversion and "terrorism"—as each government defined these evils. The Valech Commission contributed to both the Chilean and international struggle to gain support for international law in the battle against torture. But it also left questions unanswered and formed part of the ambiguous *vía chilena*—resistance to impunity and its reaffirmation; quest for "all the truth" and its partial negation.

Reconciliation without Conciliation?

The Chilean *vía de reconciliación* had (has) its advantages and its costs—some still to pay in the future. The modalities of the nineteenth century have been adapted, largely unconsciously, by personalities, factions, political parties, the Church, and the armed forces to the post-1990 context. But the *familia chilena* is more diverse, more inclusive, more informed, and more demanding than at anytime in the past. The intra-elite pacts that made "reconciliation" possible before 1925, and political accommodation feasible before 1964, face the challenge of international scrutiny, national media, and a tenacious minority that rejects reconciliation without "truth" and justice, if not repentance.

In the short term (1990–2000), the legacy of fear, the desire for social peace, and a growing economy precluded an immediate crisis. But the veil of oblivion, the deliberate repression of social memory, the presumption of impunity, and the inattention to the underlying social and political issues that provoked political rupture, had *periodically induced political breakdown* from 1818 until 1973. When the temporary coalitions that made possible "transition" weakened, when the initial policies of reconciliation were exhausted, the underlying conflicts remained, or were worsened by the trauma of the past rupture. Routinization of impunity and pacification as a political style, combined with some unique institutional aspects of the constitutional and party systems, impeded breakdown from 1932 to 1970 (see Loveman 1988). This postponement of "treatment" also made the eventual trauma more severe. Thus the political conflict of 1970–1990 was fiercer and longer lasting than any conflict in Chilean history.

After 1990, many Chileans and their friends celebrated the gradual "consolidation" of a more democratic political system. Yet many legacies of the military-imposed regime remained in place, notwithstanding important reforms that modified the 1980 constitution, the penal code, and the highly repressive national security and antiterrorism legislation. Likewise, to great extent, the *vía chilena de reconciliación política* also perdures. Impunity has not been complete, but it has been the rule. Partial truth about human rights violations has been achieved and the results of the Rettig Commission and the Valech Commission widely publicized. Still, the limitations on naming the guilty, releasing the testimony given to the Valech Commission, and prosecution of torturers are in place. The historical tensions between pragmatic and legal oblivion achieved with pardons and amnesties and justice persist. So, too, do the tensions between political reconciliation based on the need for "governability" and social peace and a policy of principled implementation of domestic and international law regarding human rights.

As the country approached presidential and legislative elections in December 2005, President Ricardo Lagos reminded Chileans of the need for reconciliation, and that the quest for justice in cases of human rights violations during the dictatorship could not go on forever. Resistance to this message came forth immediately from the human rights organizations, some of the political parties, and associations (*agrupaciones*) of victims and family members.[35]

Of course, long-term insistence on *ni perdón ni olvido* would perpetuate social and political hatred across generations. On the other hand, replication of the same old *vía chilena* would mean impunity even for crimes against humanity. Since 1990, Chileans have been caught in this bind, seeking once again to reconcile governability and "social peace" with a historical, social, and legal accounting for the conflicts and crimes of the past.[36]

Epilogue

Chileans went to the polls to elect a new president on December 11, 2005. The governing Concertación coalition presented Michelle Bachelet, a member of the Socialist party, as its candidate. Bachelet was the daughter of an air force general who had opposed the coup in 1973. The military junta ordered his arrest; he died in prison after being brutally tortured. Bachelet, and her mother, were also detained and mistreated in a notorious torture center.[37] Freed from prison, they went to Australia, then into exile in East Germany, returning to Chile in 1979. During Lagos's presidency, she had served as Minister of Health and Minister of Defense. No woman had ever served as Minister of Defense nor been elected president of Chile.

The political right, split between the UDI and Renovación Nacional parties, presented two candidates: Joaquín Lavín (UDI), who had lost closely to Lagos in 2000, and Sebastián Piñera (RN), a multimillionaire entrepreneur who sought to wrest centrist, especially Christian Democratic, votes from the Concertación. Piñera had the flash, charm, money, and political experience to mount a serious challenge to continued Concertación control of the presidency. Facing a socialist, female candidate, with a nontraditional family life, whom he sought to identify with the bitter divisions of the past (i.e., the Popular Unity government), Piñera pulled out all the stops in a campaign that promised to fight crime, create a million new jobs, improve the health care system, and commit itself to Christian Humanist ideals.

Bachelet won approximately 46 percent of the vote in December; since no candidate received 50 percent of the vote, a run-off election between Bachelet and Piñera (the second leading voter getter, 25 percent) occurred January 15, 2006. As the election approached and Piñera seemed to be gaining ground on Bachelet, newspaper articles appeared "remembering" a proposal that Piñera had offered in the Senate in 1995. Suddenly the battle between impunity, memory, and justice emerged once again as a critical issue, for Piñera, in the name of national reconciliation, had proposed an amnesty law for all persons ("authors, accomplices, and those who 'obstructed justice' [*encubridores*]") who had committed crimes from March 11, 1978 to March 11, 1990. He tied his proposed legislation directly to the 1978 amnesty decreed by the military regime, demanding that the "parade of officers before judges end" and amnesty be declared for all crimes covered by the 1978 decree law. Piñera's proposal had been rejected in 1995 and seemingly passed into oblivion along with various other proposals for "turning the page" and "not allowing the past to destroy the future."[38]

With memories fresh of the findings of the Valech Commission (the "torture commission" discussed earlier) and renewed coverage of prosecutions of human rights violations in the media, Piñera could not successfully defend his 1995 call for impunity. The resurgent battle between impunity and justice played an important role in the election of Chile's first female president. Ironically, but consistent with the historical tension between truth and "forgetting," between reconciliation *a la chilena* and the resistance to impunity, Bachelet herself was seen as "a symbol of healing in a country long divided by ideology, class and competing versions of a tumultuous recent history" (Reel 2005). Still, Bachelet's public remarks in an interview with German journalists represented a studied departure from the historical *vía chilena*:

> A country that has experienced such deep trauma as Chile can never be completely healed. I'm a doctor, so allow me to use a medical analogy to explain the problem: Only cleaned wounds can heal, otherwise they'll keep opening up again, and will likely become infected and begin to fester. It's clear to me that the truth must be brought to light. Of course, there are those—but they're a minority today—who just want to sweep everything under the rug. In a constitutional state, the government must take steps to ensure that the judiciary can operate without obstruction. The fact that I was elected shows that Chile has a mature society. And that's why most citizens insist that no one should be allowed to place themselves above the law and escape punishment.[39]

Whether Dr. Bachelet's efforts to cleanse the wounds so that they may heal will be successful remains to be seen as does whether "*echándole tierra*" (burying) the human rights violations and the tradition of impunity will be replaced, in practice, with truth seeking and the rule of law. The *vía chilena de reconciliación política* has survived many changes in government since the early nineteenth century; Bachelet's four-year presidency will likely not see a final chapter of this strongly embedded cultural and institutional pattern in Chilean politics.

Mapping and understanding continuities and change in political culture and institutions is a key concern for political science. Discovery of regularities in political life, transformation and rupture of such regularities, and explaining how and why these events occur is a challenge to social theorists and empirical research. In the writings and methodology of Vincent Ostrom, we find a nuanced blend of cultural and institutional analysis of perceived "right ways," of "what actually happens," of reasons for the gaps between norms and practice (and "trouble cases"), and of explanations for change in the behavior and "law ways" of a people. We have found this mode of analysis as useful in studying patterns of political conflict, violence, and reconciliation in Chile—"the Chilean way"—as it was for Llewellyn and Hoebel for studying the *Cheyenne Way* more than a half-century ago.

Notes

This chapter is a revised and greatly shortened version of Brian Loveman and Elizabeth Lira, "Truth, Justice, Reconciliation, and Impunity as Historical Themes: Chile, 1814–2006," *Radical History Review* 97 (Winter 2007): 43–76. Published by permission of Duke University Press.

1. This is the military version of the history of international communism's attack on Chile since before World War I. It is extensively documented with extracts from leftist politicians and the revolutionary press.

2. An emotional account of such divisions among families and the commitment by all protagonists to (their version of) *la patria* is the story of the 1891 war as remembered by the son of General Orozimbo Barbosa, the defeated commander of President Balmaceda's army. General Barbosa was killed in battle; his brother-in-law was an officer with the opposing forces, and his "favorite nephew," the son of his beloved sister, imprisoned by his own forces (see Barbosa 1929).

3. On the Ranquil uprising, see Loveman (1976, 144–45); Consejo de Defensa Fiscal, N. 165, 4 mayo, 1933; and Lúgaro et al. (2001). A more recent article in a Mapuche Indian magazine refers explicitly to the theme of *"olvido"* and *"echándole tierra"* with amnesties: "Muchos de los que sobrevivieron, chilenos y mapuche, tras duras jornadas escapando por la cordillera, terminaron dispersos en estancias o en los huertos de Neuken y Río Negro donde rehicieron sus vidas, luego de cruzar hacia el Puelmapu tras padecer indescriptibles fatigas y penalidades. Al final, tal como ocurrió muchas veces en la agitada vida política del Chile de los años '20 y '30, *el olvido y las infaltables leyes de amnistía terminaron por echarle tierra a la masacre, olvidándose de ello una sociedad entera . . . tal como antes, tal como después. . .*" (emphasis added; article

published in *Mapuche Azkintuwe*, July 2004, p. 7, http://www.mapuche-nation.org/espanol/html/articulos/art-59.htm). The most detailed account of the Ranquil incident in English is found in Klubock (2005). On the massacre at the Caja de Seguro Obligatorio (and for an anti-Alessandri frame for this event with graphic photos of the dead), see Donoso (1954, chaps. 14 and 15). For the Caja events, the congress created a joint fact-finding commission to discover the "truth" about the massacre: "a investigar la forma en que fueron muertos los prisioneros tomados en la Universidad y a establecer quién impartí la orden de hacerlos volver, cuando eran llevados a la Sección de Investigaciones, al edificio de la Caja de Seguro Obligatorio" (Donoso 1954, 275). Donoso calls his chapter 15 "El escamoteo de la verdad" ("The Illusion of Truth").

4. Whether to accept the legitimacy of the notion of "internal war" or "civil war" (or "war" at all) from 1973 to 1990 is itself part of the discourse that frames this conflict and a tactic by opposing sides in its ongoing reinterpretation. For a fascinating interpretation of this issue see Vidal (1995).

5. To anticipate the discussion of the 1990s and to stretch a metaphor only slightly: President Aylwin's minister of justice wrote that the 1980 constitution was neither legitimate in origin nor in content before the "transition to democracy." Many of the *Concertación* political leaders rejected formal democracy in the 1960s and 1970s and also the 1980 constitution later. A process of conversion and renovation made them "believers" in the "value of democracy for its own sake," and the "necessity" of accepting the 1980 constitution as the "rules of the game" in 1989.

6. A dramatic example was the reinterment, in 1922, of the remains of Balmacedista Generals Orizimbo Barbosa and José Miguel Alzérreca in the *Mausoleo del Ejército* after a mass at the Santiago Cathedral. According to an editorial in *Las Ultimas Noticias*, "the generals come to their eternal rest in the Mausoleum of the Army, wrapped in the love of all Chileans, because after thirty one years since the great catastrophe, the passions [of the past] have been extinguished, and all that remains is the serene and just appreciation for those who gave their lives in accord with military honor and an austere tradition of discipline" (cited in Barbosa 1929, 61).

7. To great extent this modality of political reconciliation paralleled, with imperfections, the sacrament of reconciliation (confession) in the Catholic Church, so integral a part of spiritual, moral life, and everyday life in Chile that its premises were taken for granted without being explicit: sin or offense against others; contrition (*arrepentimiento*) and confession; a request for pardon from those offended to those whom they offended and God; "heartfelt conversion"; and the intention not to repeat the offense. The offended, and, more importantly, God, then may forgive the sin. This model of reconciliation is implicit in most of the debates regarding amnesties and pardons from the 1850s into the 1990s. Of course, if, as occurred in 1931 and 1990, those who have "sinned" not only deny that they have done so, but justify their behavior as itself "salvationist" (of the *patria*), this model loses much of its applicability. If Ibáñez and Pinochet (and their allies) denied that they have committed wrongs, indeed proclaimed that they had acted virtuously in repressing godless subversives,

ask not for forgiveness but applause and historical recognition for their service to the *patria*, then "truth" and "justice" cannot be achieved and forgiveness and "forgetting" are not possible.

8. *Boletín de leyes* 29 (1861, 355–56, reprinted in Loveman and Lira 2001, 76).

9. "O'Higgins Bernardo—Se ordena la erección de la estatua de la Alameda, la colocacion de su retrato en la Sala de Gobierno i otros homenajes para honrar su memoria" (July 13, 1844), in Anguita (1912, 1: 435–36).

10. Reconciliation policies after each political rupture are detailed in Loveman and Lira (2000c).

11. Elizabeth Lira and I have interviewed all the members of the Rettig Commission created by President Aylwin in 1990 and various functionaries of the *Corporación de Reparación y Reconciliación* that followed up on its work. Only one of the interviewees (a prominent Chilean historian) was aware of the *juicio de residencia* of O'Higgins in 1823 and the *acusaciones constitucionales* against Manuel Montt in 1868, President Balmaceda's ministers from 1891–1893, or of Carlos Ibáñez in 1931. None of them were aware of the history of pardons and amnesties in the nineteenth century in any detail, though the Rettig Commission and the Corporación de Reparación did prepare a list (incomplete) of previous amnesties. Political exigencies of the moment prevented time and energy being dedicated to historical research on the context of previous amnesties. No attention was dedicated to discussing these precedents. Only Raúl Rettig had actually participated in previous amnesty debates, as a legislator in the 1950s.

12. There were exceptions. In 1827, for example, Francisco Antonio Pinto insisted on a letter from the mutinous military personnel requesting pardon and promising future good behavior. From 1851 to 1857, President Montt, his ministers, and the Consejo de Estado also sought formal pardon requests, promises of good behavior, and then conditioned pardons and commutations of sentences on political restraint, subject to application of the original sentence, whether capital punishment or incarceration. Part of the research for this chapter included systematic review of the minutes of the sessions of the Consejo de Estado in which pardons were debated and the conditions placed on those pardons during the 1830s–1850s.

13. For a summary of this view see Loveman (1997).

14. In an effort to equate pardons for "terrorists" (ex-MIR [Movimiento de Izquiera Revolucionaria] and Socialists who carried out armed resistance against the dictatorship and sometimes engaged in violent crimes against innocent civilians) with pardons for military personnel who had served at least ten years in prison for human rights violations, several legislative proposals emerged in early September 2005. In the meantime, President Lagos pardoned Manuel Contreras Donaire, a noncommissioned officer who had participated in the murder of labor leader Tucapel Jiménez in 1985, provoking outcries from human rights organizations and the leftist parties. See "Lagos descarta más indultos," *El Mercurio*, September 14, 2005.

15. In a longer version of this essay, we have considered important *acusación constitucional* proceedings after the civil war of 1891; the constitutional rupture in

1924–1926; and the end of the dictatorship of Carlos Ibáñez del Campo (1927–1931). In addition, we have published a book on the "Commission to Investigate the Acts of the Dictatorship" (August–December 1931)—a latter-day "truth commission," virtually forgotten in Chile, which compiled twenty-one large volumes of evidence against the Ibáñez regime (see Loveman and Lira 2006).

16. Ibáñez and party leaders negotiated this arrangement at the hot springs near Chillán. This earned the congress the disparaging nickname *"congreso termal"*—and this nickname has stuck in Chilean historiography on the period 1930–1932.

17. On the Ibáñez regime, see Flores (1993) and Loveman and Lira (2006).

18. Renuncia de Pedro Opazo Letelier, July 27, 1931. Montero had served as minister of Interior of Ibáñez until July 21, 1931, representing an effort to liberalize the regime, allow the return of some exiles, and restore relative freedom of the press. It was also an effort to demobilize professional and student groups that had carried out strikes and street demonstrations against the government for several months.

19. Ministerio de Justicia, Decreto 2676, August 4, 1931.

20. Comisión Investigadora de los Actos de la Dictadura, Acta de sesión 8a plenaria, August 18, 1931.

21. For details on the amnesties during this period, see Loveman and Lira (2001, 95–113).

22. *Cámara de Diputados*, 49a sesión ordinaria, August 31, 1931, 1765–67.

23. During his second presidential administration (1952–1958), Ibáñez was again subjected to *the acusación constitucional* procedure, making him the only president in Chilean history to face such proceedings during his term of office (see Loveman and Lira 2000a, 118–69; *Cámara de Diputados*, 22a sesión, November 27, 1956, 1393–414).

24. It must be noted that amnesties benefited workers and peasants as well as military and police officials. After World War I, labor conflicts and violence periodically produced confrontations between miners, workers, peasants, and law enforcement or the army. Amnesties in 1925 (for the bloody events at Puerto Natales in 1919 and the nitrate camp at San Gregorio in 1921), in 1934 (for the events at Ranquil in 1934, and also for all workers and leftist politicians accused of crimes against the internal security of the State), and in 1936 (for striking railway workers, among others) all evidenced the expanding clientele for amnesties and pardons in the name of reconciliation. The amnesty decree of January 1925 (DL 233, published in the Diario Oficial on January 31, 1925) was especially inclusive: *La Junta de Gobierno, de acuerdo con el Consejo de Secretarios de Estado dicta el siguiente.*

DECRETO LEY: Concédese amnistía a todos los que se encuentran actualmente procesados o pudieran ser juzgados con motivo de los sucesos ocurridos en San Gregorio el 3 de febrero de 1921 i en Puerto Natales el 23 de febrero de 1919. Se concede también amnistía a todos los que se encuentran comprometidos en los procesos acumulados por asociaciones ilícitas i de que conoce un ministro de la Corte de Apelaciones de Valparaíso, y en los procesos instruidos a consecuencia de movimientos colectivos de carácter social. Se concede igualmente amnistía a todos los que se hallen procesados o pudieran serlo por hechos cometidos con anterioridad a esta fecha contra las autoridades, contra el orden político y la seguridad interior del Estado. Decláranse amnistiados todos los que fueren responsables por delitos de carácter electoral. Rija desde su publicación en el diario oficial. Tómese razón comuníquese y publíquese e insértese en el Boletín de las leyes y decretos del gobierno Bello Dartnell C Ward José Maza.

25. An English version of the Commission's charge and its work is found on the United States Institute of Peace website, http://www.usip.org/library/tc/doc/reports/chile/chile_1993_pt1_ch1.html.

26. Cited in the introduction to the English version of the report at http://www.usip.org/library/tc/doc/reports/chile/chile_1993_introeng.html.

27. See previous note.

28. When we discussed the historical record on amnesties and the 1931 commission with members of the Rettig Commission, most were not aware of this historical legacy. Gonzalo Vial, an historian and ex-minister of education under the dictatorship, was an exception regarding the amnesties (he had written about the 1891 civil war), though he too had no immediate recollection of the 1931 commission.

29. This is a topic for another article. See Lira and Loveman (2005) for detailed analysis of the various reparation policies during this period.

30. For a summary of major episodes and tension points in civil military relations from 1990 to 2000, see Loveman (2001, 331–35, table 11–4).

31. On the Pinochet case see Davis (2003).

32. For reasons of space, and also because the Mesa de Diálogo does not neatly fall into the same patterns as the truth commissions and the *acusaciones constitucionales*, we do not include it further in this discussion. Elizabeth Lira participated as a member of this group. For a summary of the agreement reached, see "Acuerdo de la Mesa de Diálogo," *La Nación*, June 23, 2003, http://www.lanacion.cl/p4_lanacion/antialone.html?page=http://www.lanacion.cl/prontus_noticias/site/artic/20030624/pags/20030624133756.html.

33. This is an acronym for Programa de Reparación y Atención Integral de Salud. The program is described in Lira and Loveman (2005).

34. The Commission's report, the list of more than 27,000 persons recognized as torture victims, and President Lagos's speech (November 28, 2004) making public the report can be found online at: http://www.gobiernodechile.cl/comision_valech/index.asp. The entire report is available online at: http://www.gobiernodechile.cl/comision_valech/index.asp. The printed version (777 pages) is *Informe de la Comisión Nacional sobre prisión política y tortura* (Ministerio del Interior, Santiago: La Nación, 2005). A note on the imprint page claims that 33,000 copies were printed and they would be distributed without charge.

35. For example, the Fundación de Ayuda Social de las Iglesias Cristianas (FASIC), an organization created in 1975 to support victims of the dictatorship, called for the application of international law regarding human rights violations (no pardons, no amnesties) (see FASIC, "Declaración Pública," August 19, 2005, http://www.fasic.org/doc/dec050819.htm, September 20, 2005).

36. This Chilean dilemma is not theirs alone, though the particulars vary in the rest of Latin America. José Miguel Insunza, an exile in times of the Pinochet government and cabinet minister in the Lagos administration, was named in 2005 as Secretary General of the OAS. In an address to colleagues at FLACSO, Chile, in September 2005, he told his audience that a principal challenge of the OAS was to confront the "exacerbated ingovernability of the region" ("exacerbada ingobernabilidad de la region").

37. According to Bachelet, "Our room had bars on the window. We had four or five bunks, and we were eight women. The beds were full, sometimes two women slept together, we didn't all fit. . . . We were blindfolded all day, we took them off, but obviously when the guards arrived we lowered the blindfolds. If not, they beat us. . . . Bachelet's mother, Angela Jeria, was kidnapped together with her daughter and locked in a cage for five days without food. Their cellmates were raped by guards" (Franklin 2006).

38. For more on this see Loveman and Lira (2002b, 146–73).

39. Interview with Michelle Bachelet, "Only Cleaned Wounds Can Heal," *Spiegel* (March 9, 2006), by Hans Hoyng and Helene Zuber. Translated from German by Christopher Sultan. Accessed at truthout.issues, http://www.truthout.org/docs_2006/030906H.shtml.

References

Anguita, Ricardo. 1912. *Leyes promulgadas en Chile, desde 1810 hasta el 1 de junio de 1912*. Santiago: Imprenta, Litografía i Encuadernación Barcelona.
Barbosa, Enrique O. 1929. *Como si fuera hoy: Recuerdos de la Revolución de 1891*. Santiago: Imprenta Santiago.
Davis, Madeleine, ed. 2003. *The Pinochet Case: Origins, Progress and Implications*. London: Institute of Latin American Studies.
Donoso, Ricardo. 1954. *Alessandri, agitador y demoledor: Cincuenta años de historia política de Chile*, vol. 2. Mexico-Buenos Aires: Fondo de Cultura Económica.
Encina, Francisco A. 1950. *Historia de Chile desde la prehistoria hasta 1891*, vol. 14. Santiago: Editorial Nascimento.
Flores, Jorge Rojas. 1993. *La dictadura de Ibáñez y los sindicatos (1927–1931)*. Santiago: DIBAM, Centro de Investigaciones Diego Barros Arana.
Franklin, Jonathan. 2006. "Chile's Michelle Bachelet Poised for Presidency." *Women's eNews*. http://www.womensenews.org/article.cfm/dyn/aid/2532/context/cover.
Heinecke Scott, Luis. 1992. *Una larga amenaza que se cumple*, vol. 2 of *Chile: Crónica de un asedio*. Santiago: Sociedad Editora y Gráfica Santa Catalina.
Klubock, Thomas. 2005. "Ránquil: Violence and Peasant Politics on Chile's Southern Frontier." Unpublished paper, September.
Lira, Elizabeth, and Brian Loveman. 2005. *Políticas de reparación: Chile 1990–2004*. Santiago: LOM/DIBAM.

Llewellyn, Karl N., and E. Adamson Hoebel. 1941. *The Cheyenne Way: Conflict and Case Law in Primitive Jurisprudence.* Norman: University of Oklahoma Press.

Loveman, Brian. 1976. *Struggle in the Countryside: Politics and Rural Labor in Chile, 1919–1973.* Bloomington: Indiana University Press.

———. 1988. *Chile: The Legacy of Hispanic Capitalism.* 2nd ed. New York: Oxford University Press.

———. 1997. "Human Rights, Antipolitics, and Protecting the Patria: An (Almost) Military Perspective." In *The Politics of Antipolitics: The Military in Latin America,* ed. Brian Loveman and Thomas M. Davies Jr., 398–423. Wilmington, DE: Scholarly Resources.

———. 2001. *Chile: The Legacy of Hispanic Capitalism.* 3rd ed. New York: Oxford University Press.

Loveman, Brian, and Elizabeth Lira. 2000a. *Las acusaciones constitucionales en Chile: Una perspectiva histórica.* Santiago: FLACSO-LOM.

———. 2000b. *Las ardientes cenizas del olvido: Vía Chilena de reconciliación política, 1932–1994.* Santiago: DIBAM-LOM.

———. 2000c. *Las suaves cenizas del olvido: Vía Chilena de reconciliación política 1814–1932.* 2nd ed. Santiago: DIBAM-LOM.

———. 2001. *Leyes de reconciliación en Chile: Amnistías, indultos y reparaciones, 1819–1999.* Santiago: DIBAM/Centro de Investigaciones Diego Barros Arana.

———. 2002a. *Arquitectura política y seguridad interior del Estado 1811–1990.* Santiago: DIBAM-LOM.

———. 2002b. *El espejismo de la reconciliación política: Chile 1990–2002.* Santiago: DIBAM-LOM.

———. 2006. *La Comisión Investigadora de los actos de la Dictadura, 1931.* Santiago: DIBAM-LOM.

Lúgaro, Eduardo Téllez, et al. 2001. "El levantamiento del Alto Biobío y el Soviet y la República Araucana de 1934." *Anales de la Universidad de Chile,* 6th ser., no. 13. http://www2.anales.uchile.cl/CDA/an_simple/0,1278,SCID%253D216%2526ISID%253D9%2526ACT%253D0%2526PRT%253D118,00.html.

Reel, Monte. 2005. "Female, Agnostic and the Next Presidente?" *Washington Post,* December 10. http://www.washingtonpost.com/wp-dyn/content/article/2005/12/09/AR2005120902040.html.

Vidal, Hernán. 1995. *FPMR: El tabú del conflicto armado en Chile.* Santiago: Mosquito Editores.

10

Challenges Facing "State" Building in Burma

Tun Myint

The modern history of political development in Burma reveals two puzzles about governance. The first puzzle is *why and how could the British rule Burmese society for the longest period in the last two centuries while successive post-independent Burmese governments only survived for short periods?* The second puzzle related to the first is *why did successive post-independent Burmese governments fail to build a viable state in Burma?* I posit that the behavioral and social foundations of Burmese people explain these two puzzles.

Governance in modern Burmese history was a top-down exercise by the *tatmadaw* (Burmese military) and the political elites who mainly adopted the ideas of the Westphalian state model and tried to fashion *Leviathan* in Burmese society. Ordinary Burmese citizens had very little to do with state building. This is reflected in the dominant literature on state building in Burma. The literature on state building in Burma, beginning with John S. Furnivall's[1] *Colonial Policy and Practice* (1948) and Robert H. Taylor's *The State in Burma* (1987) to Mary P. Callahan's *Making Enemies: War and State Building in Burma* (2003), focuses on the political elites and the Burmese army as the state builders to explain the processes of state building in Burma.

There is no systematic political study of social, cultural, livelihood, and institutional foundations of ordinary people to explain the failures of top-down and elitist state building in Burma. The work of anthropologist Gustaaf Houtman's *Mental Culture in Burmese Crisis Politics* (1999) is the closest to explaining behavioral aspects and ordinary people's roles in the struggle for state building in Burma. This chapter differs from the literature on elitist state-building exercises in Burma. It considers citizens as the foundation for constructing productive orders of national government in Burma. We will (1) interpret and analyze the conceptual unfolding of law in the context of Burmese Dhammathats as well as the traditional social and cultural elements and (2) analyze the challenges in reconstituting Burmese society and its institutional dimensions.

Orders in Early Burmese Society

The early written works about Burmese history are *U Kula Yazawin* (*History of Kings*, written by U Kula), completed in 1721, and *Hmannan Yazawin* (*The Glass Palace Chronicle of the Kings*), written in 1829 (Tin and Luce [1923] 1960). The latter, being written by the assigned historical commission of the king, became the national archive of Burmese history. Because the king assigned the historical commission to write *Hmannan Yazawin*, Western scholars charged *Hmannan Yazawin* as a nationalistic interpretation of the history of Burma (Htin Aung 1970). The scholars who are critical of *Hmannan Yazawin* base their interpretation of Burmese history on inscriptions dating back to the Pagan era (AD 1044–1278), the first great kingdom of Burma. Before the Pagan period, there were dynasties of different regions. King Anawratha united all of those existing dynasties and established the first Burmese kingdom at Pagan in 1044 and proclaimed Buddhism as the religion of his kingdom with the help of a famous Buddhist monk named Shin Araharn (Harvey 1967, 25–27).

Burmese historians have different views about what period Burma's different kingdom began to emerge and by whom. A renowned post-war Burmese historian, U Htin Aung (1962, 4–5), in his "Introduction" to *Burmese Law Tales*, gives the account of where the Burmese people came from as follows:

> There were humans in Burma at least some five thousand years ago, but not much is known of those early humans. Later on, some Indonesian tribes seemed to have come from the West, settled for some time in coastal regions, and then passed to the East. In the early centuries of the Christian era, the Mons entered Burma from the East, by way of the region now known as Thailand, and settled in the South, founding cities and kingdoms, which originally were part of the Great Mon-Khmer Empire of Southeast Asia. The Burmese and their allied tribes bound to them by blood and a common language, left their original homeland on the south-eastern slopes of the Tibetan Highlands, and migrated across the northern hills of Burma into the Irrawaddy.

One of the pioneer works of Burmese history, on which many Western historians relied upon in studying Burmese history, is a book entitled *A*

Description of the Burmese Empire written in 1833 by an Italian missionary leader, Reverend Father Sangermano, who arrived in Burma in 1782. Sangermano (1833, 38), in his chapter on "Origin of the Burmese Nation and Monarchy," observed that it was impossible to trace back the origin of the Burmese nation and people due to the lack of historical account of the people who lived before the establishment of dynasties. Sangermano obviously failed to cite *U Kula Yazawin*, which is the account of Burmese history written in 1721.

The Emergence of the First Kingdom and Legal Development

Before King Anawratha conquered different dynasties of Burma to establish the first Kingdom of Pagan in AD 1044, Burma passed through eras of dynasties for thousands of years. Pagan is also known as the "Kingdom of Temple Builders" for its great number of temples built during the Pagan era. After Anawratha had established Pagan's power, his grandson King Alaungsithu in AD 1112–1165, began the formalization of the legal system based on customary law (Htin Aung 1962, 9). However, while legal disputes were decided according to native customary law, it was also in accordance with the spirit of Buddhist ethics. When Alaungsithu died, his decisions were collected as a work called *Alaungsithu's Pyat-hton* (or *Alaungsithu's Judgment*), which served as a code of precedent for later generations until the nineteenth century (9).

In the year AD 1173, Narapatisithu, grandson of Alaungsithu, became the king of Pagan. Like all kings of Pagan, he was a great patron of Buddhism. The king wanted a young monk, named Shin Ananda, who was then educated in India, to be the Royal Tutor. The king gave a great feast in honor of the monk and offered him the title of *Dhammavilasa*, meaning "great scholar of Buddhist scriptures." Shin Dhammavilasa[2] became famous all over the region as a teacher of other monks. He later wrote a treatise on law that came to be known as *Dhammavilasa Dhammathat*, which is one of nine highly regarded institutions of law out of thirty-six Dhammathats in Burma (see table 10.1). *Dhammavilasa Dhammathat* is the oldest-surviving Burmese law book today, although it is not a pioneer work among the thirty-six Dhammathats (E. Maung 1951, 6).

Burmese legal scholars have followed the Dhammathats and attempted to trace the legal development of Burma beginning from the first Manu Dhammathat written at the time when this world emerged according to

Table 10.1. Nine institutions of Burmese Dhammathats

Name of Dhammathat	Date	Reign of the King	Remarks
Manu	AD 540–560	First Pagan	Introduction states that it was presented to King Mahathamada by the Rishi Manu.
Dhammavilasa	AD 1200	Fifth Pagan	Introduction states that it was an abridged edition of Manu Dhammathat by Shin Dhamavilasa.
Wagaru	AD 1270	Martaban	Introduction states that it was rooted in Manu Dhammathat written at the instance of Wagaru, King of Mataban.
Pasadha	AD 1468	Taungoo	Has been considered to be of high authority in Burmese law.
Manusara	AD 1549	Pegu	Twelve legal scholars in 1549 composed this under King Sinbyumyashin.
Dhammathat Kyaw	AD 1581	Taungoo	According to its preface, is a combination and analysis of previous Dhammathats.
Pyanchi	AD 1614	Taungoo	Written by an individual named Maung Pe Thi.
Myingun	AD 1650	Konbaung	Named after the town where the Dhammathat was written.
Manugye	AD 1768	Konbaung	Drew upon all previous Dhammathats in the elucidation of legal problems.

Sources: Gaung (1898) and E. Maung (1951).

Burmese mythical tales and stories (analysis in the following section). The earliest written work by Western scholars about the sources of Burmese law and legal concept was the Jardine Prize essay entitled "On the Sources and Development of Burmese Law from the Era of the First Introduction of the Indian Law to the Time of the British Occupation of Pegu" by learned British scholar Dr. Emanuel Forchammer. It was published in 1885, one year before the British annexed the last Kingdom of Burma. In his essay, Forchammer observed:

> The development of law in Burma has not been a steady devolution. Every great Burmese or Talaing Monarch endeavored to preserve existing laws and to enact and enforce new ones suitable to the customs and usages of the people for whom they were intended. But subsequent weak rulers, or a change of dynasty, reduced the body of law promulgated by predecessors or members of subverted dynasties to a dead letter; it was set aside and then forgotten. (1885, 91)

The scholars, including Burmese legal historians and judges, rejected Forchammer's observation. Former Justice U E. Maung of Burma, in his series of lectures given at Cornell University and published in 1951, stated that Burmese law in its descent to the later part of the nineteenth century had no breaks and catastrophes. He argued that: "Dynasties passed away to be succeeded by other dynasties; kings waged war with supplanted other kings; rebellion on many occasions reared its head and pretenders had come to the rule; but there never was a revolution in the growth of Burmese law" (1951, 1).

U E. Maung's views contend that Burmese law has existed without much break and changes but steadily resonated in the sources—Dhammathats. This view was supported by the Letters Patent of the appointment of judges in the last days of Burmese monarchs in 1885, as recited below:

> In case of dispute they must, in accordance with all thirty-six Dhammathats, enquire into the causes of the people and decide between them and for this purpose they are appointed to the Courts as judges. In a lawsuit or dispute any of our subjects apply to a Judge, the Judge shall decide the matter with the Manu Dhammathat in hand first. If the required rule is not to be found therein, follow all other Dhammathats. (E. Maung 1951, 2)

The development of Burmese law may be seen as rooted in all Dhammathats written by different legal scholars appointed by different kings throughout the eras of Burmese kings. These Dhammathats were restored one dynasty after another and observed by one king after another. By this observance, the kings gained the people's support and were respected throughout Burmese history.

Bases of Orders

One of the key institutional foundations of Burmese society is the development of law and of legal concepts in parallel with the emergence of kingdoms. The development of legal theory in Burma has to be understood in the context of social meaning of rules and norms that are heavily drawn from the Buddhist concept of law and orders of life. Dhammathats written by Buddhist scholars are major sources or roots of Burmese legal theory.

Laws as Bases of Orders

Among the Burmese Dhammathats, the Manu Dhammathat is the first of thirty-six Dhammathats. Throughout Burmese history, the Dhammathats are the fundamental sources of laws. In the introduction of Manu Dhammathat, the foundation of the source of law in Burma is written:

> When this universe had reached the period of firmly established continuancy, the original inhabitants of this world conjointly entreated the great King Mahasammata to become their ruler. King Mahasammata governed the world with righteousness. Now the king had a wise nobleman called Manu, who was well versed in the law. This nobleman called Manu, desiring the good of all human beings, and being also opportuned by King Mahasammata, rose into the expanse of heaven, and having arrived at the boundary wall of the world, he there saw the natural law, Dhammathat, he committed them to memory and having returned, communicated the same to the King Mahasammata, stating eighteen branches of law.

The sources of Burmese law can be inferred as a form of natural law. "Burmese laws on the whole seem wise, and evidently are calculated to advance the interests of justice and morality" (Vincent 1874, 16). The worst insult that one could do to oneself and society is to lie or make false statements to harm others. This is reinforced by the belief in the concept of karma. To be able to capture the mentality of the Burmese in regard to law and justice, the oath of witness used in court during the Ava[3] dynasty in 1782 merits examination:

> I will speak the truth. If I speak not the truth, may it be through the influence of the laws of demerit—passion, anger, folly, pride, false opinion, immodesty, hard-heartedness, and skepticism—so that when I and my relations are on land, land animals—as tigers, elephants, buffaloes, poisonous serpents, scorpions, and etc—shall seize, crush, and bite us, so that we shall certainly die. Let the calamities occasioned by fire, water, rulers, thieves, and enemies oppress and destroy us, till we perish and come to utter destruction. Let us be subject to all the calamities that are within the body, and all that are without the body. May we be seized with madness, dumbness, blindness, deafness, leprosy, and hydrophobia. May we be struck with thunderbolts and lightning, and come to sudden death. In the midst of not speaking truth may I be taken with vomiting clotted black blood, and suddenly die before the assembled people. When I am going by water may the water nats[4] assault me, the boat be upset, and the property lost; and may alligators, porpoises, sharks, and other sea monsters seize and crush me to death; and when I change worlds may I not arrive among human or nats, but suffer unmixed punishment and regret, in the utmost wretchedness, among the four states of punishment, Hell, Prita, Beasts, and Athurakai.
>
> If I speak the truth, may I and my relations, through the influence of the ten laws of merit, and on account of the efficacy of truth, be freed from all calamities within and without the body, and may evils which have not yet come be warded far away. May the thunderbolts and lightning, the nat of the waters, and all sea animals love me, that I may be safe from them. May my prosperity increase like the rising sun and the waxing moon; and may the seven possessions, the seven laws, and the seven merits of the virtuous be permanent in my person; and when I change worlds (life after death) may I not go to the four states of punishment, but attain the happiness of men and nats, and realize merit, reward, and perfect calm. (cited in Vincent 1874, 18)

This oath of witness illustrates how Burmese are serious about upholding the truth in order to help the machinery of justice at the court. In addition, the oath conveys the social philosophy of Burmese people that is rooted in the concept of karma—such as wishing to gain good things as a result of good deeds of telling the truth and willingness to accept the bad that comes as a result of ones' lies or bad acts. I shall extend the discussion about Burmese belief in the concept of karma in the following paragraphs.

The Concept of Karma and Orders

In Burma, it is fair to state that the society is imbued with Buddha's teaching. "The one single factor which has had the most influence on the Burmese culture and civilization is Theravada Buddhism" (Kyi 1991, 66). Buddhism teaches that the sole "Creator" of an individual is the individual itself and therefore, an individual is responsible for his or her actions, which are finally judged by the karma of the individual. The similar concept of karma is found in Isaac Newton's *Third Principle of Force*, which states that when object A hits object B with certain force, object B would respond with the same amount of force that comes from object A. Therefore, all good and bad actions of individuals would result in their respective ways according to Buddha's principle of karma.

The concept of karma is a fundamental calculus of human intention and actions in Burmese society, at least among a majority of the Buddhist population. Thus, it has consequences to the ways in which orders are articulated and structured in Burma. It has both positive and negative influences on Burmese society. While the positive might be that people are tolerant of others' actions especially those of unjust actions in society, this tolerance could facilitate emergence of unjust and unproductive orders. For instance, the people in Burma tend to leave those evil doers, such as the military generals in Burma, alone under the judgment of their own karma, believing that one day in the line of their karma, justice will be served for those evil doers. At the same time, Burmese people tend to believe that the suffering under the military government is somewhat in accordance with the karma of the sufferers. However, a majority of the Burmese people have recently expressed their views through the public demonstrations of 1988 and the well-known election of May 27, 1990, in which the democratic opposition party, the National League for Democracy (NLD), won 82 percent of the parliamentary seats. The karma of Burmese people's intentions and actions has yet to become true. Until the positive side of Burmese beliefs on karma overcomes the negative side, productive orders grounded on citizens and their self-governing capacities will be locked into unproductive and unjust orders in Burma.

The Role of Governing Regimes in Organizing Orders

One of the sources of unlocking the positive side of Burmese people's karma in their political life is found in the Buddhist Burmese view of Kingship or Government or State. Burmese Buddhists consider the government or the king or the state as one of five enemies of their lives. When a Burmese worships and prays at temples and pagodas, or before going to bed as one of their daily activities, they willfully pray to be away from five enemies of life—fire-related disasters, water-related disasters, wind-related disasters, the king or State, and thieves and robbers. Therefore, it is necessary to understand the Buddhist view of Kingship or the State.

The Buddhist view of Kingship (government) does not invest the ruler with the divine right to govern the realm as he pleases, which is in contrast with the Chinese view of the legitimacy of government based on the "Mandate of Heaven." The king or government is expected to observe the Ten Duties of King or Government, the Seven Safeguards against Decline, and the Four Assistances to the People, and to be guided by numerous other codes of conducts stated in Buddha's teaching. During the people's movements in 1988, a number of speakers including a famous Burmese scholar, astrologer and novelist Min Thein Kha, widely quoted the Ten Duties of Government in his public speeches. The Nobel Peace laureate and the opposition leader Daw Aung San Suu Kyi also discussed the importance and relevance of the Ten Duties of Government to democracy in her *Freedom from Fear* (1991). Since the Ten Duties of Government or King are highly regarded by Burmese people as parameters to judge their government, it is necessary to discuss how the concept of the Ten Duties of Government work in the context of modern politics and the legal system in Burma.

The Ten Duties of Government are: charity (*dana* in Parli), morality (*sila*), self-sacrifice (*paricagga*), integrity (*ajjava*), kindness (*maddava*), austerity (*tapa*), patience (*akkodha*), nonviolence (*avihamsa*), forbearance (*khanti*), and nonopposition to the will of the people (*avirodha*). These duties are developed to provide guidance for rulership, which was often portrayed as Kingship rather than as collective decision making.

The first duty of *charity* (*dana*) demands that a ruler should contribute generously toward the welfare of the people, and makes the implicit assumption that a government should have the competence to provide adequately for its citizens. In the context of modern politics, the *dana* means that one of the prime duties of the people's government would be to ensure the economic security of the people, such as creating jobs and eliminating unemployment.

The second duty of government, morality (*sila* in Parli), is based on the observance of the Five Precepts of Buddha's teaching that entail refraining from destruction of life, theft, adultery, falsehood, and indulgence in intoxicants. The Burmese believe that the ruler must bear a high moral character to win the respect and trust of the people, thus the ruler is in a position to ensure their happiness and prosperity, and to provide a proper example as a role model of their society. When the king or the government does not observe the *dhamma* (the rule of morality or ethic), state functionaries become corrupt, and when this happens, the people are subjected to suffering.

Self-sacrifice (or *paricagga*) is the third duty of government. The *paricagga* is sometimes translated as generosity and sometimes as self-sacrifice. The former would overlap with the meaning of the first duty, *dana*, so the latter, meaning self-sacrifice as the ultimate generosity that gives up all for the good sake of the people, would appear the more appropriate interpretation. The concept of selfless public service is sometimes illustrated by the stories of the hermit Sumedha who took the vows of Buddhahood. In so doing, he "who could have realized the supreme liberation of *nirvana* in a single life time committed himself to countless incarnations that he might help other beings free themselves from suffering" (cited in Kyi 1991, 171).

The fourth duty of government is to observe integrity or *ajjava*, which implies incorruptibility in the discharge of public duties as well as honesty and sincerity in personal relations. Burmese believe that those who govern should be wholly bound by the truth in thought, word, and deed. According to the fourth duty, to deceive or to mislead the people in any way would be an occupational failing as well as a moral offense. The ruler, therefore, has to observe the truth that is "as an arrow, intrinsically straight, without warp or distortion, when one word is spoken, it does not err into two," as Buddha has compared the meaning of truth to a straight arrow (Kyi 1991, 172).

The fifth duty of government is to practice kindness (*maddava*). A ruler has to bear courage to feel concern for the people's welfare. With this courage, the ruler has the mind and heart to take care of public services. To care is to take responsibility and to dare to act in accordance with the dictum that the ruler is the strength of the needy and helpless. Not just "a few good men" but many good humans are needed in the government of the people in order to observe the fifth duty of government.

The sixth duty, austerity (*tapa*), implies that a ruler must adopt simple habits, develop self-control, and practice spiritual discipline. This duty prevents rulers from abusing public properties and taxpayers' money. This duty is to safeguard against corrupt practices of the government.

The seventh, eighth, and ninth duties—patience (*akkodha*), nonviolence (*avihamsa*), and forbearance (*khanti*)—are similar and are related in most of the interpretations in Burmese culture. Rulers must not allow personal feelings of enmity and ill will to erupt into destructive anger and violence. It is incumbent on a ruler to cultivate true tolerance, which serves him or her to deal wisely and generously with the shortcomings and provocation of even those enemies he could crush with impunity. Violence is inhumane and absolutely contrary to the Buddha's teachings. A good ruler relinquishes ill will and anger with loving kindness, wickedness with virtue, parsimony with liberality, and falsehood with truth. These are all relevant to the seventh, eighth, and ninth duties of rulers.

The most significant duty among the Ten Duties of Government is the tenth duty, which states that the ruler must not oppose the will of the people. The *avirodha*—meaning nonopposition to the will of the people—is the Buddhist endorsement of democracy. This was supported by numerous stories of the kings during the Buddha's time in the ancient world. For instance, Pawridasa, a monarch who acquired an appetite for human flesh and adopted a habit of eating it, was forced into exile because he would not heed the people's demand that he should abandon his cannibalistic habits. Another different kind of ruler was the Buddha's penultimate incarnation on earth, the pious King Vessantara. He was also sent to exile when, in the course of his striving for perfection of liberality, he gave away the white elephant of state without the consent of the people. The true meaning of the tenth duty, nonopposition to the will of people, is a reminder that the legitimacy of government is founded on the consent of the people who have the power to withdraw their mandate at any time if they lose confidence in the ability or creditability of the ruler to serve their best interest.

The Ten Duties of Government or King in the tradition of Buddha's teachings greatly influence Burmese culture. They are very different from the concept of representative democracy that is currently practiced in the majority of the world's democratic countries with the exception of the cantonal governance of Switzerland. How could the current military regime exist in a Burmese society in which the concept of the Ten Duties of Government is widely accepted? To understand the answer to this question, one must first understand the concept of karma and how it plays out in Burmese social life.

The social and legal theory discussed above still plays an important role in the daily lives of Burmese belief and practices. However, they are difficult to spell out in legal terms or to be incorporated into a rule of law system. The challenge lies before future governments and citizens in Burma to find ways to include these elements in the political and legal system.

British Laws in Burma (1886–1948)

Although Burma as a whole was eventually colonized in AD 1885, some Burmese legal scholars argue that the influence of British over the administration of Burma began in 1824 at the end of the first Anglo-Burmese war

(Maung Maung 1963, 20). Beginning from the first Anglo-Burmese war, there were three stages in which the British came into Burma and influenced the administration of the Burmese kingdoms. The first stage took place in 1824, when the British took the lower maritime areas as a result of the Yandabo[5] cease-fire treaty of the first Anglo-Burmese war. The second stage took place in 1852, when territory further north was seized and "Lower Burma" became "British Burma." The third stage occurred in 1885, when Upper Burma was annexed and the entire country was consolidated as a province of the British India Empire.

The British first arranged the administrative system in which local customary law and traditional practices were allowed to exist parallel with the British administration. The British rules immediately encompassed city administration at Mandalay where the palace of the last king of Burma was located. However, the Burmese society was not entirely shattered by the changes that took place at Mandalay. The Burmese society in rural areas, during the British rules, revolved around the family and the village. These social units survived almost at the "outside" of the British administration that was active at the capital and in the cities where most commercial activities took place. Hugh Tinker (1961) observed that Burmese people in rural villages

> were very conscious of their relationship as "sons of the village," their law was the law of custom and tradition, there were no great social differences, all bore their share in manning the village defenses and in repairing the village wells or roads; it was a democratic little world . . . and much of the tradition of past times remain alive today, village democracy, patriotism, and proud memories of independence back to the dawn of the Burmese race.

Some of these patterns of livelihoods in rural Burma are mostly retained intact by the teaching of elders and monks, and are still practiced in Burma today.

When the British established the civil service and the hierarchy of courts under the Village Act in 1886, the role of the village headman and the elders, who used to be the traditional "judges" for rural problems and quarrels, was eliminated and replaced by judges appointed by the British administration in Burma. Under the traditional system of law and justice, the aim of the village headman and elders was to keep social harmony and peace. The job of keeping social harmony and peace was not just a noble one, but it also had economic incentives for the elders who wanted

> to wax fat they must keep as many villagers as possible, and to do this they must keep the peace and reduce quarrelsome litigation to a minimum. For

this reason it will be found that in awarding punishment for an offence the elders rarely inflict the maximum penalty applicable. Because they have to live with both parties to the case their main objective is restoration of harmony, granting of just sufficient economic balm to assuage the wounded without permanently antagonizing the wonder. (Stevenson 1943, 153)

With the change in the village and agricultural land system, the role of the headman was reduced to collector of revenue and upholder of the Village Act. The British system emphasized the self-policing functions of the village, and neglected its role as a more complex social system.

The Burma Reforms Committee, organized by the British India administration in 1922, noted that

the Burmese people feel that there is too much of logic and too much of hair-splitting in the system of British law, and too many loop-holes and too many occasions for the benefit of the doubt. Therefore, the justice is not served and so the lawless people, offenders, and the clever-people enjoy the advantage of rule of law system under the British rules.[6]

This report reflects the social theory of Burmese society that values the "medium way" over the extreme view in judging things and ideas in life. The British system of rule of law was premised upon concepts of individualism rather than on the moderation of rulers working under Buddhist rules and natural law. It thus faced passive resistance throughout rural Burma. In fact, it was fertile ground for mobilizing rebellions against British rules by asserting the demand for self-governance.

Burmese Law after Independence

After Burma gained independence from Britain on January 4, 1948, it established a parliamentary democratic system in which the rule of law became an important parameter for keeping the system working. The first Burmese prime minister, U Nu, speaking to the whole nation on March 12, 1948, said, "The first essential condition for making democracy secure in our lives is to base all our activities firmly on the rule of law." With this ideology, the post-colonial government introduced the "rule of law" system by explicitly copying almost all of the rules of the governing system from the British. A Burma scholar, John S. Furnivall, pointed out that "judicial interpretation in pre-war Burma was to favour private interests over social welfare. This was a heritage from the British legal system, which had been transplanted in Burma by judges and lawyers. But judicial traditions that fortified the national solidarity of England furthered the disintegration of social order in Burma."[7] The reason why the British rule of law system failed to keep social order in Burma is because it deviated from the local social institutions, cultural beliefs, and social behaviors of people in Burma.

In the early period of newly independent Burma, the challenge of implementing rules of law was recognized by careful observers. A Burmese political leader, who wrote a note of dissent to the reorganization of the administration in 1949 that favored implementation of British style, argued:

> It has been found that the introduction of the rule of law, which is alien to Burmese tradition, has led to the disintegration of Burmese social life. Any unalloyed continuance of the rule of law will further disintegrate Burmese social life. Hence any measure to reintegrate Burmese social life will have to depend more on social sanction than on the rule of law. I do not recommend that the rule of law should be dispensed with. But the rule of law should be adjusted in such a way that it should leave the largest possible scope to the play of social sanction.[8]

Burma's post-colonial parliamentary system, based on a rule of law in British style, lasted about twelve years from 1948 to 1962. In 1962, Burma fell into the hands of the Burmese military led by the late General Ne Win. General Ne Win formulated a type of political system called the "Burmese Way to Socialism" and implemented a new "rule by law" system to replace the older "rule of law" system. In the new "rule by law" system under the socialist ideology, law is made by the authoritarian power. General Ne Win also included some of the social norms and traditional practices outside these new rules. Some social norms and traditional practices were left to be dealt with by the village headmen and abbots of Buddhist monasteries throughout the society. This dual system of the "rule by law" and the rule of the "social practices" persists today. Harmonizing the political power structures and social practices in communal life of Burmese people is a major challenge for "state building" in Burma.

Conclusion: Challenges at the Transition

The "state," conceived by the elites of the Burmese political development struggle, is largely mimicked after some concepts that do not fit Burmese cultural beliefs and behaviors. Consequently, there is no legacy of stable state structures and governments that is able to sustain a period of productive order longer than the British administrative period from 1885 to 1947. This is not to say that there are no continual existences of people's livelihoods in both rural and urban communities throughout Burmese history in a *stable and productive* manner. However, these "stable" and "productive" institutional parts of Burmese culture are largely unincorporated as an essential part of the political structure of society, namely "the constitution for governance."

Burma is now in a transition to democracy. The serious quest for this change by the Burmese people began in 1988 after the student-led popular uprising challenged the "Burmese Way to Socialism" under General Ne Win's government. On August 8, 1988, people throughout Burma marched in the streets of cities and towns demanding a more liberalized political system. The people's movement ended with the military coup on September 18, 1988. The military government known as State Peace and Development Council (SPDC) promised to transform the country to a "modern and developed" nation. In 1990, it held a democratic election. The National League for Democracy (NLD), led by Daw Aung Suu Kyi, won the election. The military government refused to transfer the power to the elected government on the grounds that the emergence of a new constitution should precede any transfer of power. Accordingly, the SPDC has single-handedly convened the National Convention that is charged to draft a new constitution.

At present, Burma is in a "constitutional moment." This constitutional moment can be considered as the juncture of both unproductive orders and productive orders. There are at least two challenges at the frontier of the constitutional moment in Burma.

The first challenge is for the emergence of a constitutional order. This challenge amplifies the historically unresolved issue of constitutional choice. The public and the majority of politicians in Burma view the constitution as a foundation for a political transformation to productive orders rather than just a foundation for a legal system. Legal systems and political systems are different. Legal systems clearly outline a set of rules or serve as a social contract that society as a whole views as parameters of civic behaviors. Political systems function on a deeper societal level. The Burmese people, who believe government is one of their enemies, consider the constitution as a means to define and limit governmental power and to maintain some level of order. They do not view a constitution as an absolute parameter of their behaviors for conducting human relationships and interactions.

Therefore, the challenge in constitutional thinking for the emergence of a new and productive order in Burma is not to equate Burma's need for broader political transition with the need for a legalistic constitution to legitimize the newly emerged government or political transition because the emergence of a new constitution does not necessarily guarantee productive orders in Burma. For the constitution to set parameters for civic behaviors, it is important in the Burmese context that the rule of law framed by the constitution reflects the social beliefs and social elements of the people. The challenge for the constitutional framers is to include the values that dominate the daily lives of people in Burma in the new constitution. If a newly emerged constitution is closer to the traditional social elements of livelihoods of different communities of Burma, it may support and lead political transformations to occur in Burma.

The second challenge is to introduce the rule of law system in Burma. The system of rule of law is important to maintain political and economic stability as well as to foster economic and social progress. Burma had a short history of a parliamentary democratic system from 1948 to 1962, in which the rule of law system began to emerge. Scholars such as Dr. Maung Maung, who served the rule by law system of General Ne Win, argued that it was difficult to discover the Burmese social elements and customary laws (Maung Maung 1963, 27). Any new government has to deal with this difficulty. One way in dealing with this difficulty is to decentralize or federalize[9] legal and political systems with polycentric orders by giving more authority to local governments, communities, and by championing citizen-sovereignty, which is understood in Burmese history as the freedom to self-govern. This freedom to self-govern, or *koh kyan mar ko phan ti maeh sate dart* in Burmese, was one of the rallying points for the Burmese independence struggle. This can be a basis for reimagining a newly productive order in Burma.

Acknowledgments

The author is grateful for a two-year postdoctoral fellowship from the Workshop in Political Theory and Policy Analysis and School of Law at Indiana University, Bloomington, from 2005 to 2007. The author would also like to thank Patty Lezotte and David Price at the Workshop for their editorial assistance with this article.

Notes

1. Furnivall's analysis of the role of local livelihood practices and institutional foundations in colonial administrations in Indonesia by the Dutch and Burma by the

British provides a crucial insight on the challenges of implanting a Western model of government on Burmese society.

2. "Shin" is the title used to address a monk.

3. The Ava dynasty is one of the early dynasties that started establishing relationships with India and Italy in the further west. During this period, Italian Reverend Father Sangermano visited and established a mission in Burma in 1782, and later wrote one of the earliest works by western scholars entitled *A Description of the Burmese Empire* (1833).

4. Nat(s) is the term that refers to the goddesses or spirits of different kinds. Some people still believe in different nats in Burma today.

5. The name of the village where the cease-fire treaty was signed after the first Anglo-Burmese war.

6. See Burma Reforms Committee, *Record of Evidence*, II, p. 73, Rangoon, 1922.

7. See Furnivall's foreword to *Burma's Constitution* by Maung Maung (1961, xi). Furnivall made earlier analysis of British Burma and the effect of the British rule on Burma in his seminal work, *Colonial Policy and Practice* (1948, 216, 297, 470).

8. See *The First Interim Report*, Administration Reorganization Committee, Rangoon, 1949. Especially see Bo Khin Gale's note of dissent in this report.

9. The term "federal" here means a power and authority-sharing system between the union government and state, division, and local governments. In the military regime's view, the term "federal" is misunderstood as "disintegrated" while in practices in other federal republics in the world, it means the opposite. This notion of interpretation of language "federal" is perhaps the most important "trap" in reconciliation of views in Burmese politics between the regime and other parties.

References

Callahan, Mary P. 2003. *Making Enemies: War and State Building in Burma*. Ithaca, NY: Cornell University Press.
Forchammer, Emanuel. 1885. "On the Sources and Development of Burmese Law from the Era of the First Introduction of the Indian Law to the Time of the British Occupation of Pegu." The Jardine Prize Essay. Rangoon, Burma: Rangoon Government Press.
Furnivall, John S. 1948. *Colonial Policy and Practice: A Comparative Study of Burma and Netherlands India*. Cambridge: Cambridge University Press.
Gaung, Kinwun Mingyi. 1898. *A Digest of the Burmese Buddhist Law*. Rangoon, Burma: Superintendent Government Printing.
Harvey, G. E. 1967. *History of Burma: From the Earliest Times to 10 March, 1824, the Beginning of the English Conquest*. London: Cass.
Houtman, Gustaaf. 1999. *Mental Culture in Burmese Crisis Politics: Aung San Suu Kyi and the National League for Democracy*. Study of Languages and Cultures of

Asia and Africa Monograph Series No. 33. Tokyo University of Foreign Studies, Institute for the Study of Languages and Cultures of Asia and Africa.

Htin Aung, M. 1962. *Burmese Law Tales*. London: Oxford University Press.

———. 1970. *Burmese History before 1287: A Defense of the Chronicles*. London: Oxford University Press.

Kyi, Aung San Suu. 1991. *Freedom from Fear*. New York: Penguin Books.

Maung, E. 1951. *The Expansion of Burmese Law*. New York: Cornell University Press.

Maung, Maung. 1961. *Burma's Constitution*. 2nd ed. The Hague: Martinus Nijhoff.

———. 1963. *Law and Custom in Burma and the Burmese Family*. The Hague: Martinus Nijhoff.

Sangermano, Reverend Father Vincentius. 1833. *A Description of the Burmese Empire: Compiled Chiefly from Native Documents*. London: Santiago de Compostela, Susil Gupta.

Stevenson, H. N. C. 1943. *The Central Chin Tribes*. Bombay: Times of India Press.

Taylor, Robert H. 1987. *The State in Burma*. Honolulu: University of Hawaii Press.

Tin, Pe Maung, and G. H. Luce. [1923] 1960. *Hmannan Yazawin—The Glass Palace Chronicle of the Kings of Burma*. Rangoon, Burma: Rangoon University Press.

Tinker, Hugh. 1961. "A Short Survey of Burmese History." *The Guardian* (English-language monthly magazine), Rangoon, Burma, December.

Vincent, Frank, Jr. 1874. *The Land of the White Elephant: Sights and Scenes in South-Eastern Asia: A Personal Narrative of Travel and Adventure*. New York: Harper & Brothers.

11

American Experience in Metropolitan Governance

Vincent Ostrom

I have been asked to make a presentation on patterns of metropolitan government in the United States. Before such matters can be explored with mutual understanding, it is first necessary to recognize that we confront a basic problem of how we think about a system of governance in human societies. My presentation is based upon a presupposition that two fundamentally different approaches are possible. One might be called a state-centered, or government-centered, approach. Historically, the English-speaking world has tended to use the term *government* rather than *state*. The opposite tendency exists in other languages. In the German language, for example, reference to *der Staat* is pervasive. A political order would be referred to as a *Staatsordnung*. Much the same tendency occurs, however, whether reference is made to "the government" or "the state." There is a presumption that the government governs society or equivalently that the state rules over society. Discourse among the English-speaking countries is increasingly using the term *state* with a presupposition that nation-states are the basic reality in the modern political world.

Another way of conceptualizing how some human societies are governed, especially those that conceive of themselves as democracies, is to think of them as self-governing societies rather than state-governed societies. The distinction was explicitly recognized approximately one hundred and fifty years ago when Tocqueville wrote his account of *Democracy in America*. He characterized three types of political orders. "In some countries," Tocqueville asserts, "a power exists which, though it is in a degree foreign to the social body, directs it, and forces it to pursue a certain track" ([1835–1840] 1945, I:57). This is the circumstance where we could speak of "the state" or "the government" as ruling over society. Tocqueville recognizes an intermediate condition that he considers as applicable to some European countries where "the ruling force is divided, being partly within and partly without the ranks of the people" ([1835–1840] 1945). We can then imagine the crown and the bureaucracy as representing the state; and parliamentary institutions and institutions of local self-government as occurring within the ranks of the people as members of society. Tocqueville then goes on to assert: "But nothing of the kind is to be seen in the United States; there society governs itself for itself" ([1835–1840] 1945). This third type is what I would characterize as a self-governing society (V. Ostrom [1971] 2008b).

I would further infer that Tocqueville's interest in doing a study of democracy in America was stimulated by this distinction between a state-governed society and a self-governing society. At the end of his first chapter on the physical features ("exterior form") of the North American continent, Tocqueville presents his analytical task in the following observation:

> In that land the great experiment of the attempt to construct society upon a new basis was to be made by civilized man; and it was there, for the first time, that theories hitherto unknown, or deemed impracticable, were to exhibit a spectacle for which the world had not been prepared by the history of the past. ([1835–1840] 1945, 25)

This might be viewed as a key transitional paragraph where an author is indicating to a reader the essential thrust of what is to follow. If we follow this clue, Tocqueville is indicating that (1) a great experiment was occurring on the North American continent to construct society on a new basis, (2) that such an effort drew upon theories "hitherto unknown or deemed impracticable," and (3) that this experiment exhibited "a spectacle for which the world had not been prepared by the history of the past." In other words, something had occurred in the patterns of human governance that might be characterized as intellectually revolutionary in proportions.

But these developments drew upon ideas and experiences that had been generated in European circumstances. These tendencies were most strongly manifest in the United Provinces, in the Swiss Confederation, and in the revolutionary struggles of the Puritans and Independents in England and the Presbyterians in Scotland, and more generally in the tradition of the free cities of Europe. Northern Italy, in particular, was the homeland of many of the free cities of Europe that became centers of European enlightenment and of republican traditions of self-governance.

If we take the essential core of Tocqueville's analysis, we see that the basic presuppositions applicable to self-governance were derived from Jewish and

Christian theology. So far as Tocqueville is concerned, religion is "the first of their political institutions" even though "[r]eligion in America takes no direct part in the government of society" ([1835–1840] 1945, 305). In American experience, the basic conceptions that informed American democracy gained expression in Puritan theology that "corresponded in many points with the most absolute democratic and republican theories" ([1835–1840] 1945, 32). The kernel of that theology, and associated political theory, was the concept of covenant. The Puritans drew upon the concept of covenant to relate themselves to God, the eternal, and to constitute themselves as a church organized in self-governing congregations and as a civil society constituted in self-governing communities. These communities were organized in accordance with explicitly stated rules establishing the terms and conditions of governance binding upon all in the same way that God's commandments were binding upon all who partake in a covenantal relationship with God. Covenantal principles of being bound by mutual consent grounded in the fundamental moral precept that one should do unto others as you would have others do unto you, became the basis for organizing self-governing congregations in the Congregationalist tradition and self-governing communities in a republican and democratic tradition.

Acting in relation to covenantal arrangements for specifying the terms and conditions of governments is what Tocqueville refers to as "the law of laws" ([1835–1840] 1945, 56) and as the "sovereignty of the people" ([1835–1840] 1945, 55). Gratian, the great Italian student of canon law, had much earlier recognized that the principle of all law, as he conceptualized law, is "the timeless principle that we should do unto others as we would have them do unto us" (Tierney 1982, 13). The golden rule, thus, is the foundation for a method of normative inquiry that enables human beings who use that method to formulate, use, apply, and enforce mutually agreeable rules of law that meet standards of fairness and justice. Gratian understood that such a method could be used to harmonize and resolve contradictions, anomalies, and conflicts of law to create a "concord of discordant canons" as he characterized his codification of canon law. This same method can be used for processing conflict and achieving conflict resolution and building the corpus of law in a self-governing society.

It was the application of this method of normative inquiry—this law of laws—that came out of the townships in New England and was used to organize the counties, the states, and the Federal Union in what became the United States of America. Thus, the Constitution of the United States was, as Tocqueville asserts: "in fact nothing more than a summary of those republican principles which were current in the whole community before it existed, and independently of its existence" ([1835–1840] 1945, I:59).

The principles used to constitute republican institutions of government are reasonably well understood as those principles apply to constitutional government. The basic challenge in creating a system of constitutional government is (1) to specify the terms and conditions of government by processes of constitutional deliberation and choice conducted through popular initiative and referenda, and not controlled by the narrowly-construed instrumentalities of government and (2) setting those terms and conditions of government so as to achieve an enforceable system of constitutional law where everyone exercises basic prerogatives of government and no one exercises unlimited authority. These conditions can be met through three types of provisions. The *first* pertains to the constitutional authority of persons and citizens to exercise basic inalienable rights to govern their own affairs and participate in an open public realm (*res publica*) subject to correlative limits upon the authority of specialized instrumentalities of government. The *second* pertains to a division of labor allocating specialized and limited authority to legislative, executive, judicial, and other specialized instrumentalities of government subject to correlative constraints or veto capabilities. The *third* type of provision is to establish methods for citizens to participate directly or indirectly in the formal structures and processes of governance. The election of representatives to exercise limited prerogatives of government is a mode of indirect participation. Service on juries is a mode by which citizens participate directly in the judicial instrumentalities of government. If such structural arrangements are applied to all units of government in highly federalized systems of government where each unit of government functions as a self-governing republic in a complexly organized system of compound republics, the aggregate effect is to create an open public realm where all authority is subject to limits and no one exercises unlimited authority. The aggregate system manifests equilibrating tendencies where "power" is used "to check power," as expressed by Montesquieu ([1748] 1977, 200) through "opposite and rival interests," as expressed by Madison (Hamilton, Jay, and Madison [1787–1788] 1941, 337). Such systems manifest emergent properties by the way that the parts interact with one another rather than being subject to control by a single dominating part. Among these emergent properties is the achievement of civic education, error-correcting capabilities, and innovations and change in the evolution of human civilization.

Intellectual traditions of the late nineteenth and twentieth centuries are apt to focus upon "republican principles" as these apply to the representative character of central governmental institutions to the neglect of "*res publica*"— the open public realm—that is constitutive of any republic. It is this emphasis upon representation principles in the organization of central governments to the neglect of "*res publica*"—the open public realm—that has given rise to a state-centered mode of analysis. This mode of analysis has come to dominate the presuppositions that have applied to governmental reform and administrative reorganization both in the United States and in Europe (V. Ostrom [1973] 2008a).

Woodrow Wilson in *Congressional Government*, for example, explicitly builds upon a state-centered mode of analysis. He assumes that any system of government is to be characterized by "the essential machinery of power" where "[t]here is always a centre of power" (1956, 30). The basic task of inquiry then is to determine "where in this system is that centre? in whose hands is self-sufficient authority lodged and through what agencies does that authority speak and act?" (1956, 30). Wilson viewed Congress as "the predominant and controlling force, the centre and source of all motive and of all regulative power" (1956, 31) in the American system of government. *American government* from this perspective was *Congressional government*.

Constitutional limits such as those associated with a separation of powers and an equilibrating system of checks and balances, according to Wilson, had "proved mischievous just to the extent to which they have succeeded in establishing themselves as realities" (1956, 187). These checks and balances, thus, are construed as the primary source of institutional failure in the American system of government. Wilson asserts that "the more power is divided the more irresponsible it becomes" (1956, 77). Wilson views the natural tendency, then, in any system of republican government "to exalt the representative body, the people's parliament, to a position of absolute supremacy" (1956, 203). Representative government and bureaucratic administration in a unitary republic became the essential components of what is presumed to be the appropriate way to constitute a democratic system of government.

These basic principles, derived from a state-centered political theory, were relied upon in formulating principles of governmental reform and administrative reorganization for creating metropolitan governments. Fragmentation of authority and overlapping jurisdictions were viewed as the primary source of institutional failure in American local government. Each metropolitan area was viewed as a unified whole requiring a unity of power that could address all metropolitan problems in a comprehensive way. The appropriate mode of metropolitan government, viewed from this perspective, was to merge all existing units of government into a single unit of metropolitan government where legislative authority would be exercised by a self-sufficient legislative body and an executive apparatus would be organized in a bureaucratic command structure accountable to a single unified metropolitan chief executive officer (E. Ostrom 1972).

When reference is made to metropolitan government, accompanied by a presupposition that governments govern, there is a strong tendency for an exclusive and unitary instrumentality of government to be identified as "the" metropolitan government. Such a government would exercise supreme authority over a metropolitan region. This approach might be contrasted to the conceptualization of a metropolis constituted as a compound republic composed of diverse self-governing communities of relationships conducted in accordance with covenantal principles (Bish 1971; Bish and Ostrom 1973). To pursue this inquiry further, I shall shift from this issue of how we think about and constitute systems of governance to another theoretical issue pertaining to a theory of goods. Work on the theory of goods in contemporary economic theory enables us to make basic distinctions between private market economies and public economies (V. Ostrom, Tiebout, and Warren 1961). After pursuing this analysis and its implications for metropolitan governance, I shall in conclusion return to some of the implications that follow from the constitution of self-governing societies as against state-governed societies.

The Theory of Goods and the Organization of Public Economies

When we think of goods in the context of market relationships, two basic characteristics usually apply. One of these characteristics pertains to exclusion. Exclusion occurs when a vendor can exclude a potential customer from acquiring that good and enjoying it unless the potential customer meets the terms and conditions of the vendor. This is usually specified in price so that pricing is normally associated with market arrangements where the principle of exclusion prevails. Another characteristic of many goods subject to market transactions is that such a good is subtractable in consumption. When a good is subtractable in consumption, its consumption by one individual or one family means that the good is not available for others to use or consume.

There are, however, circumstances where contrary conditions apply. In some circumstances, exclusion cannot feasibly be achieved or is considered undesirable. The contrary condition to subtractability in consumption is where jointness of use prevails. When goods are fully subtractable in their use or consumption, no jointness of use prevails. We may have circumstances however where jointness prevails with partial subtractability. Under such conditions, congestion can be expected to occur beyond certain thresholds so that when increasing demand occurs that demand is accompanied by increas-

| | | Jointness of use or consumption ||
		Alternative use	Joint use
E X C L U S I O N	Feasible	*Private goods:* bread, shoes, automobiles, books, etc.	*Toll goods:* theaters, night clubs, telephone service, toll roads, cable TV, electric power, library, etc.
	Infeasible	*Common-pool resource units:* water pumped from a groundwater basin, fish taken from an ocean, crude oil extracted from an oil pool, etc.	*Public goods:* peace and security of a community, national defense, mosquito abatement, air pollution control, fire protection, streets, weather forecasts, etc.

Figure 11.1. Types of goods.
Source: V. Ostrom and E. Ostrom (1977, 12).

ing congestion such as occurs in many public facilities like streets, highways, parks, and so forth.

We can array these different characteristics as in figure 11.1. The rows represent the circumstances where exclusion is feasible or infeasible. The columns represent a dichotomization of jointness of use such that jointness does not prevail and goods are subtractable as against the circumstance where jointness prevails. When we array these basic characteristics in the simplified device of a 2x2 table, we can derive the following types of goods. Goods subject to exclusion and subtractable in use are easily subject to market arrangements as private goods. Goods that are subject to joint use, but where exclusion is feasible, can be defined as toll goods. In such circumstances, market arrangements are feasible as with a tall bridge, a toll road, or a theater. Jointness of use occurs, but it is feasible to levy a charge for each user of that joint facility. Problems arise in such circumstances with regard to regulating the patterns of use that do not arise in the consumption of goods that are fully subtractable.

We may, however, have goods where exclusion is infeasible, and these are the types of goods for which we rely upon forms of association that have the essential characteristics of a "government." A class of events viewed as goods have the characteristics that exclusion is difficult to achieve (infeasible) and where the use by one is subtractable, at least in part, from its use by others. These can be identified as common-property or common-pool resources. A standard example might be a fishery. Each fish captured is fully subtractable. Anyone who catches a fish precludes anyone else from capturing that particular fish. But fish occur in fisheries where exclusion is difficult to achieve. Problems of collective organization arise when demand exceeds supply. Unless appropriate measures are taken, the exploitation of a fishery may yield what has been identified in the literature as a "tragedy of the commons" (Hardin 1968). In the extreme case, this may mean the destruction of the fishery.

An analogous pattern is operable in the use of many public facilities. Streets, highways, and public parks, for example, may be subject to congestion as demand exceeds the supply. Problems of congestion may become such that some patterns of use will drive out other patterns of use to a point where a public facility, not properly maintained and regulated, may become a public bad rather than a public good (Buchanan 1970).

Where exclusion of individuals from access to a good or service is infeasible and where conditions of jointness exist in either the use of a good or service or a common-property resource or facility, a latent community of interest exists on the part of all of those who make joint use. In this circumstance, a puzzle arises because anyone within the domain of that latent community of users cannot be excluded and thus will enjoy whatever service, resource, or facility is available. If choice is a purely voluntary matter, some individuals will have an incentive to enjoy that which is available without assuming a proportionate share of the burden for making the service available or for managing the resource or public facility. This is what gives rise to the need for collective organization and collective decision-making arrangements so that actions can be taken on behalf of the community of users when exclusion is infeasible.

Collective organization, however, can be achieved in relation to identifiable communities of users where a fit can be achieved between the jointness of use and the domain that pertains to resource, facility, or good or service in question. To have recourse only to the central authorities in a state will fail to proportion supply and demand and coordinate the management of the resource, facility, or service to the patterns of use that might appropriately be made. Both the material conditions of the natural world and preferences and ways of life in human communities are sufficiently diverse so as to require diverse regimes rather than uniformity of optimal results are to be achieved.

These problems of collective organization that derive from the failure of exclusion and/or jointness of use pertain to the organization of consumption in a public economy. The task is how to resolve the hold-out or free-rider and devise an alternative to the pricing mechanism to cover costs in the provision of public goods or services (Olson 1965). Taxes serve as substitutes for prices. The compulsory nature of a tax means that payment is required without regard for the preferences of those who make joint use of a public resource, facility, or service. The constitution of collective decision-making arrangements thus requires recourse to diverse decision structures having reference to voting, representation, and decision rules for translating and aggregating individual preferences into collective decisions.

The critical aspects of collective organization in a public economy then turn upon the collective organization of consumption functions pertaining to the failure of exclusion as applied to individuals and to jointness of use as among some community of users. In a world where domain of the relevant resources, facilities, and services may range from neighborhoods to global proportions, many different communities of interest amenable to collective organization may exist. A public economy might, thus, have recourse to many diverse and autonomous forms of collective organization pertaining to the diverse, overlapping communities of interest having to do with different resources, facilities, and services that are subject to jointness of use.

When appropriate forms of collective organization are achieved for resolving the problems of jointness of use in a public economy, a variety of options become available for organizing the management or supply of such goods or services. A collective consumption unit, organized to take collective decisions, can employ its own staff as a production unit. Alternatively, it might contract with a private vendor or the staff of some other collectivity to supply the service. In such a case, it might function as a consumer cooperative where its own staff functions more as a buyer responsible for monitoring the services supplied by vendors. Or, it might rely upon some combination of using its own staff to supply some services in coordination with other vendors supplying other services.

The availability of choice to collective consumption units in arranging the supply of public goods and services carries radical implications. The possibility of collective consumption units contracting with alternative vendors to supply public goods and services means that quasi-market conditions can exist in a public economy. This opportunity is enhanced with increasing fragmentation and overlap among the governmental jurisdictions that function in the public economy of a metropolitan region. The circumstance that distinguishes quasi-market arrangements in a public economy from a standard market arrangement is that transactions occur between collective consumption units and production units rather than between individuals and firms as buyers and individuals or firms as sellers in standard market arrangements.

As soon as such arrangements are recognized as possible, then patterns of coordination in systems of governance become achievable through diverse processes associated with competitive rivalry, cooperation, and conflict and conflict resolution apart from principles of order associated with superior-subordinate relationships inherent in bureaucratic organization. Contractual arrangements are themselves institutional arrangements that cannot only function to exchange goods and services in market economies but to constitute forms of economic organization and power structures in systems of governance. When metropolitan regions are organized as compound republics, the configuration of organizational arrangements in the public economy of a metropolitan area yields emergent properties where contractual arrangements become constitutive of multiorganizational arrangements amenable to a great variety of productive potentials (Gregg 1974).

The possibility also exists that contractual arrangements can be used by some to exploit others as in the organization of cartels. The productive potential that arises from multiorganizational forms in the governance of a metropolis thus requires more careful attention to monitoring arrangements and to institutional arrangements for processing conflict and conflict resolution than might otherwise be the case in a private market economy. Nonetheless, alternatives are possible in organizing patterns of governance in metropolitan areas by multiple, overlapping jurisdictions as distinguished from a simple unitary structure.

Critical Assessment and Performance Evaluation

Numerous studies have been done to assess performance of more highly fragmented, as against more highly integrated, metropolitan areas in the United States. These studies are more fully reported in an Italian-language publication, *Il governo locale negli Stati Uniti*, prepared by the Olivetti Foundation (V. Ostrom, Bish, and E. Ostrom 1984; see also English version, 1988). Quasi-market conditions can feasibly exist in the public sector allowing for a mix of different organizational arrangements including units of government, voluntary nonprofit associations, private enterprises, administrative agencies, and judicial instrumentalities. Potential for privatization exists in the public sector; but we must approach those potentials with caution informed by appropriate analytical capabilities. Viewed from such a perspective, a highly federalized system of metropolitan government accompanied by extensive fragmentation of authority and overlapping jurisdictions can be expected, on theoretical grounds, to be at least as efficient and equitable as a system of metropolitan government marked by a unity of power and highly-integrated, bureaucratic, command structure.

- In the metropolitan areas that have been studied, the largest police departments consistently respond more slowly, face higher crime rates, and satisfy their citizens less effectively than smaller- to medium-sized departments serving matched neighborhoods (E. Ostrom 1983). In the most consolidated metropolitan areas, it takes more full-time officers on the force to support each officer actually on the street patrolling at any point in time. The more consolidated metropolitan areas employ nine hundred and fifty full-time officers for every one hundred officers on the street, compared with a working force of six hundred and fifty officers for every one hundred officers on the street in the less consolidated areas. New York City is the extreme case, employing (at the time of the study) three thousand full-time officers for every one hundred officers patrolling streets (Parks and Ostrom 1981).
- In another study, the performance of police departments was evaluated using the dual measures of police response capabilities (the number of police cars on the street per officer employed) and police crime performance (the number of clearances of crimes by arrest per officer). In a study of eighty metropolitan areas, it was found that the efficiency of the very best departments was greater in metropolitan areas with the largest number of police departments. The best departments in the least consolidated metropolitan areas performed better than the best departments in the most consolidated metropolitan areas (Parks 1985).
- An in-depth analysis of the effect of the structure of organizational arrangements at the metropolitan level revealed rather complex relationships. The highest police efficiency is achieved in metropolitan areas where there are only a few agency-producing radio communications and homicide investigations while direct services such as patrol are simultaneously supplied by many agencies exercising a high level of autonomy (Parks 1985).
- There is, thus, no single optimal scale of organization for the supply of all police services in a metropolitan area (E. Ostrom, Parks, and Whitaker 1975). Rather, organizing metropolitan areas so that diverse scales of operation exist for different types of services enhances the overall performance level in metropolitan areas. Fragmentation and overlap can enhance performance when the characteristics of particular services, and needs and resources of diverse communities being served, are taken into account.

Conclusion

If we are to understand the patterns of governance in democratic societies, much greater attention will need to be given to maintenance of an open public realm than to representative institutions as these apply to the organization of the central instrumentalities of government. By the open public realm, I mean *res publica*—the public thing—where ordinary people, as citizens, function in the governance of public affairs. The critical level pertains to the neighborhood, village, or town where people build the bonds of community, learn both how to govern their own affairs and to relate to one another in the governance of community affairs. Tocqueville was correct in recognizing that "Town meetings are to liberty what primary schools are to science; they bring it within the people's reach, they teach men how to use and how to enjoy it" ([1835–1840] 1945, I:61). It is in the context of village or town affairs that people learn how to govern their own affairs in a public realm that is open and accessible to each individual. It is in such circumstances where individuals have enduring relationships with one another, where each has a known individuality grounded in a cumulative assessment, and where the method of the golden rule is the foundation for a community of understanding that does not tolerate direct action against unknown persons in the name of "proletarian justice." When the governance of democratic republics is identified with a mere handful of governors, the multitudes of citizens lose their sense of reality about how ways of life in self-governing societies are based upon that fundamental political process that we learn by doing unto others as we would have others do unto us.

This principle is not confined to American experience in metropolitan governance. Gratian long ago understood how to build a system of jurisprudence and create concord among discordant canons by the use of such a method. The grandeur of Rome and the Roman law needs to be contemplated in relation to the place of the free cities of Italy in the emergence of the European Renaissance and the development of modern civilization. American experience in metropolitan governance would suggest that self-governing urban villages nested in self-governing communities functioning in self-governing metropolitan regions can function in a self-governing nation and become a part of a self-governing European Community. The traditions of the self-governing cities of Italy, liberated from the predations of imperial armies, offer the possibility of contributing to the building of a European civilization that is measured by their enhancement of self-governing capabilities. Such an edifice can be fashioned not by recourse to principles of dominance and force but by using the method of normative inquiry inherent in the golden rule to fashion processes of deliberation and choice that apply to all aspects of human relationships. It is by the use of such a method that human beings come to understand what it means to be self-governing so that freedom and order can coexist with one another. By such methods we learn to draw upon one another's ideas and experiences and open new horizons to human understanding and development.

Bibliographical Note

This chapter was initially presented at the Fourth International Conference on Urban Government, Milan, Italy, January 30, 1987. The theses advanced in this chapter draw heavily upon Harold Berman's *Law and Revolution* (1983), Brian Tierney's *Religion, Law and the Growth of Constitutional Thought, 1150–1650* (1982), Hans Albert's *Freiheit und Ordnung* (1986), and long conversations and discussions with Daniel Elazar and other colleagues in the Workshop in Covenant and Politics of the Center for the Study of Federalism (Elazar and Kincaid 1980). A fuller elaboration of these arguments is available in V. Ostrom (1986; see also chap. 2 in this volume).

These formulations are consistent with more traditional analyses offered by Montesquieu ([1748] 1977), Alexander Hamilton and James Madison in *The Federalist* ([1787–1788] 1941), and especially Tocqueville's work both in *Democracy in America* ([1835–1840] 1945) and *The Old Regime and the French Revolution* ([1856] 1955). The latter is an important complement to *Democracy in America* because it demonstrates the strong predatory tendencies in state-governed societies. On local government in the United States, see V. Ostrom, Bish, and E. Ostrom (1984).

References

Albert, Hans. 1986. *Freiheit und Ordnung: zwei Abhandlungen zum Problem einer offenen Gesellschaft*. Tübingen, Germany: J. C. B. Mohr.
Berman, Harold J. 1983. *Law and Revolution: The Formation of the Western Legal Tradition*. Cambridge, MA: Harvard University Press.
Bish, Robert. 1971. *The Public Economy of Metropolitan Areas*. Chicago: Markham.
Bish, Robert, and Vincent Ostrom. 1973. *Understanding Urban Government: Metropolitan Reform Reconsidered*. Washington, DC: American Enterprise Institute for Public Policy Research.
Buchanan, James M. 1970. "Public Goods and Public Bads." In *Financing the Metropolis*, Urban Affairs Annual Review, vol. 4, ed. John P. Crecine, 51–72. Beverly Hills, CA: Sage.
Elazar, Daniel J., and John Kincaid, eds. 1980. "Covenant, Polity, and Constitutionalism." *Publius* 10(4) (fall): 1–185.

Gregg, Phillip M. 1974. "Units and Levels of Analysis: A Problem of Policy Analysis in Federal Systems." *Publius* 4(4) (fall): 59–86.

Hamilton, Alexander, John Jay, and James Madison. [1787–1788] 1941. *The Federalist*. Ed. Edward Mead Earle. New York: Modern Library.

Hardin, Garrett. 1968. "The Tragedy of the Commons." *Science* 162:1243–48.

Montesquieu, Charles-Louis de Secondat, baron de. [1748] 1977. *The Spirit of Laws: A Compendium of the First English Edition*. Ed. with introduction, notes, and appendices by David Wallace Carrithers. Berkeley: University of California Press.

Olson, Mancur, Jr. 1965. *The Logic of Collective Action: Public Goods and the Theory of Groups*. Cambridge: Harvard University Press.

Ostrom, Elinor. 1972. "Metropolitan Reform: Propositions Derived from Two Traditions." *Social Science Quarterly* 53(3) (December): 474–93. Reprinted in Michael D. McGinnis, ed., *Polycentricity and Local Public Economies: Readings from the Workshop in Political Theory and Policy Analysis* (Ann Arbor: University of Michigan Press, 1999, 139–60).

———. 1983. "A Public Choice Approach to Metropolitan Institutions: Structure, Incentives, and Performance." *Social Science Journal* 20(3) (July): 79–96.

Ostrom, Elinor, Roger B. Parks, and Gordon P. Whitaker. 1975. "Defining and Measuring Structural Variations in Interorganizational Arrangements." *Publius* 4(4) (fall): 87–108. Reprinted in Michael D. McGinnis, ed., *Polycentricity and Local Public Economies: Readings from the Workshop in Political Theory and Policy Analysis* (Ann Arbor: University of Michigan Press, 1999, 265–83).

Ostrom, Vincent. 1986. "Constitutional Foundations for a Theory of System Comparisons: An Inquiry into Problems of Incommensurability, Emergent Properties, and Development." Paper presented at the Radein Research Seminar, Milan, Italy, February 14–25, 1987.

———. [1973] 2008a. *The Intellectual Crisis in American Public Administration*. 3rd ed. Tuscaloosa: University of Alabama Press.

———. [1971] 2008b. *The Political Theory of a Compound Republic: Designing the American Experiment*. 3rd ed. Lanham, MD: Lexington Books.

Ostrom, Vincent, Robert Bish, and Elinor Ostrom. 1984. *Il governo locale negli Stati Uniti*. Milano, Italy: Centro Studi della Fondazione Adriano Olivetti, Edizioni di Comunità.

———. 1988. *Local Government in the United States*. San Francisco, CA: ICS Press.

Ostrom, Vincent, and Elinor Ostrom. 1977. "Public Goods and Public Choices." In *Alternatives for Delivering Public Services: Toward Improved Performance*, ed. E. S. Savas, 7–49. Boulder, CO: Westview Press. Reprinted in Michael D. McGinnis, ed., *Polycentricity and Local Public Economies: Readings from the Workshop in Political Theory and Policy Analysis* (Ann Arbor: University of Michigan Press, 1999, 75–103).

Ostrom, Vincent, Charles M. Tiebout, and Robert Warren. 1961. "The Organization of Government in Metropolitan Areas: A Theoretical Inquiry." *American Political*

Science Review 55(4) (December): 831–42. Reprinted in Michael D. McGinnis, ed., *Polycentricity and Local Public Economies: Readings from the Workshop in Political Theory and Policy Analysis* (Ann Arbor: University of Michigan Press, 1999, 31–51).

Parks, Roger B. 1985. "Metropolitan Structure and Systemic Performance: The Case of Police Service Delivery." In *Policy Implementation in Federal and Unitary Systems*, ed. Kenneth Hanf and Theo A. J. Toonen, 161–91. Dordrecht, the Netherlands: Martinus Nijhoff.

Parks, Roger B., and Elinor Ostrom. 1981. "Complex Models of Urban Service Systems." In *Urban Policy Analysis: Directions for Future Research*, ed. Terry N. Clark, 171–99. Beverly Hills, CA: Sage. Reprinted in Michael D. McGinnis, ed., *Polycentricity and Local Public Economies: Readings from the Workshop in Political Theory and Policy Analysis* (Ann Arbor: University of Michigan Press, 1999, 355–80).

Tierney, Brian. 1982. *Religion, Law and the Growth of Constitutional Thought, 1150–1650*. Cambridge: Cambridge University Press.

Tocqueville, Alexis de. [1835–1840] 1945. *Democracy in America*. 2 vols. Ed. Phillips Bradley. New York: Alfred A. Knopf.

———. [1856] 1955. *The Old Regime and the French Revolution*. Trans. Stuart Gilbert. Garden City, NY: Doubleday, Anchor Books.

Wilson, Woodrow. 1956. *Congressional Government: A Study in American Politics*. New York: Meridian Books.

Index

absolutism, 17, 86, 88–89, 93
Akhtar, Shabbir, 70–71
Ali, Yusuf, 69
Allende, Salvador, 153, 166–67, 170
Alternative Dispute Resolution (ADR), 49. *See also* conflict resolution
Alzérreca, José Miguel, 176n6
Amin, Idi, 79
Anglo-Burmese War, 193–94; Yandabo cease-fire treaty, 194
antarctic resources, 50
Araharn, Shin, 184
aristocracy, 13
Arrow paradox. *See* impossibility theorem
Asad, Muhammad, 69, 71–72
Ashby, W. R., 7, 22–24
Australia, 173
Austria, 92
authoritarian regimes, 85, 145, 167
autocratic regimes, 8
Aylwin, Patricio, 167
Aztec civilization, 103

Bachelet, Michelle, 173–74
Bagehot, Walter, 3, 18
Balkanization. *See* tragedy of the commons
Banda, Hastings, 145

barbarism, 104
Barbosa, Orozimbo, 175n2, 176n6
Bengal, 100
Berman, Harold, 48–50
Böhm, Franz, 112
Boulding, Kenneth, 29, 36
British India Empire, 194; Burma Reforms Committee (1922), 195
Buddha, 73
buddhism, 103; in Burmese society, 184–85, 188, 190–91, 195; principle of karma, 188–90; Ten Duties of Government, 191–93; view of kingship, 191
Bull, Hedley, 51
Buonarroti, Filippo, 88
burden-shredding, 125–26
Burkhardt, Jacob, 103
Burma, 4; Ava dynasty, 189; Burmese Way to Socialism, 196–97; Dhammathats, 183, 185–88; first Burmese kingdom of Pagan, 184–85; formalization of legal system, 185, 187; Great Mon-Khmer Empire, 184; influence of British administration on, 194; legal theory in, 188, 193; National League for Democracy (NLD), 190, 197; state building in, 183, 196; State Peace and

Development Council (SPDC), 197;
Village Act (1886), 194–95. *See also*
buddhism

California water "industry", 4
Callahan, Mary P., 183
Canada, Confederation (1867), 97;
opening of Welland Canal, 100
canon law, 50, 203
capitalism, 113, 120
cartels, 210
Carter, Stephen, 59
Catholic Church, 49–50, 86; in Chile,
153, 157, 159, 172, 176n7
Cattaneo, Carlo, 6, 86, 90–98,
100–102, 105; conception of the
individual, 101–2, 104; conception
of the state, 101–4; features of the
city, 98–100
Cavour, Camillo, 90, 96, 105
centralized economy, 15, 115, 117–18
checks and balances, on concentrated
powers, 7, 14–15, 30–31, 39, 45, 47,
91, 126, 204–5
Chile, 4; amnesty decree (1978),
153–55, 168–69, 171, 174; Battle of
Lircay (1830), 160; Caja de Seguro
Obrero massacre (1938), 158, 176n3;
civil wars, 152–53, 156–60, 167;
Commission to Investigate the Acts
of the Dictatorship (1931), 165, 169;
Constitution (1833), 157, 160–61;
Constitution (1980), 167, 169–70,
172; general amnesty (1861), 160;
National Commission on Political
Imprisonment and Torture, 162, 168;
National Truth and Reconciliation
Commission, 162, 168; *la patria*,
156–58, 162, 164, 166–67; political
repression in, 158, 164–65, 168–69;
Ranquil massacre (1934), 158,
175n3, 176n3; suppression and
reconstruction of social memory, 159,
161–63, 172; UDI party, 169, 173;
Valech Commission, 171–73
China, 25, 58, 103–4
Cold War, 167
collective action, 31, 41–42, 66–69,
75–76, 78, 80–81, 112, 208–9
collective authority, 31
collective choice, 5, 40, 76, 85–86,
91–92, 104
collective consumption unit, 21, 209
collective security, 71. *See also*
disarmament
common-pool resources, 207–8; "free-
rider" problem, 41–42, 66, 81–83,
136–37, 139, 145, 208; management
of, 21–22, 41, 50, 135–36, 209
common-property management,
135–36, 142
Commons, John R., 3
communism, 168
communitarian view of society, 88
community-based organizations, 52, 57
community of understanding (ethical
consensus), 19, 32–34, 37–40, 42,
49, 53, 67–68, 94, 97–98, 212
compound republics 12, 14, 98, 204,
206, 210. *See also* patterns of order,
polycentric
conflict resolution, 21, 49–51, 53–54,
57, 203, 210; in Chile, 152, 156–62,
165–66, 170, 172–73; in Malawi,
126, 144; peace-building, 57, 59
Confucius, 73, 103
Congregationalist tradition, 203
Congress of Vienna, 85–86
Constant, Benjamin, 87
constitutional choice, theory of, 5, 42,
86, 99, 197, 204
constitutional law, 6, 14, 38–39, 42,
204
constitutional monarchy, 88, 90, 93
constitutional rule, 11, 14–16, 20, 157
constitutionalism, 87, 98, 157, 204

constructivism, 76, 151
Coordination game, 66, 77, 79
Cornell University, 187
covenantal relationships, 19, 33, 46, 203, 206
Cuban Revolution, 167
cybernetics. *See* requisite variety, law of

democracy, 13–15, 59, 87, 197; Buddhist endorsement of, 193; constitutional, 11, 88; liberal, 89, 96, 105; social and cultural foundations of, 47–48, 88
democratization, 85–87, 105
Descartes, René, 113
despotism, 89
development assistance, 56, 59
Dhammavilasa (Ananda), Shin, 185
diplomacy, 49, 57
disarmament, 82
dispute resolution. *See* conflict resolution
division of labor, in rule-making, 14, 16–17, 31, 38–40, 204–5
Donaire, Manuel Contreras, 177n14

economics, discipline of, 112. *See also* Freiburg school of economics
Egypt, 116
electoral reform, 86
Encina, Francisco, 160
England, 87, 196, 202; constitution of, 18
environmental activists, 53, 67
environmental destruction, 68
equilibrating structures. *See* checks and balances
equity jurisprudence. *See* Alternative Dispute Resolution
Esack, Farid, 66, 74–75, 80–81
Eucken, Rudolf, 112
Eucken, Walter, 3, 7, 111–20; framework of economic orders (*Ordnungstheorie*), 115–17, 120; "Great Antinomy", 113–14, 118–20;
  implementation of economic policy (*Ordnungspolitik*), 117–18
Europe, reconstruction of (19th century), 86, 89, 92
European Union, 8, 25, 50, 212
European Renaissance, 212
evangelical Christians, 58, 69
exclusivism, religious, 68–70, 72, 74
externalities, 55; negative, 56, 58; positive, 56

faith-based organizations (FBO), 55–59; political activism of, 57–58
Faustian bargain, 34–35, 42
federalism, 104–5. *See also* United States, federalism
The Federalist, 6, 12, 46–48, 53
Ferrara, Francesco, 96
Ferrari, Giuseppe, 96
feudal laws, 50, 99
fisheries resource governance and management (RGM), in Malawi, 126–28, 133–34, 136, 139, 141, 144–45
Forchammer, Emanuel, 187
Foucauld, Charles de, 69
France, 17, 87, 90, 96, 116; coup d'état, 94–95; revolutionary bourgeoisie, 95
freedom, meaning of, 35
free trade, 86, 90
Frei, Eduardo, 166, 170
Freiburg school of economics, 111–12, 116–18; concept of economic constitution, 116
French Revolution, 47, 54, 86–90, 95
Furnivall, John S., 183, 195

Game theory, 66, 75–78, 105. *See also* Coordination game; Harmony game; Prisoner's dilemma
Garibaldi, Giuseppe, 97
Germany, 85, 116; post-World War II, 111–12

Ghazali, Abu Hamid, 69, 71
global ethic vision, 67, 75, 82
golden rule, 6–7, 13, 20–22, 24–25, 53–54, 203, 212–13
governability. *See* conflict resolution
governance, bottom-up (Malawi), 125, 133–34; global, 48, 53, 59; Ostrom's evaluation of, 5–7, 212; policy networks, 52–53, 56–57, 59; principles of, 3, 51–52; top-down (Burma), 183; top-down (Malawi), 140–41. *See also* self-governing societies; state-governed societies
Gramsci, Antonio, 95
Gratian, 20, 203, 212
Greenfield, Kent R., 92
Gregory VII (Pope), 50
Grew, Raymond, 87
Guizot, François, 87, 90
Guzmán, Jaime, 169

Hamilton, Alexander, 3, 12, 47–48, 53, 85; general theory of limited constitution, 47
Hardin, Garrett, 41
Harmony game, 66, 77–80
Hayek, F. A., 3, 112
Hegel, Georg Wilhelm Friederich, 90
Hensel, Paul, 3
Herder, Johann, 103
heterogeneity of society, 102, 104
Hobbes, Thomas, 3, 6, 12–13, 15–17, 22, 29, 31–33, 37, 46; laws of nature, 22, 29, 34, 36, 46–48; methodological individualism, 46; natural punishments, 6, 13, 15, 30, 54
Hobbesian state, 45, 47–48
Hoebel, E. A., 48–49, 153–54, 175
Holocaust, 167
Holy Roman Empire, 8, 50, 98
Hooghe, Liesbet, 52
Houtman, Gustaaf, 183

Htin Aung, U, 184
human beings, fallibility of, 11, 35–36, 151–52
humanitarian relief, 56, 59
human rights, 50, 53, 59; organizations, 53, 58, 171, 173; violations of, 153, 162, 167–70, 172, 174
Hume, David, 3, 6, 20, 40
Hutchison, T. W., 112

Ibáñez, Carlos, 164–67, 169, 176n7, 177n11, 178n15
ideas, nature of, 65–66
imperialism, 82
impossibility theorem, 32
inclusivism, religious, 68–69, 71–74
India, 15, 58, 103
Indiana University, 4, 151
individualism, 195
institutionalism, 111
Insunza, José Miguel, 180n36
interest groups, 53, 57
International Criminal Court (ICC), 53
international law, 50–51, 53, 170–72
international realism, 45–48
International Religious Freedom Act (1998, U.S.), 58
Internet, 50, 171
interorganizational level of analysis, 29–31, 40–42
Interreligious Liberative Collective Action (ILCA), 65–69, 74–76, 80
Islam, laws of, 57; mosques, 57; theology, 74. *See also* Quran
Italy, 25, 85–87, 164, 202, 212–13; Constitution of Sicily (1812), 89; eras of civil evolution, 98; free cities of, 88, 99, 212–13; *incivilmento*, 87, 89–91, 102; Lombard Plain, 102; revolts (1821, 1832), 94; revolts (1848), 93–94, 96; unification of, 85–88, 90–93, 96–98, 105

Jackson, Andrew, 90
Jacobinism, 88–89, 92
Japan, 102
Jay, John, 47–48
Jiménez, Tucapel, 177n14
jurisprudence, private-law versus public-law, 17

karma, as impediment to self-governing societies, 8. *See also* buddhism, in Burmese society
Keller, Nuh, 70
Kha, Min Thein, 191
Knitter, Paul, 66–68, 72, 74, 76–77, 80–82
Küng, Hans, 66–67, 80
Kyi, Daw Aung San Suu, 191, 197

labor relations, 116
Lagos, Ricardo, 170–73
language, for ordering relationships, 29, 32, 46, 54, 101–2, 152; personification of theoretical concepts, 120–21
Lao Tsue, 103
Lavín, Joaquín, 173
Leviathan, 3, 4, 12, 48, 183. *See also* Hobbes, Thomas
liberation theology, 65, 71
liberalism, 48, 86–87, 89, 92
Liberia, 100
Lira, Elizabeth, 152–53
Llewellyn, Karl, 48–49, 153–54, 175
logical positivism, 151
logic of situations, 21–22

Madison, James, 3, 12, 14, 25, 47–48, 204
Malawi, Area Fisheries Associations, 129, 131–32, 137, 139–41, 143, 147n8; Beach and River Village Committees, 129–33, 136–37, 139–41, 143–45, 147n8; Department of Fisheries, 127, 129, 132, 134, 137, 139–42, 145–46, 147n8; Fisheries Act (1974), 126; Fisheries Conservation and Management Act (1997), 126–28, 143; government of, 5, 125–27, 129, 133, 138, 140, 145–46, 147n8; Lake Chiuta Fisheries Association, 129, 131–33, 137, 139–40, 142–43; National Fisheries and Aquaculture Policy, 128, 131; *Nkatcha* net fishing, description of, 128
Mali, 147n6
manorial laws, 50, 99
market economy, 15, 36, 112, 115, 117–18
Marks, Gary, 52
marxism, 118
marxist dictatorships, 54
Massi, Nixon K., 141–42
Massignon, Louis, 69
Mastnak, Tomaz, 66
Maung, Maung, 198
Maung, U E., 187
Mazzini, Giuseppe, 88–89, 96–97, 105
means-end calculations, 36
Mennonites, 57
merchant law, 50
Mill, John Stuart, 87, 90, 103
monarchical states, 85
monarchy, 13
monetary system, 116
monopoly power, 12–13. *See also* sovereignty, theory of
Montero, Juan E., 165
Montesquieu, Charles-Louis de Secondat, baron de, 12, 14–15, 104, 204
Mont Pelerin Society, 112
Montt, Manuel, 167, 170, 177n11, 177n12
moral judgment, basis for, 33. *See also*

community of understanding; golden rule
Mozambique, 130, 132, 142, 145; Chief Nsiya, 142, 147n7
Murad, Abdul Hakim, 74

Napoleon III (Louis Napoleon), 94–95
Nasr, Seyyed, Hossein, 73
nationalism, 86–87, 93, 158
Netherlands, the, 46; United Provinces, 202
network governance approach. *See* governance, policy networks
New England, self-governing communities in, 4, 203
Newton, Isaac, 190
Nietzche, relativism of values, 73
nongovernmental organizations (NGOs), 56
nonprofit associations, 210
normative theory, political science, 151
Nu, U, 195

O'Higgins, Bernardo, 160, 177n11
Olivetti Foundation, 210
Olson, Mancur, 81
ordinary law, versus constitutional law, 38
Ordo-liberalism. *See* Freiburg school of economics
Oregon, local democracy in, 4
Orwell, George, 65
Ostrogorski, Moisei, 36

Paine, Thomas, 87
Palmer, R. R., 87
Papal Revolution (1075–1122), 49–50
paradox of revolt, 89, 91, 93, 95, 97, 105
patterns of order, 3–5, 11–18, 20, 119, 209, 212; eternal, 30, 33; hierarchical, 3, 4, 6, 11–13, 30; monocentric, 30; polycentric, 3, 4, 6–8, 11, 30–42, 46, 51, 90–91, 118, 125, 137, 198, 205, 210
perennialist school of religion, 73
Pérez, José Joaquín, 160
Peru, 160
Pickthall, Marmaduke, 69
Piñera, Sebastián, 173–74
Pinochet Ugarte, Augusto, 168–71, 176n7
Pinto, Francisco Antonio, 177n12
Pisacane, Carlo, 95
Pius VII (Pope), 87
pluralism, legal, 48–49, 58; religious, 69, 72–74, 82, 159
Portales, Diego, 167
postmodernism, 68, 74, 76
prerogatives of rule, 29–30, 34, 36–38, 41
Prieto, Joaquín, 167
Prisoner's dilemma, 22, 66, 75, 78–82
private corporations, 52, 57, 210
proselytism, 58, 66. *See also* faith-based organizations
public accountability, 13, 37, 39–40, 53, 154, 163–64
Puritanism, 19, 203

Quakers, 57
Quran, 69–74

Rahman, Abdul, 58
rational choice theory, 54–55
Reformation, 5
regulation and adaptation, 22–23. *See also* requisite variety, law of
religion, as political institution, 18, 54–59, 91, 203
renewable natural resource (RNR) burdens, 127, 134
representative government, 87–88, 90–91, 204–5. *See also* liberalism
requisite variety, law of, 7–8, 22–25

res publica (open public realm), 14, 35, 204, 212
Rettig, Raúl, 166, 177n11
Rettig Commission, 167–69, 171–72, 177n11, 179n28
Robespierre, Maximilien, 87
Roman Empire (Augustan), 116
Rousseau, Jean-Jacques, 104
royal laws, 50
rule by assembly. *See* democracy
rule by law, Burma, 196, 198
rule of law, 13, 15, 19, 31, 38–40, 42, 86–87, 126, 161, 174, 193, 195–96, 198, 203
rule-ordered relationships, 12, 19, 22–23, 25
rule-ruler-ruled relationship, 19, 21
Russia, 58

Sangermano, Vincentius, 185
San Martín, José de, 160
Schillebeeckx, Edward, 66
Schuon, Frithjof, 73
Scotland, 202
secularization, 86
self-governing societies, 11, 14–20, 24–25, 35, 37, 39, 42, 47, 51, 54, 87, 90–92, 94–95, 100, 102, 105, 144, 201–3, 206, 212–13
sexuality, 74
Shakir, Zaid, 71, 74
Siedentop, Larry, 101
Smith, Adam, 3, 6, 20, 56
socialism, 113, 120
social justice, 65, 67
soteriology, 69
South Africa, apartheid system, 76, 78–79
sovereign power, 6, 15–17, 20, 36. *See also* Hobbes, Thomas
sovereign states, 45
sovereignty, popular, 19, 86–87, 94, 198, 203; theory of, 12–13, 30–31, 51

Spain, 89, 97, 164, 170
state, definitions of, 5, 12, 45–46, 101, 104, 201
state-governed societies, 11–12, 14, 16, 25, 90, 201, 205–6
stateless societies, 17
Switzerland, 17, 46, 93, 112, 193, 202

Taylor, Robert H., 183
Thailand, 184
theory of goods, 206–8; jointness of use, 206–9; principle of exclusion, 206–9; private goods, 207; subtractability, 206–8. *See also* common-pool resources
Thirty Years War, 8
Tiebout, Charles M, 51
Tierney, Brian, 20
Tinker, Hugh, 194
Tocqueville, Alexis de, 3–4, 8, 15, 18–19, 37, 46–48, 54, 87–91, 94, 96, 101, 103, 201, 203, 212; law of laws, 19, 21, 24, 203; three types of political order, 15–16, 201–2
tragedy of the commons, 7, 22, 41–42, 208. *See also* common-pool resources
Treaty of Münster. *See* Treaty of Westphalia
Treaty of Osnabrück. *See* Treaty of Westphalia
Treaty of Westphalia, 45–46
tsunami, Indonesia (2004), 58

Uganda, 79
United States of America, American Revolution, 86; civil war, 97; Congress of, 18, 205; constitution of, 45, 47–48, 203; democracy in, 16, 18, 88, 90–91, 201–3; federalism, 6, 12, 18, 47; nullification controversy, 90. *See also* Tocqueville, Alexis de
Universal Declaration of Human Rights, 167

University of Berlin, 112
University of Bonn, 112
University of Freiburg, 112
urban law, 50
user groups, Lake Chiuta fisheries, 130, 136, 141, 144
utility functions, 55

veto capabilities, 14–15, 31, 39, 204. *See also* division of labor
voluntary associations, 52–53
voluntary self-regulation, 50, 52. *See also* commons management

Warren, Robert, 51
Weber, Max, 5
Westphalian state system, 45–46, 183
Whitehead, Alfred, 69
Wilson, John, 146n5
Wilson, Woodrow, 3, 18, 205
Win, Ne, 196–98
women's rights, 74
World Parliament of Religions, 68
World War II, 167

Zalaquett, José, 168

Contributors

Barbara Allen is professor, former chair of the Department of Political Science, and former director of women's studies at Carleton College, Northfield, MN. She is a contributing editor to the Martin Luther King Jr. Papers Project at Stanford University. She has written extensively on the political thought of Alexis de Tocqueville and Martin Luther King Jr. Her book, *Tocqueville, Covenant, and the Democratic Revolution: Harmonizing Earth with Heaven* (2005), examines the covenant idea in politics and its influence on American federalism. Professor Allen joined her students in a multimethod, eight-year study of election campaign news and political advertising, the 2004 portion of the project for which she and Carleton College colleague Gregory Marfleet were awarded the American Political Science Association Rowman and Littlefield Innovations in Teaching Award in 2005.

Stephan Kuhnert is founder and chairman of Kuhnert Management Consulting. He has developed strategic and organizational solutions for numerous governmental, corporate, educational, and human-service organizations. Kuhnert earned his master's degree and doctorate in Economics from the University of Marburg, Germany. He has held leadership positions in consulting firms and government organizations. His scientific interests include entrepreneurship, innovation, economic development, and American federalism. His research has resulted in three books and sixteen articles.

Brian Loveman came to the Department of Political Science at San Diego State University in 1973 after receiving an M.A. (1969) and Ph.D. (1973) from Indiana University and B.A. in history and political science from the University of California at Berkeley (1965). His major fields of interest are

Latin American politics, inter-American politics, international relations, U.S. foreign policy, and human rights. Among his recent publications are *Addicted to Failure: U.S. Security Policy in Latin America and the Andean Region* (2006), *Strategy for Empire: U.S. Regional Security Policy in the Post-Cold War Era* (2004), *Políticas de reparación: Chile 1990–2004* (2005, with Elizabeth Lira), *For la Patria: Politics and the Armed Forces in Latin America* (1999), *Las suaves cenizas del olvido: Vía chilena de reconciliación política 1814–1932* ([1999] 2000, with Elizabeth Lira), *Las ardientes cenizas del olvido: Vía chilena de reconciliación política, 1932–1994* (2000, with Elizabeth Lira), *Las acusaciones constitucionales en Chile: Una perspectiva histórica* (2000, with Elizabeth Lira), *Leyes de reconciliación en Chile: Amnistías, indultos y reparaciones 1819–1999* (2001, with Elizabeth Lira), *Historia, política y ética del verdad en Chile, 1891–2001: Reflexiones sobre la paz social y la impunidad* (2001, with Elizabeth Lira), *Chile: The Legacy of Hispanic Capitalism* (2001), and *Arquitectura política y seguridad interior del estado 1811–1999* (2002, with Elizabeth Lira). He teaches classes in Latin American politics, inter-American relations, comparative politics, politics of the developing nations, international relations, and environmental politics. He served (2001–2005) as the Fred J. Hansen Chair for Peace Studies and is working on research projects funded by the Ford Foundation and the William and Flora Hewlett Foundation on Andean regional security policy, human rights in Latin America, and judicial reform in Chile in comparative perspective.

Anas Malik is assistant professor of political science at Xavier University in Cincinnati. He received his Ph.D. in political science and master's in economics from Indiana University, Bloomington. Born in Pakistan and raised in Libya, he speaks Urdu and Arabic, and has conducted fieldwork in Jordan and Pakistan. His research interests are in political Islam, international political economy, and development.

Michael D. McGinnis is professor of political science at Indiana University, Bloomington. From 2003 to 2005 he served as codirector of the Workshop in Political Theory and Policy Analysis. He is editor of three volumes of readings from the Workshop and coauthor of *Compound Dilemmas: Democracy, Collective Action, and Superpower Rivalry*. His current research focuses on the contributions of faith-based organizations to the design and implementation of global conflict policy.

Tun Myint is assistant professor of political science at Carleton College, where he also teaches in the Environment, Science, and Technology Program. He left Burma after the military coup on September 18, 1988, that cracked down on the people's movement for democracy in which he was involved as a student activist. After winning a scholarship from the United States Information Agency-funded Burmese Refugee Scholarship Program, he came to Indiana University, Bloomington, in 1993 where he earned a B.A. in political science and East Asian studies, M.P.A. at SPEA, and Ph.D. in law and social sciences jointly conducted at the School of Public and Environmental Affairs and Indiana University School of Law. He was a research associate at the Workshop in Political Theory and Policy Analysis at Indiana University where he engaged in teaching and research on democracy and environmental governance with a regional focus on Southeast Asia. He has published articles on the effects of opportunities for participation and social learning on environmental governance in case studies featuring the Mekong and Rhine Rivers.

Vincent Ostrom is Arthur F. Bentley Professor Emeritus of Political Science and founding director of the Workshop in Political Theory and Policy Analysis at Indiana University, Bloomington. Professor Ostrom has been a fellow of the Social Science Research Council and the Center for Advanced Study in the Behavioral Studies, contributed to the drafting of the Alaska Constitution, has received honors from the American Political Science Association, and was a co-recipient of the Atlas Economic Research Foundation's Lifetime Achievement Award. He has been president of the Public Choice Society and has served on the editorial boards of *Constitutional Political Economy*, *International Journal of Organization and Behavior*, and *Publius: The Journal of Federalism*. His books include *The Meaning of American Federalism: Constituting a Self-Governing Society* (1991), *The Meaning of Democracy and the Vulnerability of Democracies: A Response to Tocqueville's Challenge* (1997), *The Intellectual Crisis in American Public Administration* ([1973] 2008), and *The Political Theory of a Compound Republic: Designing the American Experiment* ([1971] 2008).

Filippo Sabetti is professor of political science at McGill University. He is the author or editor of twelve books dealing with theories and practices of self-government in Canada and Europe.

Mark Sproule-Jones is the Foundation Chair in Urban Studies at McMaster University. He has held the L. G. Pathy Chair in Canadian Studies at Princeton University. His previous appointments include positions at the Universities of British Columbia, Victoria, Auckland, Australian National, and Indiana. His work on institutional analysis and design led to new governance arrangements for the Fraser River, for Hamilton Harbour, for the Great Lakes, and for solving urban problems in Hamilton and western Lake Ontario. His publications include seven books, eight monographs, and more than seventy research papers.

Jamie Thomson has, first as an academic and then as a consultant, conducted applied research on common-pool resource governance and management problems and on special districts in eleven African and Asian countries over the past thirty-five years. Results of that work have appeared in a dozen articles and numerous consulting reports prepared for the United States Agency for International Development, the World Bank, and the Asian Development Bank. Thomson was a founding member of the International Association for the Study of Common Property and continues as a member of the successor organization. He is currently retired and planning research to be conducted in France on renewable natural resource governance and management problems within special districts.